Work's a
BITCH

and then

You Make It Work

Work's a BITCH

and then

You Make It Work

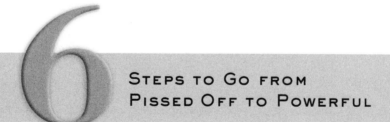

6

STEPS TO GO FROM
PISSED OFF TO POWERFUL

ANDREA KAY

STEWART, TABORI & CHANG | NEW YORK

Published in 2008 by
Stewart, Tabori & Chang
An imprint of Harry N. Abrams, Inc.

Library of Congress Cataloging-in-Publication Data

Kay, Andrea, 1954-
   Work's a bitch and then you make it work : 6 steps to go
from pissed off to powerful / by Andrea Kay.
      p. cm.
   ISBN 978-1-58479-708-1
      1. Career changes--United States. 2. Vocational guidance—
United States. 3. Job hunting--United States. I. Title.
   HF5384.K395 2009
   650.14—dc22   2008027905

Edited by Rahel Lerner
Designed by Susi Oberhelman

Printed in the United States of America

10   9   8   7   6   5   4   3   2   1

HNA ▮▮▮▮▮
harry n. abrams, inc.
a subsidiary of La Martinière Groupe

115 West 18th Street
New York, NY 10011
www.hnabooks.com

Visit Andrea Kay at www.andreakay.com

Contents

Introduction: We Begin Right Where You Are   9

P A R T   I :
A Day in the Life of You (And How You Got Here)   13

P A R T   I I :
A *New* Day in the Life of You (And How You Get There)   39

Step 1
Take Your Pick: Disillusionment or Naked Truth   41

Step 2
Enough Already: Lay Down Your Cell Phones
and BlackBerries   85

Step 3
Have a Brush with Greatness (Even If No One Notices)   113

Step 4
Prepare for Hurricanes, Sinkholes, and Mañana   153

Step 5
Develop a Sixth Sense   189

Step 6
Go Twist and Shout and Shake Things Up   219

Summary: All's Well That Intends Well   257
Acknowledgments   259
Index   260

We Begin Right Where You Are

The words "work" and "enjoy" are rarely used in the same sentence these days. You're more likely to hear "work sucks." Or "work's a bitch."

It's no wonder. If you've been at it a while, you've worked your butt off to help create the most productive economy in the world. You've been asked to do more with less, yet may receive less in return—including shouldering more of the cost of health care. All the while you see companies' stock values soar—some showing record earnings—and CEOs' salaries skyrocket. (I hate to add salt to the wound, but did you know that many CEOs earn more in one day than the average worker earns in a year?)

Add to all that the fact that your company may ask you—nicely, you'd hope, but not necessarily—to plug into company business 24/7 by way of beeper, BlackBerry, or e-mail. What kind of life is that? With your work life being such a drag, your overall life may not be so hot, either. They tend to bleed over into each other.

And while we're at it, let's not forget that you may be one of those people whose job doesn't exist anymore or is filled in some far-away land. And what about all the talk about quality, quality, quality, while it seems nearly every corporate decision is based on profits, profits, and more profits? How can you feel good about your work?

I haven't even touched on one of the top reasons people grimace in pain at the thought of work (or claim to in some surveys): bosses. Inept managers and leaders who lack integrity seem to overpopulate the workplace. Then add in the fact that you feel helpless to do anything about it. And if you're looking for a job, you have undoubtedly run into one annoying scenario after another—the most notorious being silence on the other end—no phone call, no letter saying "thanks, but no thanks," no nothing.

If any of this sounds familiar, you've got what I call a bad case of Career Rage. You're pissed off, and it's understandable. With all that

I've listed here, and more that I haven't even touched on, you may feel that you can never get ahead. What's the point of trying to find work you'd enjoy, developing the skills to get along with others, and working toward a career dream, when so much of the workplace is broken?

In the short run, no one can turn around the crumbling of trust in the workplace and, in some cases, in corporate leaders. Nor will anyone quickly alleviate the daily stress of life compounded by a workplace that seems to treat people like inventory. But you can take steps to get out of the self-defeating cycle that has eliminated the phrase "enjoy work" from your vocabulary. Yes, work can be a bitch. But there is hope—and there's even more. You don't have to suffer, feel helpless and betrayed, and wake up feeling crappy about your career and your future. There's a way to go from being pissed off to powerful. And you owe it to yourself to discover it.

Just so you know, I am not going to try to fill your head with a bunch of rah-rah happy talk and here's-how-you-deal-with-stress-and-stay-positive-and-turn-these-difficult-times-into-an-opportunity-for-growth jazz. That stuff is well meaning. But we're way past that.

I'm not giving up, though. And neither should you. This is your career—where you spend half or more of your life. How you feel about your work and career affects your relationships at home. Your future. Your potential income. Children you might have and the attitudes they develop as they observe and mimic you. The way you operate in the world and treat everyone who crosses your path. And someday, how you'll look back at your life. Please don't waste it being pissed off.

If it's any consolation, I'm ticked, too. I'm ticked that workers and job hunters feel so helpless, and I'm ticked that injustices and some situations in the work world have deflated the spirit of workers. I'm upset that the odds seem so stacked against you that you wonder, "Why bother?" I'm disturbed when I get e-mails like this one from a worker somewhere in America saying, "In this country it's not possible anymore to do what you want or what you're good at." I'm shocked by the number of discouraged twenty-somethings who have already lost faith in their ability to make a difference through their work.

I don't blame you for feeling frustrated. But to feel powerful about your career, you have to feel powerful about yourself. So let's begin with where you are right now.

The first section of this book starts there. It's your chance to vent. Then we'll move on to the meat of the book—the steps you can take at work and in life to help you go from being pissed off to powerful. From time to time we'll touch upon laws, education, policies, and business practices that affect you. But this isn't a book about social and economic-policy analysis and who's right or wrong. It's a book about what you can do *despite* what's wrong and broken. It's also a workbook that makes you think, so get ready to do some work.

You might be a wee bit skeptical at this point. The work world and all those forces you don't control loom large. But the workplace is not like the weather, which everyone complains about but figures there's nothing they can do about. In the case of your career, there's plenty you can do. Let's begin.

PART I

A Day in the Life of You

(AND HOW YOU GOT HERE)

I t all started on a sizzling hot day in July 1988. The mail carrier walked into my office, looking burdened by the heavy gray sack on his shoulder and the promise of the U.S. Postal Service letter carrier patch on his sleeve: his pledge to deliver in rain, sleet, snow, and eighty-five-degree temperatures. In this case, he was also delivering my first Career Rage letter.

Addressed to "Ask Andrea," as my column was called back then, my first piece of mail thrilled me. Someone had actually read what I had to say! "They're probably writing to thank me," I thought. "How nice to be appreciated." I gently slit open the top of the number-ten envelope and unfolded the two-page typed letter inside.

"Dear Andrea, What planet do you live on?" it began. It went on: "What kind of moron would advise people to negotiate their salary? You have to take what you can get if you want to get anywhere. As you sit there in your ivory-tower office making the big bucks, perhaps it would help if you got a dose of the real world." The writer then told me about his real world. I'd go on, but you get the picture.

In *my* world, I was collecting zero dollars per column for the privilege—which it was—of writing approximately 650 words in the newspaper. The editor had told me, "Let's try it and see how it goes."

The letter really bothered me at the time, but that was 20 years ago. Compared to the mail I get today, that was a love letter. Many of the issues people write about now are similar; some are brand-new. But I must say you do seem madder in the last ten years. Today, it's more like foaming-at-the-mouth, seething outrage.

This outrage rears its head in the most unlikely of places. In 1998, my second book, which was about resumes, had just come out, and I was giving a talk at a bookstore. A man in the back of the standing-room-only audience began heckling me. People started shifting uncomfortably in their seats as he went on his verbal rampage. A few people stood up and began circling the man. I scouted the audience for some brawny security-guard-looking types, but there were none. After all, who heckles the author of a harmless resume book? One really upset worker, that's who.

It's not that the relationship between you and your company or boss has ever been a bed of roses. In fact, people were not only throwing fits about working conditions back in post–Civil War days, but they were killing each other over them. Let's take a quick look at what came before you, to better understand how you and other workers got to such an angry place today. Even if you don't like history much, stick with me here. This will help you get to the next part—the part where you can turn your wrath into something more productive.

Quick History Lesson

Back in the late 1800s, when mass production was developing, work became more dangerous, was often monotonous, and was often carried out under harsh conditions. It was then that some nasty events took place, says James McBrearty, economics professor at the University of Arizona's Eller College of Management. Some of the highlights of the era were the Molly Maguires, who were upset about bad working conditions and who intimidated, beat, and killed mine owners in the anthracite coal mines of eastern Pennsylvania. Then there was the Great Railway Strike of 1877, in which workers protesting a wage cut were killed, and federal troops were called in. There was Chicago's Haymarket Square Riot, where workers were striking for an eight-hour day; someone threw a bomb into a group of policemen who were trying to break up strikers, and several people were killed.

And if you think working long hours is a recent phenomenon, until the early 1920s steelworkers worked twelve-hour shifts six days a week.

In the early 1900s, unions came into power, says Tom Chacko, professor and chair of management at Iowa State University. The relationship between workers and management succeeded in some cases and didn't in others. In 1956, when the number of white-collar workers surpassed the number of blue-collar workers, America became more of a white-collar nation, according, once again, to Professor James McBrearty. Workers often thought they would move up the socioeconomic ladder—or that at least their children would be able to. And that is what many people saw as the American Dream. More on that later.

Which brings us to today.

Today our economy is based on delivering services rather than manufacturing products. Unions, which negotiate wages and benefits for their members, don't have the numbers or the clout they used to. Since 1980, unions have lost nearly 5 million members, says Gary Chaison, professor of industrial relations at Clark University. In the 1950s, unions represented 35 percent of workers. Today it's 12 percent.

Today, workers are faced with what those in labor and management circles call "givebacks"—a term that refers to wages and benefits employees have but management wants to reduce or take away entirely. Things like health care and pension plans. Of course, as you may have experienced, this is also happening to workers who don't have unions backing them.

Although you may never have worked for a company that fit this exact description, until the mid-seventies companies generally had a paternalistic view of their relationship with workers. Companies took care of workers through benefits, and workers basically had a position with the company as long as they did a good job, explains Professor James McBrearty. It was "a fair day's pay for a fair day's work, including decent fringe benefits, of course," he says, "symbolized by the likes of IBM." Companies like IBM took care of people from womb to tomb, he says. "IBM never laid anyone off for lack of work. They might make you take a different job with them and you may have to relocate. But they took care of you. You had job security, health-care programs, and pensions fully paid for by the company. Life was good!"

The shift away from this became more pronounced in the early 1980s, with the sharp recession of '81/82, McBrearty explains. But the view of what work is supposed to be and how people want to be treated hasn't really changed. The work relationship is one of exchange, says Professor Tom Chacko. The worker gives his or her time, talent, skills, knowledge, and education. And the employer provides an interesting place to work, a salary, and bonuses. But when one party feels there's an imbalance in the relationship, they sever the relationship. (Or, as many of your letters to me say, you're so mad about how the relationship is playing out, you want to get the hell outta wherever you are.)

As the employer is putting more of the onus on you—everything from figuring out your career path to covering your own health insurance—that balance keeps getting, in your eyes, less balanced. Your letters tell the story this way:

- "I give my all, then get laid off—three times now."
- "They expect me to answer my phone at 2:00 in the morning, in case the client has a problem."
- "They're bringing in someone from the outside instead of promoting from within."
- "My work isn't fulfilling."
- "My boss doesn't give me feedback. I don't know where I stand."
- "I should get promoted, but they won't give me anything concrete about how to make that happen."
- "I'm disappointed by the lack of creativity in my job. My time is consumed with meetings and conference calls."
- "My best skills aren't being used."

What do all of these remarks have in common? Something is not fair. The balance is way off. Any trust that did exist is evaporating or gone. You entered the work relationship thinking, "You, the employer, are going to give me certain things in exchange for what I do as well as I can." Remember the "fair day's pay for a fair day's work" concept? As Chacko puts it, "As long as there's mistrust, nothing works."

Factor in the feeling you're being lied to, and it gets even worse. I keep a file called "Lies My Company Told Me." Tucked away in it are the things clients tell me and the things readers who work in companies or are job hunting write to me about. Here are some samples:

"Lies My Company (or Potential Companies) Told Me"

- "They told me I'd get a review at the end of the year. That was two years ago. Never happened."
- "My boss told me we'd meet to discuss [fill in the blank] and he's cancelled the meeting every month now for the last year."
- "They told me I'd be doing one job and traveling only once a month. It's not the job they hired me for, and I'm gone three weeks out of the month."

- "They said they'd get back to me in two days. That was a month ago, and they won't return my calls."
- "They told me I'd have an office, and a year later I still am in a cubicle."
- "I trusted them with my pension. Now, twenty-five years of savings is all gone."
- "Their mission statement says they care about people. Two of my co-workers landed in the hospital last week. One had a heart attack. They couldn't care less if I drop dead, as long as they make their numbers."

Notice a trend here?

Of course the lies, perceived unfairness, and broken contract of the relationship between workers and companies create stress. It's enough to age you prematurely. In fact, if you want to see just how working in a stressful office environment can age you, go to a Web page created for that sole purpose. It's called Age-O-Matic.com, and it promises to help you "find out what your soul-sucking job is doing to you." You upload your photograph, and then, to measure how bad things are, you pick answers from such multiple-choice selections as "I'd rather *eat maggots, sleep with a hippo* or *get an eyeball tattoo* than work."

But many people stay put because they see no way out. In the book *Toxic Work*, author Barbara Bailey Reinhold reports that "an estimated twenty million Americans are staying in jobs they hate in order to keep their health insurance—when research indicates that career dissatisfaction is more likely than anything else to make them need to use it."

To be fair, some companies do appreciate their workers—and show it—and their workers appreciate their jobs and employers. *Fortune* magazine's 2008 list of "100 Best Companies to Work For" offers examples of such mutual admiration between management and employees.

Take the number-one-ranked company on *Fortune's* list, Google, a company that continues "to mint millionaires as the stock cracked $700," according to *Fortune*. But it's not just giving stock options to workers that helps land a company on the list. The online mortgage lender Quicken Loans was number two. Described by a worker as "ethically driven," the company avoided the subprime crisis "by sticking with lower-risk, traditional loans," says *Fortune*.

Genentech, ranked number five, is known for its perks, which range from doggie day care to an on-site farmers' market. Number-eight-ranked Qualcomm, headquartered in San Diego, is quadrupling the size of its popular on-site primary-care clinic. Accounting firm Plante & Moran, ranked forty-fourth, encourages employees to bond, and last year over twelve hundred workers (that's 80 percent of all employees) gathered together to "amp it up."

General Mills earned sixty-ninth place, in part because of its formal phase-back to work following a leave-of-absence benefit. King's Daughters Medical Center in Ashland, Kentucky, ranked sixty-third, with such benefits as on-site child care, subsidized gym membership, adoption aid, job sharing, compressed workweek, and telecommuting.

But a company doesn't have to be large to be a great place to work. Planet Dog, developers of innovative, premium products "made for dogs, by dog lovers" based in Portland, Maine, was named one of America's Best Places to Work in 2008 by *Outside* magazine. Ranked second in the small-sized category, they only have 44 employees, not including the 30 dogs that accompany their owners to work. It was recognized for providing a great work environment that not only allows for quality of life and balance, but that also promotes environmentally friendly business practices. (More on other such companies that didn't make *Fortune*'s list in Step 5.)

But the news isn't so cheery at many other organizations—maybe yours.

For starters, you may have lost trust in your institution because of some naughty executives involved in illegal dealings or shady financing. Many say this perceived trend of increased bad behavior is based on a lowering of ethics due to deregulation or the way executives are compensated. But the point is, *you* got screwed.

Or, because of broader issues companies face or choices they make, your career has been damaged, derailed, or deported to another continent. Due to competitive pressures, your company may have merged with another firm, been acquired, or gone bankrupt. Perhaps the industry you've worked in has totally evaporated or been replaced by automation. Maybe your benefits have been reduced or your salary hasn't kept up with inflation.

Whatever the issues are, if I could sum up your general reaction, it would go something like this: You're mad as hell, and you don't want to take it anymore. Am I close?

To help you vent I've provided this space for you to get it off your chest. Go ahead, fill it in.

I'm mad because:

_____

_____

_____

_____

_____

_____

Many of my clients and readers are relieved to learn that they are not alone in feeling this way. So let's look at what your colleagues have to say.

You're Not the Only One Who Feels This Way

For the record, let me say that I am certain I haven't covered every issue you're upset about. I've tried to touch on the ones I hear about most often, that come up again and again, and that seem to have the greatest impact on people in today's workplace.

You're going to have to figure out how to deal with some issues yourself. Like the fact that nearly 60 percent of workers surveyed by CareerBuilder said they experience road rage during their office commutes. It does make me wonder whether people are getting in their cars and yelling, honking their horns, and giving obscene hand gestures because they're mad about their careers. Nevertheless, some self-control would be nice.

Also, for the record, let me say that life in this day and age is not easy. Besides work, people feel stress from information overload, family responsibilities, illness, money, and too much stuff to do, to name a few. These concerns are compounded by workplace problems such as:

- Losing your way of life after working for a company like General Motors or Ford for decades
- The prevailing hiring practice of "employment at will"
- Feeling bad about the work you produce because you're asked to compromise quality so the company can make more money
- Business decisions that are focused on the short term at the expense of people and doing good work
- Being turned down for jobs because you're not bilingual
- Corporate untouchables who seem to get away with anything

Here, in your words, are the things you've told me make you red in the face with fury, and, in some cases, ready to resign your hopes and dreams. This is your section to bitch and moan. Enjoy it while you can.

You're pissed because:
"I HAVE NO LIFE."

Over the last five years, a growing number of workers have been telling me they feel pressured or are required to be plugged into their company 24/7 by way of beeper, BlackBerry, or phone.

You don't need a survey to know this. Just have a meal with someone who makes himself available at all times, even if it's not required. His cell phone starts humming, ringing, or vibrating on the table while you've barely started your salad. But to drive the point home, let's look at a couple surveys.

In a 2006 survey conducted by Korn/Ferry International, 81 percent of more then 2,300 global executives said they are connected to work through a mobile device such as a cell phone, PDA, laptop, or pager all of the time. Another 2006 survey, conducted by Hudson, found that workers are clocking in when they should be tuning out. At the end of the year, nearly 25 percent of those surveyed hadn't taken any vacation time. When workers do go away, 72 percent of them connect with the office; 87 percent of managers stay in touch to some extent when they're supposed to be unwinding; and 38 percent of workers and managers said they return from vacation no more relaxed, or even more stressed, than when they left, as a result of work they missed.

In "Extreme Jobs: The Dangerous Allure of the 70-Hour Work-week," published in the *Harvard Business Review* in 2006, the Center for Work-Life Policy reported that 35 percent of high-income earners work more than 60 hours a week; 10 percent work more than 80 hours. The research revealed that 60 hours or more of work per week is often spent on activities that require tight deadlines, attending work events outside regular work hours, being available to clients twenty-four hours a day, and/or large amounts of travel. Over two-thirds of the workers studied do not get enough sleep, and half don't get enough exercise. Their sex lives, their ability to have strong relationships, and their relationships with their children also suffer.

Or take my client, the poster child for the Worker Who Has No Life. He is asked to travel three weeks out of the month while managing a global organization of hundreds of people. He takes calls from clients and managers six to seven days a week, until 1:00 a.m. (He's not officially required to do this but feels he must.) He was on the verge of a breakdown, couldn't sleep, and complained of his heart pounding so fast that sometimes he couldn't catch his breath. I couldn't convince him to take even one day off to see the doctor and chill out. He felt it would be more stressful to have to return to the phone calls and e-mails that would await him.

I have lost count as to how many people tell me they are craving control over their time. It gets to be more every year. And just as many ask me: Isn't part of the purpose of work to make it possible to enjoy life? What life?

You're pissed because:
"MY BOSS IS AN INCOMPETENT IDIOT/JERK."

There have always been idiot and incompetent bosses. Are there more nowadays? Is it harder to get rid of them? Do companies put up with worse behavior? Your letters seem to suggest as much.

OK, let's start by looking at what a 2006 Hudson survey found: Only 67 percent of employees rate their managers favorably, while 92 percent of managers consider themselves to be excellent or good bosses. Surprised? Probably not. Part of the reason managers don't know how folks really feel is that only 26 percent of the workforce is ever given the chance to formally review their managers' performance, the survey found. And unless there is a way to keep their managers from knowing who said what, most workers I know aren't going to take the risk of telling their managers what they really think.

When some workers who weren't too thrilled with management did make their feelings known on the company bulletin board, they felt the sting of retribution. The workers wouldn't even identify themselves or their place of work in the e-mails they sent me—for fear of more retaliation. But apparently someone posted a column I wrote about how people feel about their bosses for all to see.

"It created such a stir—all the managers took it personally and were very offended," writes one of the workers. One manager called each employee into the office or on the telephone "asking if we knew

---

**"There are simply times when an asshole
must be called such to his or her face."**
—Amy in Washington

Amy wrote me after reading a column I wrote on how to handle rude employers with tact and diplomacy. She described my column as "all in all, a good article expressing valid points of view and courses of action to be taken by employees when faced with the overbearing pompousness all too common in the American workplace."

But, she continues, "There are simply times when an asshole must be called such to his or her face. Due to the corporate strategies allowed to run rampant in this country . . . workers are intimidated, lied to, manipulated into unsafe environments, suffer privacy violations, and bullied . . . by employers who think that just because they can offer a job to someone, they have the right to play God over that person inside and out of the company. I personally choose not to commit violence, but I will honestly tell you that I fully understand those who do!"

> **"They sent him to Kellogg School of Management for a week. It will not do any good, because he cannot be trained."**
> —Sam

Sam and his wife work for a large government agency. "We both pride ourselves on our work. However, we have the prototypical idiot boss. He lacks basic intelligence, has limited reasoning abilities, no common sense, and cannot absorb new information.

"Last week it took him 15 minutes to change the bag in the shredder, five minutes to fail at opening the plastic bag and then ask for my help, and another ten minutes to fit the bag on a frame and put it back in the shredder . . . They sent him to the Kellogg School of Management for a week. It will not do any good, because he cannot be trained." Sam says even though the agency prides itself on doing excellent work, it allows such ineptitude to exist because "it is less work to let him flounder than it is to demote him."

who put it on the wall. He did this after telling people it was 'insubordination' and that 'employees will be fired.'"

My column described the biggest frustration people report having at work as "idiot bosses." Definitions ranged from "not having a clue as to how to do their jobs" and "not being able to solve problems when you come to them with issues" to "being insensitive to people around them." Accounts of insensitivity include a manager who berates employees in front of others to exert power, and a supervisor who subjects her staff to daily details of her in vitro process.

One of the workers who wrote me, referring to one particular manager, said, "Rather than taking a look at himself and perhaps not wanting to be the type of manager in your article, he has made the situation at work unbearable [and] many of us do not want to continue working there."

In my own very unscientific poll, which I conducted on my Web site, I asked the question, Have you become more frustrated and angry at work in the last year? Everyone who responded said yes. Fifty percent said it was because their boss was an idiot.

Some disgruntled employees hate their bosses so much that they write disparaging things about their *dead* bosses on the Web site Legacy.com, which carries death notices and obituaries.

"I had to listen to [the details of] her sex life."
—Kathy on the East Coast

"My so-called manager loved to belittle me and the other women in the office in front of other people; it made her feel powerful. To top it all off I had to listen to [the details of] her sex life [after] her boy-toy would come over every weekend."

You're pissed because:
"I TRIED TO DO THE RIGHT THING, BUT . . ."

It seems quite a few people have discovered irregularities at their companies. They involve financial records or safety, environmental, or ethical violations. Many who speak up are branded as (the nice name) whistle-blowers. The not-so-nice names? Tattler, rat, snitch.

Those who reveal company violations are often discredited, says James Helmer, a Cincinnati attorney. "The company will overturn every rock it can to dishonor you and paint you as the worst employee they ever had." Companies file counterclaims against workers who go public, charging defamation. Some people lose their work friends. A former New Jersey worker who complained about unethical practices at the company reported in a *Wall Street Journal* article: "It's like I've got the bubonic plague."

Others get demoted or are forced out of their jobs after the company tries to discredit them. A woman who worked as a zookeeper spoke up when a co-worker was attacked by a bear, and she told me she was demoted the next day. When she refused the demotion, she was suspended without pay.

This despite the fact that people in the organization and society are probably better off as a result of someone's speaking up. "Loyalty is more highly valued in business than in any place but the Mafia and the military (where followers in both must be prepared to kill for the boss)" writes Michael Lewis in *The New York Times Magazine*.

Whistle-blowers are supposed to be protected by law. When I once wrote about a government bill being passed for whistle-blower protection, I heard from Ron, who said, "Hell, I work for the federal government, and I'm scared to report any wrongdoing for fear of reprisals."

"When I asked my boss for guidance, he instead fired me and kept the thief."
—Anonymous e-mailer

"As the manager of a retail shop, I wanted to fire a worker who was stealing hundreds of dollars in cash and merchandise every week. When I asked my boss for guidance, he instead fired me and kept the thief. When another worker protested the thief being allowed to continue work, that worker was told by my boss he did not care how much the thief stole, and if she didn't like it she could leave."

You're pissed because:
"THE COMPANY CHEATED AND STOLE FROM US."

A couple of years ago I started cutting out news stories about the shameful things occurring at companies and trusted institutions. I'd find an article about an ousted official here and there. A leader of a company accused of sheltering taxes illegally or employing creative accounting. A CEO convicted of fraud or tampering with something he wasn't supposed to be tampering with being led out of the company in handcuffs. An analyst who failed to disclose stock deals or who publicly recommended buying stocks he privately ridiculed. An inquiry or investigation into a company's shady bookkeeping practices or an executive accused of stealing millions. The pile of articles got so big that it became a fire hazard, so I had to stop collecting them.

It's no wonder WashingtonPost.com referred to the business pages as reading "like the crime blotter." One ticked-off reader of my column put it this way: "Leadership isn't black-and-white—it's green."

No one knows for sure how many scandals and management fiascoes have occurred in the last five to ten years, or if it really has gotten worse or just seems that way (more on this in Step 1). But I, for one, do know that hardworking people have had to bear the brunt of bad, uninformed, or, in some cases, corrupt and criminal managers.

The subprime mortgage market crisis that began to unfold in 2007 is one example of "leaders who are paid first and foremost to manage risk" who "have been caught either unaware or uninformed about giant risks their companies took," writes Jenny Anderson in *The New York Times*. "Never in the history of Wall Street have so many who are so senior fallen so fast."

And just as upsetting is that workers have become so cynical and distrustful, having lost their faith in the workplace and the integrity of corporate leaders. They don't feel they can believe in anything. And people need to believe in something.

You're pissed because:
"COMPANIES DON'T CARE. THEY TREAT US LIKE INVENTORY."

According to *USA Today*, on August 29, 2006, four hundred workers at RadioShack received an e-mail stating, "The workforce reduction notification is currently in progress. Unfortunately your position is one that has been eliminated." The company spokesperson said officials had told workers in a series of meetings that layoff notices would be delivered electronically. But still, what were they thinking?

Another article in *USA Today* talked about a British store clerk who was fired by text message. I don't even know how to retrieve a text message, but I know it's not a good way to tell someone he just lost his job.

Sometimes companies have to make tough calls. Even governments lay people off. In January 2007, the Libyan government announced plans to lay off four hundred thousand people—more than a third of its workforce—to ease budget pressures and stimulate the private sector.

> **"It's like the company wants him to die and just go away."**
> —Paula in South Carolina
>
> Paula wrote me about her 77-year-old father, who had worked for a large retailer for 13 years. After he suffered a heart attack at work, he was rushed to the emergency room. His employer told Paula "that he would not only have his job when he returned but be allowed to transfer to a store closer to me, where he moved in after his surgery. After three months' leave, the company said they didn't have a job for him at this time; 'sorry, we cannot help you.'"
>
> She goes on to explain that the managers have said to her father, "Can't you make it with your Social Security? You really don't need to work, do you?" Paula adds, "It's like the company wants him to die and just go away."

It's never easy to lose your job, even when circumstances are beyond anyone's control. But after it happens to you a few times or you get treated so poorly in the process, it makes you cranky.

You're pissed because:
"WE WORK HARDER AND GET LESS, WHILE CEOS KEEP MAKING MORE."

It's not that companies shouldn't profit and CEOs shouldn't make good salaries. But it's a hard pill to swallow when, well, you feel you're working your tush off and getting less for it, and—even though it's not fair to generalize—you read about executives who bilk their companies and leave workers high and dry or walk away with millions in severance packages after losing gobs of money.

As I mentioned earlier, many CEOs earn more money in one day than the average worker earns in a year. And while employees are working hard to help create the most productive economy in the world, in many cases they are getting less in the way of benefits while companies' earnings soar and some CEOs' make tremendous salaries without being tied to performance.

This doesn't seem to be changing. One headline, for a 2007 ExecuNet newsletter about trends for the year, read, NEW WAR FOR TALENT YIELDS BETTER PAY PACKAGES.

The article goes on to say that with executive talent in high demand for the fourth consecutive year, companies will continue to add more incentives, including bigger bonuses, to their compensation packages to lure top talent from competitors and keep key leaders from walking out the door.

On January 8, 2007, *The New York Times* reported that "Robert L. Nardelli's unceremonious departure from Home Depot may spell the end of the era of supersized pay packages for chief executives of public companies, but a new refuge for lavish compensation and private jets is emerging elsewhere." It went on to say that businesses owned by private equity are now offering "compensation on a previously unimaginable scale to the chief executives who run the once-public companies that the firms have bought out" and that the "imperial chief executive officer is still very much alive and well in the private realm."

So, what's it like for the average worker? Incomes have been stagnant for most workers since 2000—except for those at the top of the wage distribution, according to the Economic Policy Institute (EPI). Wages simply haven't kept up with inflation. Since 2000, the typical working family's income has fallen 5.4 percent after adjusting for inflation, representing a three-thousand-dollar loss in annual income, the institute reports. Many workers write me to say, "I feel like no matter how hard I work, I can't get ahead."

I hear from people in various professions about this issue. But to use one example, let's look at teachers' paychecks. A 2006 article in *The New York Times* discussed an American Federation of Teachers survey of teacher salary trends. It found that the average teacher's salary increased by only $1,000 from 1994 to 2004, with the average annual salary for teachers being $46,597. For the first time since 1982, teachers' salaries on average were less than those of government workers.

Extreme income inequity is only part of the issue. People are also frustrated at having to shell out more money from their paycheck to pay for health care. Granted, the cost of employees' health care has

> "As long as everyone's wages are rising and the standard of living is going up, tolerance for certain people making what might seem like rapacious pay packages is higher," says Ross Eisenbrey, vice president of the Economic Policy Institute. "But when times are bad and people see these giant severance packages and $40 million golden parachutes for CEOs leaving companies after they've lost billions, they resent that."

gone up drastically. Starbucks spends more on health benefits than on coffee beans.

Health-care coverage through an employer has declined from 61.5 percent in 1989 to 55.9 percent in 2004, according to the EPI. And those of you who do get coverage are paying a larger portion than ever before, with your share rising from 14 percent in 1992 to 22 percent in 2005, says the EPI.

Health policies introduced by the Bush administration in early 2007 don't help the problem, says Elise Gould, an economist with the EPI. The policies "are about shifting risk onto the individual. As the employer market erodes, more individuals must seek insurance on their own if they want any kind of health security. Those unlucky enough to be unhealthy today or to get sick tomorrow will find it very difficult to find affordable insurance in the private market," Gould contends.

Even an economic boom—when stocks are doing well and corporate profits are high—doesn't necessarily benefit all workers. As the EPI points out, how important is the Dow Jones Industrial Average to the average person? "Fewer than half of Americans own any stock at all, and the richest 20% of the population owns 90% of all stock market wealth."

You're pissed because:
"THEY THINK THEY OWN US."

Yes, companies can and do monitor e-mail, phone calls, and, in some places, more. Some even track workers' whereabouts via the Global Positioning System. While many companies have legitimate and legal reasons for doing this, it certainly doesn't build trust. Such tactics also tend to generate angry workers, who feel they have fewer rights and more rules that impinge on personal choice.

One reader of the Stanford University Web site, the Stanford Daily Online, upset about employer practices that dictate what employees do in their off-hours, commented that after the eight hours spent at work, "The rest of our lives belong to us."

Some people are peeved about organizations that dictate what they can display in their offices and cubicles. Such companies include the Hearst Corporation, which limits personal knickknacks and vacation photos in its offices in Manhattan, according to a *New York Times* article. Hearst's policy "specifies limiting 'the amount of personal items, stacks of paper and other materials'" and "bans carrying in 'furniture or lighting without prior approval.'" At Calvin Klein, executives "decreed there could be no desktop displays of photographs, mementos, toys, awards, plants or flowers, other than white ones."

Such policies have apparently spread in the last decade. The *Times* article cites a 2006 Steelcase and Opinion Research survey that "found that only 40 percent of companies encourage employees to personalize their work space." A decade ago, that number was 56 percent.

Job hunters are pissed because:
"COMPANIES TREAT US LIKE CRAP."

Job hunters aren't feeling so great about their treatment in the job-hunting world, either. Whether they're hourly workers or executives, the consensus is, "companies treat us like crap." Complaints range from receiving bad references from former employers to getting bad interviewers. The number-one complaint? "No one gets back to me." It doesn't matter whether you applied for a job electronically or by mail or had an actual interview—there's silence on the other end.

Being a job hunter can be lonely. It gets lonelier when you reach out and there is dead silence. But really, what can you expect if you're communicating with a computer? Even so, impersonal process or not, a response would be nice.

There was a time when you sent off your resume to a search firm or employer and you could "pretty well count on getting a letter back, even if it simply said, 'Thanks, but we don't have anything,'" says Dave

Opton, CEO of the online executive career site ExecuNet. Of course, that's all changed. Now that you can send out hundreds of resumes via your computer, "the recruiting world is overwhelmed," says Opton, and, even with autoresponders, "from the job seeker's perspective it is just a big, black void in cyberspace. Or best case, they feel they get a response that is only a half-step removed from 'Dear Occupant.'"

This, he says, is especially true for seasoned executives who haven't been shopping for a job in a long time and whose "expectation and experiences belong to times that are no more. It is a real shock and a deep disappointment."

"No phone call, no postcard, not even a mass e-mail saying 'no, thank you.'"
—Doug in California

"Employers think nothing at all about simply ignoring the job seekers . . . No phone call, no postcard, not even a mass e-mail saying, 'no, thank you' to the ones who spent gas, money, and time coming in . . . When employers discover that they're winding up with people who treat them just as the employer treated them in the hiring process—for example, by leaving a job with nary a day's notice—perhaps things will change."

One job hunter told me the highlight of his week was the day he got a response from a company he had contacted about a position. The letter had the typical rhetoric: "Thank you for your interest in our company. Although we don't have an appropriate opening for you at this time, we would like to keep your information on file." He was overjoyed just to know that someone had taken the time to acknowledge him.

Besides being overwhelmed by the volume of responses they receive to job postings, some companies don't manage the interview process well, says Louise Kursmark, owner of Best Impression, an executive resume service. In a survey she conducted of her clients and others, she found that, on average, 66 percent of candidates received one response to every ten job applications they submitted. And they weren't "blasting their resumes all over the place," she says, but carefully selecting jobs for which they felt they were well qualified.

Fifty percent of her respondents also said the company had actually done something during the interview process that made them decide they would never work there. Half said it had to do with how they were treated, including being kept waiting or shown a lack of respect. Respondents also complained of interviewers being disorganized, unprofessional, or confrontational and taking phone calls, glancing at e-mail, or allowing interruptions during the interview.

Then there's job hunters' rage over "digital dirt digging." This practice of employers and recruiters using search engines such as Google to dig up information about a job applicant is seen at best as unfair, as expressed by this woman in an audience I spoke to, who asked me, "What do you think of these employers who search the Internet for information on you, then use it against you?"

Others see this practice as unethical, even illegal. The editorial board of Stanford University's Stanford Daily Web site posted com-

> **"Some of these jerks . . . believe they should continue to torment employees even after they've left the company, by means of horrible references."**
> —John

"I'm the one they're asking to invest a significant portion of my irreplaceable time into improving their bottom line. I've worked for more than my share of jerks . . . Some even believe they should continue to torment employees even after they've left the company, by means of horrible references, or interference with unemployment benefits."

"The feeling is *anger*, which is white-hot and molten."
—Walter in Connecticut

Walter, who describes himself as a "high-tech American" with several college degrees and more than a decade of experience, wrote: "I have been seeking work continuously since 9/11. Over 239 weeks since my last paycheck . . . unemployed because my employer's facility in the World Trade Center burned on the evening of 9/11. I am a victim of offshoring since that crime. The feeling is not a mere lack of rationality. The feeling is *anger*, which is white-hot and molten."

ments to that effect, referring to employers who use Facebook.com, a site "expressly set up for personal, non-commercial use," and whose "popularity lies in its ability to foster a vibrant online community that taps into our society's confessional culture."

The board members concede that while employers can Google you, surf your Web site, and read your blog, and "such extensive background checks are distasteful, they are not illegal. This information is public and freely available to all, including nosy corporate recruiters." But, says the site, dredging up private information on Facebook is unethical.

An older generation of workers also has cause for concern about the use of digital dirt digging—even though it may not involve the embarrassing photographs or public nudity that some Web sites feature. ExecuNet's 2006 research revealed that more than 35 percent of executive recruiters who used the Internet to research candidates eliminated someone from consideration based on information they uncovered online. That figure is up from 25 percent in 2005.

And while we're on the subject of older workers, let's not forget discrimination. Employers have biases about all kinds of things, including age—even with the available number of workers shrinking (this does seem to be changing, though; more on that in Step 6).

Many older workers believe they have been discriminated against, and many more older workers who haven't yet run into such treatment expect it to happen to them. Other times it really happens. Disenchanted at 54, Robert Aspland summed up the feelings of many older workers when he was quoted in a *New York Times* article about American workers flocking to job fairs for skilled workers looking to work for Irish companies. For someone like him in America, he said, "getting a full-time job with benefits that also pays a living wage is like a pipe dream . . . these days."

Summing up the feelings of so many older job hunters, Sharon, who is trying to find work in the southern United States, wrote, "Very few employers know the difference between an educated, experienced professional and a turnip."

CHANGE CAREERS? WHO NEEDS THE AGGRAVATION?

You can make a career change at any age. I've helped and heard from hundreds of people who have changed careers successfully at 35 and 65. But because of negative experiences in the job hunt, many career changers—especially older ones— have given up.

Gabriella, who lives in Canada, wrote in response to my column on looking for a new job when you want to change careers: "My resume with my credentials puts me into the category of overqualified, but in reality employers feel something must be wrong with me. Why would anybody give up a high-profile professional job with high salary to 'downgrade' herself? I can't even get the interviews to explain myself. Radical change in a career is not celebrated but looked at with suspicion."

What Worries Me Most

Remember the very unscientific survey I told you I conducted on my Web site, asking people if they were more angry at work than they used to be? Everyone who responded said yes. When I asked why—besides idiot bosses, co-workers who frustrate them, and working too much—respondents said they were more angry because they feel out of control, with little hope for the future. This worries me. If there's one thing humans need, it is hope.

It feels good to vent. After all, you've encountered idiot bosses, raw deals, unjust policies, arrogant and reckless leaders, and employers who don't "know the difference between an educated, experienced professional and a turnip," as Sharon so eloquently put it.

Now that you've gotten that out of your system—somewhat—let's see what we can do about getting some hope back into your life.

PART II

A *New* Day in the Life of You

(AND HOW YOU GET THERE)

Step 1

Take Your Pick: Disillusionment or Naked Truth

Y ou should not have to pay a ticket when you park at a busted parking meter and don't know that it's busted. And yet, in at least one city (which will go unnamed), if you do park at a broken meter, tough luck. You fess up and pay up.

I know this because I once parked at a meter in this particular unnamed city I was visiting. And when I returned to my car, tucked under the wiper blade, like a smooshed butterfly with its wings flapping in the breeze, was a ticket for $15. Just ten minutes before, I had forked over more than my fair share, depositing 75¢ in coins. The meter had flashed a mishmash of letters that didn't spell anything, but since it took my money, I figured all was well, and this grouping of incomprehensible letters meant "A-OK" in local parking-meter lingo.

The accompanying flimsy piece of orange paper anticipated my protest of innocence. In so many words it said, Even if the meter is broken, that's no excuse.

This seems unfair. Their equipment is broken; they should not only fix it, but they should also certainly not make me suffer because of their inoperable machinery, right? What incentive do they have to fix it if they can keep collecting money from people who don't speak local broken-meter lingo?

All of this pissed me off, and therefore I refused to pay this ticket and have been driving around as an outlaw ever since.

When I made the decision not to pay—that is, *never* to pay—this ticket, I entered the Pissed-off Vortex. It's hard to get out of it. I insist on gripping for dear life to my belief that I am right and they are wrong and to stand my ground from now until eternity. I warn others about this city's parking policy in the event that they drive there and park at a meter. I curse this city whenever I see its name on a map.

Do I feel powerful? Not really. In fact, just the opposite. Small, inconsequential, and powerless. And, I might add again, pissed. And unless I want to risk being hauled off to jail, I can't drive within an 80-mile range of this unnamed city. Maybe even the entire state, for all I know. I am not only pissed *and* powerless, I am also limited in where I can go. I have sunk deep into the Pissed-off Vortex.

What would it take for me to feel powerful and free to drive wherever I want again?

First, I'd have to face reality. That includes the fact that this city can apparently create whatever policy it wants and is not budging when it comes to this particular one—even though it is unfair and causes suffering to innocent people.

Second, I'd have to entertain a new approach. In this case, I'd need to pay the darn ticket, which by now has accrued late fees amounting to over one hundred dollars.

It's really my choice, isn't it? Which bugs me, too.

This feels a lot like how you may be operating at work. Pissed off and powerless—due to one or more of the unfair issues we talked about in Part 1. Who does your pissed-offness hurt? It's obvious (or maybe it's not): you. But trust me, it's obvious to everyone around you.

People at your work and home and those you deal with in your job search get a taste of your pissed-offness all your waking hours— when you walk around the office, during meetings and phone calls, and outside the office. Just as I limit my ability to get around, you limit your abilities and opportunities to get ahead at work and in your career. As a result of your anger, you're not doing your best work; you're too busy being mad. And because of that, you may not be getting promotions or good assignments, because everyone notices your bad attitude. And who wants to be around that? If you're job searching, your anger may cost you first or second interviews, let alone offers. I don't mean to alarm you, but some people may be avoiding you. You may be giving off mad vibes. Others won't want to refer you to their contacts—and on and on it goes. See how that works? You, too, have now entered the Pissed-off Vortex.

Before we go any further, let me say that anger is not necessarily a bad thing. It can motivate you to do many things for the better. But you need to learn how to use your anger wisely so it doesn't rule you, your life, and your relationships at work and home. Otherwise, you'll find yourself spinning and swirling in the Pissed-off Vortex.

In order to get *out* of the Pissed-off Vortex, the first step is to look at the way things are (like 'em or not). The most pervasive, overarching how-things-are-like-'em-or-not issue facing you and me is this: Life includes both suffering and joy. I would venture to say that most philosophers would agree with me on this point.

Since work is part of life, you will also encounter both suffering and joy within your work life. The degree to which you will suffer will vary. Sometimes it will be intolerable. Bully bosses, discrimination, and criminals posing as senior managers can make your life hellish. But this book is not intended to offer strategies for dealing with bully bosses, discrimination, issues related to illegal practices, extremely hostile environments, or workplace violence.

But there's plenty of other stuff that can add up to bad days at the office and a lamentable career outlook. Interacting with certain customers and co-workers, bosses that can't think their way out of a paper bag, managers who don't keep promises, employers who reward losers and ignore hard workers, corporate decisions that affect your livelihood, poor references, not knowing where you stand, interview processes that resemble a meandering maze without end, and people who don't do what they say they will can all make work . . . well, since we're getting right down to it, a bitch.

So even though the things that are happening to you may not be illegal, they are circumstances and realities that exist, and as a result, you may feel that you suffer unfairly. They will come into play throughout this book, and I will refer back to them throughout these six steps.

Let's look at twelve of these realities. I call them the Naked Truths of Work and Career.

NAKED TRUTH #1

The workplace is not a democracy.

Employers have the power to hire and fire you and do all kinds of things in between.

For example, you may be more qualified than the next guy and the better person for the job you're interviewing for, but the offer still goes to John Junior, the less qualified person, with no job experience and only a bachelor's degree. You may be saying, "That's because they can get away with paying him less." Perhaps. But it doesn't matter why. It's the employer's prerogative to pick whomever they want.

You might be the person next in line for a promotion and for the title of vice president, but the company brings in Olivia Outsider from a competitor to fill that nice corner office with the view. That's their right.

You might work at a company that limits the knickknacks you can hang on the outside of your cubicle. They can do that.

You might have been the most loyal, dependable worker the company ever had in the 20 years you put in, and the company can still decide to close your division. The company has the power to do all this and more.

As a result of their right to do these kinds of things, you might get angry—you might even hurt your chances in job interviews or your relationships at work because of your anger—and suffer. This brings me to the next Naked Truth.

NAKED TRUTH #2
You can be fired pretty much at any time and for any reason— as long as the reason isn't prohibited by law.
This is because all states recognize at-will employment relationships in some form.

So, you can be fired pretty much any time your boss pleases—as long as the reason doesn't involve such things as discrimination, retaliation, prevention from vesting in a pension or other benefit plan, belonging to a union, being pregnant, or making a workers' compensation claim.

The top ten "strange but true reasons used to fire someone," according to Working America, an affiliate of the AFL-CIO, include working too many hours, smoking, holding a second job, and not asking the boss for permission to go on a date.

There is a grassroots effort to pass national legislation to end at-will employment (more on this in Step 6). And getting fired at will may not necessarily be as definitive as you'd think, according to employment attorney Randy Freking of Freking & Betz in Cincinnati (more from him in Step 6, too). But at this point in time, Naked Truth #2 does seem to prevail.

Let me add that what is and isn't prohibited by law and what constitutes discrimination also seems to be changing. There has been a growing focus on "family-responsibility" discrimination, which has to do with workers suing employers for alleged mistreatment due to family-caregiving responsibilities. If you want to know more about this, see the Center for Work Life Law's Web site: www.uchastings.edu/?pid=3624.

But despite any changes on the horizon, the current prevalence of at-will employment relationships might cause you to get mad and suffer.

NAKED TRUTH #3
You are not owed a good job and security for life.

Nowhere in the U.S. Constitution, the Declaration of Independence, or the Bill of Rights does it say you are owed, let alone have the right to, a good job. People seem to mix up some of the phrasing from the Declaration of Independence, which does say, "We hold these truths to be self-evident, that all men are created equal, that they are endowed by their Creator with certain inalienable Rights, that among these are Life, Liberty and the pursuit of Happiness." But there's nothing in there about a right to a good job.

As a worker, you are entitled to a safe workplace free of discrimination. If you want more details about legal rights regarding unions, overtime pay, family and medical leave, and unemployment, there are many sources of information. One place to start is this page on the Working America Web site: www.workingamerica.org/issues/yourrights.cfm.

Getting back to my point, as a result of the fact that no one owes you a good job and security for life, and that employers may decide not to hire you or to fire you or eliminate your job, you might get upset and suffer.

NAKED TRUTH #4
A lot of managers don't know squat about how to manage and lead.

People who have the title of manager or supervisor or who, in their job description, reign over others are not required to have special training. Any fool can do it.

Take the manager who fired his people using a puppet. Or the president of a company who got drunk at night, dictated memos into a tape recorder detailing his disgust for people who leave dirty dishes in the sink and put their feet on furniture, then gave them to his secretary to type up and distribute to his staff the next morning. We could spend all day on the topic of bad managers, but we won't.

The point is, a lot of people aren't very effective managers and leaders, yet they hold sway over you and also do the hiring. You might be ignored, treated unfairly, or mismanaged. And as a result, you may get upset and suffer.

NAKED TRUTH #5
You are not entitled to a creative job with high wages.
Despite what many twenty-somethings think and are not afraid to declare publicly, you are simply not entitled to a creative (or not-so-creative) job that comes with good pay.

The 2006 documentary *Generation Next* includes a discussion among employees of the Los Angeles advertising agency Muse, sitting around a conference table. The agency's owner, Mr. Muse (yes, that's his real name), asks his young employees why they expect vacation time after working at the agency for only a few months. One young woman replies, "We're used to a microwavable world, where we get it *now*. We expect to be millionaires by the time we're forty." Another worker pipes in, "Thirty." An employee of a different company says, "We feel we're entitled to creative jobs with high wages." How disappointed and pissed off many of them must be.

When surveyed, most all workers say they want jobs that allow them to think creatively (more on this in Step 5). But you may not have that at this point. And no one along the way will be ensuring that you get everything you want in your career. The facts are, you are not entitled to a creative job with high wages, you may not get the salary and benefits and creative responsibilities you expect, and you may not be surrounded by fun co-workers. Therefore, you might get mad and frustrated and suffer.

NAKED TRUTH #6
Technology, a machine, or someone overseas may replace you or affect your wages.
To begin with, the whole issue of "offshoring," or offshore outsourcing, and of how many jobs and whose jobs are going elsewhere is quite complex. Economists have trouble explaining it in simple terms. And

I'm not an economist, so don't ask me to explain it. When I've talked to economists about how many jobs have gone elsewhere, the responses are based on a million caveats.

L. Josh Bivens of the Economic Policy Institute (EPI) put it this way: "The short answer is we don't (and nobody does) have good numbers on the number of jobs offshored to where, and what kind of workers they are." The simple answer is it's happening, and the way it's affecting "the U.S. economy and U.S. workers is wages, not jobs," he says.

Others offer their opinions. According to *BusinessWeek*, work processes that were outsourced offshore in 2005 included customer care, for which businesses spent $41 billion; manufacturing, $170 billion; logistics and procurement, $179 billion; and information technology, $90 billion.

Your work could also be replaced by a machine, which can do what you do cheaper. And it's not just low-skill jobs, but decent-paying middle-class jobs that are being replaced by machines driven by technology.

"Automation has more of an impact than offshoring," says Ted Balaker, author of the study "Offshoring and Public Fear: Assessing the Real Threat to Jobs." Academic studies forecast that the number of additional jobs that will be "offshorable" over the next two decades is in the neighborhood of 25 to 40 million, says the EPI's Bivens. If you want to know more about it, here are the sources he cites:

- www.foreignaffairs.org/20060301faessay85209/alan-s-blinder/offshoring-the-next-industrial-revolution.html
- www.petersoninstitute.org/publications/wp/wp05-9.pdf

We also know that countries like China and India have a lot of highly educated workers who will work for lower wages. And this is the case in other countries as well, with young people around the world increasingly getting not only more education than Americans, but a better education, says the report "Tough Choices or Tough Times" by the New Commission on the Skills of the American Workforce: "American students and young adults place anywhere from the middle to the bottom of the pack in all three continuing comparative studies of achievement in mathematics, science and general literacy in the advanced industrial nations."

While this is happening, the global economy is evolving, with more and more work ending up in digitized form. This means, according to the report, "employers everywhere have access to a worldwide workforce composed of people who do not have to move to participate in work teams." This increases the number of American workers at all skill levels "in direct competition with workers in every corner of the globe." And these workers are better skilled and less expensive.

It may also seem that things are more volatile and that more companies are laying off workers. But it's not a simple picture to paint one way or the other. For one thing, mass layoffs have always happened. Today, they tend to affect more people and get lots of media coverage, which can make things seem more unstable.

The point is, offshoring, automation, and the drive for higher productivity and lower costs are happening. No one is absolutely sure how much offshoring and automation is taking place. It just might affect you. As a result, you might get angry and suffer.

NAKED TRUTH #7
Most people ignore you until they need you (or until you offer them money).
Although this dynamic has been around forever, it seems worse these days. Or maybe people are just more obvious about it. It's why job hunters don't hear back from employers, and in general, why others ignore your e-mails and phone calls. They simply don't need you when you have come calling. Do you have a better explanation?

Once, out of sheer etiquette, people were more likely to acknowledge you even if they didn't need you. But now they think they're too busy to be that polite or, because of technology, they can ignore you and get away with it. ("I didn't get your e-mail—it must have gone into my junk mail.")

Although most people respond when they think you're offering them money, even that's not always the case. Several times in the last few years I was in search of contract help for a particular project, and the person I contacted never responded to my inquiry. I learned later they felt they were just too busy to get back to me. Whatever the circumstances, you might be one of the culprits. Think about it. If you are now job hunting but used to be gainfully employed, how many times did you blow someone off?

But now that you're on the receiving end, don't be too hard on yourself. Most of us walk around believing that others should treat us considerately. The problem is you will be disappointed and mad when people don't.

As a result of this observation—that most people ignore you until they need you (so when *you* need them they ignore you)—you might get upset and suffer.

NAKED TRUTH #8
Some people will try—and get away with—highway robbery.
There has always been and there will always be white-collar crime and mismanagement. That's because there will always be people with greed flowing through their veins who are willing to break the law. They may think that the benefits are worth the risk and the chances of getting caught are low. Or that somehow they are justified. Or that they can't compete unless they cheat. Who knows—they might just get a kick out of trying to beat the system.

It seems that there is more of this going on these days. That may or may not be the case. This perception of increased white-collar crime could be due to how much has been written about the high-profile cases of corrupt corporate leaders in the past ten years.

One former federal prosecutor I spoke with who was involved in these types of cases said proven fraud and other shady practices in the past ten years have affected larger numbers of people. Thousands of workers have lost their jobs overnight. Stock prices have been influenced, which can affect retirement money tied up in those stocks. That brings to bear on shareholders. It all has a ripple effect on society.

The bigger the company, the bigger the crime. As the former prosecutor put it, the magnitudes of the crimes morph, getting bigger because there are bigger companies with larger amounts of money available, which leads to bigger crimes and bigger losses to victims.

Going back even further, many people have forgotten about the savings and loan crisis of the 1980s and '90s, in which more than a thousand savings and loan institutions failed due to mismanagement and criminal activities.

Brian Walsh, a senior legal research fellow at the Heritage Foundation, says there has been a big push to go after white-collar crime since the Enron incident in 2001. He claims the government has become more heavy-handed and aggressive in its investigatory techniques, policies, and practices. As a result, as he put it, because the law is now "so full of technicalities and traps for the unwary," it can be hard to establish who has and hasn't really committed a crime.

People do things in a business environment without even being aware that what they are doing is illegal. And since companies accused of crimes don't want to go to court, they'll "plead out," meaning, guilty or not, they'll agree to something less than the maximum possible punishment and forfeit their right to a trial by jury.

That's not to say that the accused senior executives are necessarily angels. But, says Walsh, "There's strong pressure today to convict the CEO even if she or he had no actual knowledge of embezzlement being committed by the CFO."

It's not always CEOs and presidents who commit crimes, either. It can be supervisors of finance departments or plant managers. There are also violations and abuses by government workers of all stripes. Take the $146 million that government employees spent in a year on business for first-class airline tickets, violating government policies that require them to fly coach, according to a Government Accountability Office report in 2007.

On the other hand, according to Dr. Patricia Harned, president of the Ethics Resource Center, the 2007 National Business Ethics Survey of nearly two thousand employees in U.S. public and private companies shows that "despite new regulation and significant efforts to reduce misconduct and increase reporting when it does occur, the ethics landscape in American business is as treacherous as it was before implementation of the Sarbanes-Oxley Act of 2002."

More than half of those employees surveyed over the year said they had personally observed violations of company ethics standards, policy, or the law. "It is fair to say that we have an ethics crisis in America," Harned says.

Another recent phenomenon that can affect the statistics: the so-called deferred prosecution agreement. This is an agreement that lets a company that's been caught doing something illegal pay money and enter into a monitoring agreement with the Justice Department, avoiding criminal prosecution.

The agreement "allows the government to collect fines and appoint an outside monitor to impose internal reforms without going through a trial," and in "many cases, the name of the monitor and the details of the agreement are kept secret," according to a 2008 *New York Times* article. The tactic, which some say is basically "the promise, in effect, of a get-out-of-jail-free card," was rarely used in the past, but usage has skyrocketed in recent years, says the article. And the Justice Department has "put off prosecuting more than 50 companies suspected of wrongdoing over the last three years."

These agreements make white-collar crime even more difficult to track.

All things considered, the statistics about whether there's more crime or not can get murky. But there's no question that some people are guilty, and their actions have caused others to suffer, which contributes to the overall contempt you may feel toward corporate leaders.

But let's look at the nuances of this picture before we scorn and vilify *all* corporate leaders (we don't need to add more aggravation to our lives unnecessarily). Personally, I am sickened by the thought of a trusted leader taking advantage of his or her position to lie and steal. I am appalled by individuals at any level of a company who treat their customers and workers with disregard in any form. I'm horror-stricken when I pick up the paper and read about yet another scheme someone cooked up to increase profits, scam customers, and cheat workers. I think we should stuff all these double-dealing crooks into a helicopter and drop them on their own island to live with and scam one another. So don't get me started.

The sad fact remains that some brazen people will cheat and act in their own selfish interests. Others will mismanage. Depending on the situation, if this happens, there may be actions you can take. But as I've indicated before, I'm not offering strategies related to legal issues. That's somebody else's expertise. The point is, cheaters and those who mismanage can affect your career, livelihood, and future. You might get very angry and, therefore, suffer.

Business *is* personal.

People decide who they want to hire, fire, do business with or help based on business needs. But ultimately, people make such decisions based on how they *feel* about someone. You see this all the time. You've probably done it yourself.

I know when I've needed help on a project, I've picked the most capable person I *liked*. Why wouldn't you want to work with someone you found pleasant to hang around and share your Taco Bell lunch with?

Like it or not, employers who are thinking of bringing you on board will consider personal information they find out about you on the Internet or elsewhere. But people are also willing to do more for others they know—and like. People tell me stories all the time about how they overlooked a mistake committed by someone they knew; went out of their way to help someone they knew; did favors for an associate, peer, or client; or gave a better price to someone they liked or with whom they had a good relationship. On the other side of the coin, look at how difficult (or so it seemed) it was for New York governor Eliot Spitzer to find support when, in 2008, his alleged involvement with a high-end prostitute became public. His past business dealings and his aggressive tactics and style with foes and even colleagues were reportedly the reasons many people didn't go out of their way to help him. He resigned.

A week later, after Lieutenant Governor David A. Paterson had been sworn in as governor, Paterson himself revealed that he had had several extramarital affairs. But "reaction to the revelations in Albany was generally supportive, in part because the new governor, a former state senator, has a deep reservoir of good will among lawmakers," stated *The New York Times*.

Business also feels personal to you because work is a huge part of how most of us define ourselves (more on this in Step 3). But for the point I'm making here, because business is personal, someone may not want to hire you or do business with you or go out of their way to help you or support you for personal reasons. Therefore, you may get angry and suffer.

Nurses, teachers, police officers, firefighters, artists, and writers don't usually make the big bucks.

"There is extreme income inequality in this country," wrote Ben Stein in his that's-the-way-it-is voice in a 2006 *New York Times* article. The top 1 percent of income earners in the United States earn roughly 20 percent of total U.S. income. And the top 5 percent of wealth holders have about 50 percent of all wealth.

You can reach that top 1 percent by working in a field where "torrents of money are sloshing through and you can grab a handful as it goes by"—like finance—Stein says. In other words, "You make money by making money for people who already have money." Or you give them the illusion that you're helping make them money.

The Bureau of Labor Statistics seems to be in agreement. In a report issued in September 2007, the bureau revealed that investment banking paid an average weekly salary of $8,367, compared to the average $841 for all private-sector jobs. And the more money you make for others, the more you get in return. The chief executive of Goldman Sachs Group made record profits for the company in 2007—and got a record $67.9 million bonus.

Other ways to make bigger bucks? "Making people feel and look better, learning how to draw their wills, learning how to make complex things like computer parts in ways that lead your employer to make money and reward you with stock options," says Stein in the *Times*. The key, usually, is having skills that add value.

Generally, the more valued in the marketplace (and, sometimes, the more specialized) those skills, the more you get paid. A surgeon is higher paid than a general medical practitioner. The more training it takes to do what you do—which usually means you're more specialized and the work is more difficult—the more you tend to get paid.

This is not to say that you should go back to school to study law or electrical engineering. And it's not to say that teachers or firefighters, for example, don't have value. Of course they do. It is to say that there are many noble, interesting professions that, based on economics or other issues, do not get paid the big bucks. You still may want to be in one of those professions, nevertheless.

Although I won't go into depth on this issue, I'll offer ideas on things you can influence when it comes to getting more money for the work you do (see Step 6). I bring up the issue of income inequality here to say it's a reality. Professions that may not directly contribute to the financial wealth of others (or make people feel and look better) or that don't require extensive or difficult training are typically not highly paid. You may be mad about this inequity and, therefore, suffer.

NAKED TRUTH #11

Government regulations, laws, and bureaucratic policies are not going anywhere soon.

This stuff is worse in some professions and industries than others, but everyone deals with it to some degree, and detests it. It slows down interview processes. What should be a simple, everyday decision can take forever and a day. Some of my clients who work in larger companies where bureaucracy is thick wait months for someone in an office somewhere to approve a request to bring in a three-foot bookcase or a functioning chair or to transfer an employee to a new role. It took a year and a half for the landlord of my three-story building to fix a gaping hole in the ceiling of my office, and I don't work in a large corporation.

Paperwork and administrative decisions made by someone far removed from your everyday work can get in your way of doing the job you thought you were hired to do. Take nursing. Most nurses get into the profession because they want to care for patients. And many want to leave the profession—where they are sorely needed—because, in part, they feel they can't give safe, competent care due to cutbacks in staff, resources, education, and benefits. Many also face mounting paperwork that keeps them from patient care or deal with increasing regulations from government and watchdog agencies.

Teachers, some of the most dedicated professionals you'll ever meet, are dropping like flies. Morale is low and frustration is high. Many blame government policies such as No Child Left Behind, saying a policy intended to be about school quality is now about statistics and that it has created unrealistic expectations and punished teachers for not meeting those expectations. As a result, many say, "It's just not worth it."

One law—the Sarbanes-Oxley Act of 2002—has caused all types of ruckus. Enacted in response to the major corporate accounting scandals, it established new or enhanced corporate governance that many people say is not only a government intrusion but a major source of worker stress.

As one of my clients who sees firsthand what it takes to comply says, "The law has created mounds of paperwork, and has increased stress put on workers by superiors, who want 100 percent assurance on everything. It's killing people in the process. It's expensive and takes away from meaningful tasks. Compliance costs hit small- and medium-size companies extremely hard. In the end, the same people who would break the previous law will also violate Sarbanes-Oxley."

In Step 6 I'll talk about things you can do to shape and influence policies that affect your work and career. But the point I want to make here is that if you choose to work in an organization—or even if you work for yourself but depend on others' organizations in some way—red tape, rules, laws, and administrative systems exist. By their very nature, to one degree or another, they will get in your way, frustrate you, and slow down your progress. As a result, you may suffer. You may even decide that it's just not worth it.

NAKED TRUTH #12

People rarely act the way you want them to act.

This is hardly news, I'm sure. But I bet you still fight this. That is, if you oversee staff or work on teams, with clients, or with anyone, for that matter. You probably say, "Why can't they just [fill in the blank]?" a dozen times a day, right?

To name a few of these "Why can't they just . . ." moments, there's the co-worker who comes in late. People who don't double-check their work before they send it out. Individuals who don't do what they said they are going to do. Managers who don't tell you what's going on. People who don't respond to e-mails or voice mails. Callers who can't get to the point and who leave five-minute voice mails. People who can't confront others. Managers who can't lead. People who can't admit mistakes.

Why *can't* they just . . . whatever? People have their own good reasons for doing what they do (don't *you*?). This may slow you down, get in the way of something getting done, screw up projects, and waste time—it may even cost you a job or a client. As a result, you may get frustrated and mad and suffer.

These Naked Truths may not seem fair. And there are probably more that I haven't thought of. But they are the way things are as we sit here today. And some of them simply won't change. Throughout the book I'll show you ways you can influence some of these issues. I can't twist your arm into accepting the Naked Truths as the way things are for now, but I wouldn't be doing my job if I didn't try to persuade you further to examine how you think about and react to them. After all, this book aims to help you develop some peace of mind and become more powerful in your life and career.

So with the goal of feeling less helpless, betrayed, and crappy about your career and future in mind, here are your choices in dealing with these Naked Truths.

Option 1: Scornfully Snub the Naked Truths

You know you are doing this when you start your sentences with "They shouldn't do" or "They shouldn't say" when, in fact, they *are* doing or saying just that. Continuing down this path—scornfully snubbing the Naked Truths—will motivate you to keep doing the same thing (and justify it), which will lead to your being disillusioned, stuck, pissed off, and powerless.

For example, let's say you think that people should call you back within 24 hours (or at least in your lifetime) after you've left a message, because you *believe* that people should treat you considerately. But they don't call tomorrow, the next day, the next week, or ever.

As a result, you think, "That jerk never called me back. Come to think of it, neither did that other jerk." So now you're mad. And now you may do one of two things: stop contacting anyone else (Why bother?—they're all jerks who don't return phone calls, right?) or call up those jerky people and give them a piece of your mind.

Now I agree that not responding to your phone calls is down-right unprofessional, witless, and inconsiderate. But if you choose to scornfully snub the Naked Truth (which, in this case, is either that most people ignore you until they need you, or that they simply don't treat everyone considerately), here's what you're basically saying: "This is just totally unacceptable—just terrible. They shouldn't treat me this way." And you will keep saying that and keep on being very mad much of the time, and then react accordingly. And here's what you're doing as a result: ensuring that no one will ever call you again. You will surely suffer.

Option 2: Work With—Not Against—the Naked Truths

This is an excellent choice if you're tired of being mad and you're sick of suffering. When you choose this option, it basically allows you to say: "Mmm, that's a shame." Or: "It's disappointing that things are that way." Or: "These are unfortunate circumstances."

Now you're getting somewhere, and you're ready to go on to the next part, in which you are basically saying: "I need to look at how I can change what I'm doing to make this work better or so I'm not affected in such an adverse way."

Although it seems pretty basic, this is not necessarily easy to do. So I have an exercise to guide you and help you work *with* these Naked Truths. The exercise has four steps. First you'll be looking at what you believe and how it's affecting what you do. Then you'll come up with a more productive way of looking at the situation, which will foster more productive behavior or, at least, different choices.

The four steps of this exercise can help you get on with your career on *your* terms. I call it my "Think About How You Think" exercise.

Please find a quiet place to do this exercise, away from phones and other interruptions. And give yourself a decent chunk of time to complete it.

Also, please note that doing this exercise will not keep you from ever being angry or suffering. You live on planet Earth and you're human. So you will go on interpreting things that happen to you based on what you believe. Things will still happen that you won't like because

> *"Anybody can become angry, that is easy; but to be angry with the right person, and to the right degree, and at the right time, and for the right purpose, and in the right way, that is not within everybody's power, that is not easy."*
>
> —ARISTOTLE

of your beliefs, and you will get mad. Remember what I've talked about—that the most pervasive how-things-are-like-'em-or-not issue facing you and me is this: Life includes both suffering and joy. So, things are going to happen at work and in your career that may upset you.

Doing this exercise can, however:

1. Help you become more aware of what you believe and how that affects what you *do*—giving you time to pause and, then, the wherewithal to change your beliefs and actions
2. Help you change your anger into something productive that can lead to getting what you want
3. Significantly shorten the amount of time you spend being mad and suffering
4. Motivate you to take actions that lead to better outcomes and to feel more powerful about your career and life

. . . .

"Think About How You Think" EXERCISE

STEP 1: PICK THE NAKED TRUTH—OR TRUTHS—THAT APPLY TO YOU.

Go back to Part I, page 20 and look at what you wrote down that pisses you off. Let's say you wrote, "I'm pissed because my boss is a jerk." If your boss is a jerk, it's likely because of Naked Truth #4: A lot of managers don't know squat about how to manage and lead. So write that in the space below.

If you wrote, "I keep getting laid off," it's likely that it happened (and therefore you are pissed) because of Naked Truth #1: The workplace is not a democracy. Or because of Naked Truth #2: You can be fired pretty much any time and for any reason—as long as the reason isn't prohibited by law. Or because of Naked Truth #3: You are not owed a good job and security for life. Or because of Naked Truth #6: Technology, a machine, or someone overseas may replace you or affect your wages. Or, finally, because of Naked Truth #9: Business *is* personal.

Write here the Naked Truth or Truths that apply to you (if you came up with another one, write that):

_____

_____

_____

_____

_____

_____

STEP 2: DECIDE TO START WHERE THINGS ARE, NOT WHERE YOU THINK THEY SHOULD BE.

Like my parking ticket, no matter what you are pissed about, you're enraged in part because it seems unfair. If you want to break the Pissed-off Vortex cycle, though, you have to decide that you're going to start where things are—as unfair as they seem—not where you think things *should* be.

This is not to say that you will roll over and do anything to go along, that you'll give up, or that you'll lower your standards of how you work or conduct your job search. But before you move forward, you have to understand where things are. Then you'll have the awareness and means to decide what to do next. Right now, you're so pissed you can't think straight. Your anger controls you. So, in the space below, write what angers you and what you understand about it.

If you are mad at your boss, you might write:

- I understand that a lot of managers don't know squat about how to manage and lead, and my boss is one of them.

If you have lost your job to technology, a machine, or someone from another country, you might write:

- I understand that technology, a machine, and people in other countries with cheaper labor are replacing some jobs, and that has happened to me twice in my career.

If you are constantly frustrated because people around you cover up and deny mistakes, you might write:

- I understand that people don't necessarily act the way I want them to, and the two groups that report to me cover up errors and don't meet their commitments every day of the week.

If you are mad because you have been turned down for interviews and jobs as a result of something you posted on the Internet, you might write:

- I understand that business is personal and that companies have the right to hire who they want, and because of something I once posted on the Internet I am running into problems.

Write here what you see, accept, and/or understand is going on in your particular situation that is disappointing or unfortunate, but is happening anyway:

_____

_____

_____

_____

_____

_____

Having written that, can you feel yourself moving out of the vortex just a teensy-weensy bit? Do you feel *some* relief?

When you accept facts, you can stop fighting them, says clinical psychologist Carolyn Kaufman. And because you're neither using energy to try to change the thing nor attempting to defend against it in any way, you will no longer experience stress over it, she says. I'd add to that, you can also stop your suffering.

To summarize what the late psychotherapist Albert Ellis said: To be happy, you have to accept. Until then you're going to be angry, angry, angry.

STEP 3: DISASSEMBLE YOUR PISSED-OFFNESS.

This step involves four questions. Once more, so it's easy to refer to, rewrite here what you are pissed about:

_____

_____

_____

_____

_____

Question #1: What *exactly* does or did this person do or what *exactly* has happened to you that has you so ticked?

If you haven't already gotten specific, add more detail:
If it's a person who's making you crazy, what *specifically* does (or did) this person *do* that upsets you? Or what, specifically, has happened to you or continues to happen to you as a result of an event or situation?

EXAMPLES:

- My boss doesn't realize how much I know; she still sees me as a 22-year-old neophyte who doesn't know squat and puts me down in front of others.
- My boss cancels every meeting we schedule to talk about my performance or says I'll get a raise, then comes up with some excuse about why he can't give it to me.

- The software developers who work for me never make the deadlines and our clients are mad as hell—at me.
- I never hear back from companies after I send in my resume, so I'm always sitting around waiting to hear from someone.
- I was fired from my last job and can't get a good reference.
- I didn't get the promotion I deserve, even though I work endlessly.

Write here what exactly this person does or did or what exactly has happened to you that has you so ticked:

_____

_____

_____

_____

_____

_____

_____

Question #2: With that in mind, what do you *believe* about this treatment, event, or situation?

EXAMPLES:

- How dare they Google me! They shouldn't use online information against me.
- I believe it's up to your manager to get to know you, what you can do, and what you need in your career, and to guide you to get there. Mine doesn't do that.
- Everything is about who you know. Since I don't know anyone, it will be impossible to find a new job.
- I believe bosses should do what they say they'll do. Since my boss doesn't keep his promises, I'm screwed and I'll never get anywhere at this company or in my career.
- Getting fired is the worst thing that can happen. Since I was fired I'll never get another decent job.

- I believe companies should respond to you when you go to all the trouble of writing a letter and mailing a resume. Since no one responds to my resume, I'll never get anywhere in my job search.
- The people who work for me should have more integrity and tell me what's going on and not cover up their mistakes.
- You can't be an artist *and* pay the bills.

Keeping in mind what you wrote in Question #1, write here what you believe about this treatment, event, or situation:

_____

_____

_____

_____

_____

Question #3: How is your belief about this person, event, or situation affecting you, and specifically, what do you *do* as a result of your belief?

EXAMPLES:

- Since my boss doesn't appreciate me or know how to manage, I complain to everyone about her, and she and I constantly butt heads. If she doesn't leave soon, I will.
- I work 80 hours a week to prove how much I am worth to the company and that they can't live without me.
- Because my boss doesn't keep his promises or his appointments to discuss my performance and since I believe I'll never get anywhere at this company, in meetings I sit and stew or doodle on my pad. I am sick of being ignored, so I just ignore him.
- I keep sending out more resumes, figuring eventually someone will give me a chance to just interview.
- I rag about my boss, spewing hateful denunciation about her online and on company bulletin boards.

- I sit there in meetings and ask my staff, "Why can't you meet a deadline?" I want to squash them like bugs. I've fired a few.
- I've given up looking for a decent job; I figure I'll never find another one with the same benefits and pay.
- I am staying in my crummy career that I hate.
- I've given up my dream of going to art school.

*Based on what you wrote in Question #2, write here how your belief about this person, event, or situation is affecting you, and specifically, what you **do** as a result of your belief:*

_____

_____

_____

_____

_____

_____

Question #4: How do the actions you just described affect your career and your life?

EXAMPLES:

- I am constantly frustrated by and angry at how my boss dismisses me. I am sarcastic and figure, "Why bother?" because whatever I do will never be appreciated.
- People in my department have quit, telling human resources that I've become intolerable to work for.
- My friends and family are sick of my complaining and even avoid me. My wife forbids any discussion of work at home.
- Since I work so much and take calls at home, on weekends, and even on vacation, I hardly ever see my kids.
- I dread going to work, am bored, and am biding my time.
- I wake up at 3:00 every morning and can't go back to sleep. My health is affected. I have headaches and have developed ulcers.

- I have lost hope that I will ever have a creative career.
- I put my career at risk by saying negative things about my boss online, not contributing, and exhibiting a lousy attitude, which everyone probably notices.
- I question whether I'm any good at anything and walk around in a state of self-loathing. My confidence is the lowest it's ever been.

Write here how the actions you just described affect your career and your life:

_____

_____

_____

_____

_____

_____

_____

_____

STEP 4: REASSEMBLE YOUR POWER.

This step involves five questions.

Question #1: How else *could* you look at this situation?

EXAMPLES:

- I could consider whether I'm doing something that makes my boss see me the way he does.
- I could decide to be more assertive about getting a performance review.
- I could accept that what I posted on the Internet was immature and easily misinterpreted, and look for ways to build a better online reputation.
- I could decide my relationship with my boss is a two-way street.

- I could decide that since companies probably get hundreds of resumes, maybe just sending out resumes isn't the best way to conduct my job search.
- I could entertain the idea that maybe I'm doing something that's making my staff not tell me the truth about what's going on.
- I could decide to examine my priorities and how to change my work habits.
- I could ignore what others are saying about my career dream and decide it's my life—I'll do whatever it takes to get what I want.

*Write here how else you **could** look at this situation:*

_____

_____

_____

_____

_____

_____

_____

Question #2: If you looked at your situation like that, what else could you *do*—other than what you listed in Step 3, Question #3? In other words, how *else* could you react to the person, event, or situation?

EXAMPLES:

- Instead of waiting around for my boss to meet with me, I could write up my own evaluation, setting my own goals, and give him a copy, saying I'd like to set a time to get his feedback; I could follow up until he does keep the appointment.
- I could start a blog or personal page on the Internet that creates a new, positive image and shows me as a professional instead of a rebel.

- I could talk to someone else about my future at the company—even seek out a mentor or coach.
- I could stop sending out resumes and focus on a strategy that gets me in front of people who do the hiring.
- I could ask my staff for feedback on what's not working that's leading to missed deadlines and what would help them.
- I could set a deadline for getting a raise; if it hasn't happened by then I could put into action a job search for a position that's better suited to me with a higher salary.
- I could decide not to take my computer with me on vacation and not to take calls at home after 9:00 p.m.
- I could talk to other artists and see what is realistic and how they have created careers, as well as explore commercial avenues that may allow artists to make more money.
- I could ask other people I've worked with to be my reference.

Write here what else you could do—other than what you listed in Step 3, Question #3—if you looked at your situation differently:

_____

_____

_____

_____

_____

_____

Question #3: What do you *give up* if you decide to look at your situation differently and then act differently?

EXAMPLES:

- I give up blaming someone else.
- I give up feeling sorry for myself.
- I give up feeling so defeated and helpless.
- I give up sitting around my apartment half the day in my pajamas in front of the computer.

Write here what you give up if you decide to look at your situation differently and then act differently:

_____

_____

_____

_____

_____

Question #4: What do you *gain* if you decide to look at your situation differently and then act differently? (Based on what you want your life to be like, is it worth it to choose to look at this differently?)

EXAMPLES:

- The prospect of having a job that I like more and that pays better.
- A career I would enjoy.
- A better salary.
- More responsible, challenging work.
- More control over my career and future.
- More insight into what I need to do to be valued.
- A new group of people who can help me in my career.
- Peace at home and more enjoyable time with my family.

Write here what you gain if you decide to look at your situation differently and then act differently:

_____

_____

_____

_____

_____

_____

Question #5: What can you start doing differently today to get that?

EXAMPLES:

- I can create and follow a daily schedule of job-hunting activities that includes going to professional association meetings, volunteering for a group or cause I believe in, and asking people to meet to get their advice.
- I can take a course in new technology that will give me a leg up on other job hunters or make me more valuable to my present employer.
- I can talk to a co-worker who understands my responsibilities and set up an arrangement in which she handles my clients' calls when I'm on vacation. I can also introduce her to my clients so they have a relationship.

Write here what you can start doing differently to get what you want:

_____

_____

_____

_____

_____

_____

Now that you've gone through all that, can you see how what you *think* and *believe* and then what you *choose* to do because of your beliefs affects your career and life? How, if left unexamined, those can lead you down the path of career grimdom, feeling you are stuck in impossible circumstances? Assuming you're open to trying out this approach with these four steps, here are strategies that will come in handy along the way. For the most part, they are new ways of thinking that replace old beliefs and actions that tend to perpetuate suffering. I call these Attitude Implants.

. . . .

Attitude Implants

Go first

People become my clients in one of two ways. They have either been told by their companies to clean up their act or else (so they seek my help to clean up their act), or they come to me on their own because they hate their lives so much (due to something in their career) they can't stand it anymore.

Every couple weeks we meet, and they tell me about work. Larry tells me about the four knuckleheads he dealt with that week that didn't follow through on what they said they'd do. Or the moron who didn't double-check the details of a report fraught with errors before it got distributed to a hundred people. Kate, a senior executive, tells me about her boss, who put her in charge of a breakfast, telling her to make sure the milk is nonfat and the berries are organic, and who called daily to make sure she was on it. Leo is livid about the fact that Jackson made him look bad in a meeting in front of everyone. Jeanine complains about a supervisor who "kisses his boss's butt." Several people tell me about co-workers having affairs with the boss or stealing their ideas. Charles moans about how he's having zero luck finding a job. Bruce wails about clients who muck up his work. And half the people I talk to are upset because they are over 45 and can't get anywhere in their career or job search. That type of thing and worse.

My clients will go on to tell me how they just couldn't take it anymore and how they let so-and-so have it—on the phone, in an e-mail, or in person—and how it occurred to them halfway through their ranting that this probably wasn't the best approach, even though they were completely justified. Or we'll discuss how badly companies treat them by never returning calls or responding to their e-mails. I suggest an idea of what to do next, or we discuss how brooding about their boss's treatment isn't getting them anywhere and how they might instead initiate a conversation with the boss.

"But why do *they* get to act the way they do?" many clients say to me at this point in our conversation. "Why do I have to be the one to change or always take the high road?"

Good point, but not really relevant.

First, I tell the person sitting in front of me (and I will tell you) that you *don't* have to be the one to change. But, the person or institution you're frustrated with isn't the one who came to get coaching. You are. (That other person may need help in other ways, but that's another story.) This is not to say that the other person's behavior is "right." But he didn't call me for help—you did. And you're the one reading this book—not the other person. So you're the one who will be doing the changing.

Second, you don't control what this other person says or does, only what you say or do. So quit dwelling on it.

Third, if you keep acting the way you are acting, and the other person or entity keeps acting the way they are acting (and why wouldn't they?), nothing changes. If you want something to change, you have to go first. Remember what Newton said: For every action, there is an equal and opposite reaction.

DON'T THROW PITY PARTIES

This is when a group of people are all a-clatter about how so-and-so did this or that and how that makes them mad. Pity parties take place at lunch, over coffee, in office kitchens, hallways, bathrooms, and elevators. They're held at home with family members or friends. Pity parties can have a significant influence on co-workers and the general attitude and tone at your office.

A 2007 study published in *The New England Journal of Medicine* found that obesity can spread from friend to friend, similar to a virus. One person gains weight; close friends tend to gain along with them. These scientists believe that social networks may influence types of behavior. I don't know of any academic studies of pity parties, but my unscientific opinion is that when you stand around complaining with a bunch of other people, it influences you. Pity spreads like a virus.

Other people hold individual pity parties when trying to fall asleep. They replay situations in their head and how they are right and someone else is wrong.

While you may have plenty to be mad about, just remember you do have options: You can take the road of pity or the road that moves you forward.

Embrace a little realistic gloom

People generally tell you that you should be optimistic and upbeat to get what you want. Many psychologists say optimism is critical to mental health. Some studies show that optimists live longer, healthier lives than pessimists. Being optimistic may also help some people cope with adversity. This all seems sound. But degrees of pessimism appear to have advantages, too.

Writer Bob Morris tells of a dinner he was having with friends in Los Angeles and how things got tense after he casually told them he wasn't hopeful about being able to sell the sitcom he had been invited to pitch to four networks. His friends told him he'd never get anywhere with that attitude. He explained, "I know what the odds are." They told him that he should "be positive and it will happen."

"What is so bad about being a little negative?" he asks. "It isn't defeatism. It's defensive realism." It's a "sound way to manage your own expectations." With his preferred "cold shower of negativity," Morris explains, he won't be disappointed and depressed when, because of things well beyond his control, the situation doesn't work out. He cites Daniel Gilbert, author of *Stumbling on Happiness*, saying "it is actually the depressed people who are less deluded about reality."

So what's wrong with a little realistic gloom when it comes to getting what you want at work and in your career? Or put more optimistically, what's wrong with being realistically optimistic? Of course you must do everything in your power to get what you want or to change something. But it's reasonable to hope for the best *and* allow for the possibility that things won't go as you planned or hoped.

One of my clients had been out of work for six months and was desperate to get a position he had learned about. He was very qualified for it, but there was strong competition. We spent hours preparing for the interview. But I warned him repeatedly: Don't count on getting the offer. A zillion things you don't control could happen. It may take months before they make a decision. The company could go bankrupt. They could get bought by a government-owned corporation in Dubai. The manager could choke on a peach pit and die. They could scrap the position. They might offer it to someone the manager meets on an airplane on his way to Tasmania. *Anything* could happen.

Follow up, I insisted. Do whatever you can to remind them how interested and qualified you are, I urged. But please make other plans while life goes on.

It took the company three months longer than it originally said it would to hold interviews. They put the decision on hold for another month after that. The person my client interviewed with originally left the firm, so he had to start from scratch. This went on for nearly six months. Then he got a call that the search was back on and he was in the running. He had three more interviews—and then they put the search on hold indefinitely.* Naked Truth #11 was in full force.

Defensive realism leaves room for making alternate plans and lets you suffer less and move on faster when things don't work out.

NUDGE AWAY THE GRUDGE

Grudges can stick like chewing gum to the bottom of your shoe, sinking into the sole deeper and deeper. A grudge is a result of conditioning, says psychologist Larina Kase. You and so-and-so interact, there's a negative consequence from something that person does, and now you've learned to associate that person with a bad feeling or result.

You may be holding a grudge against a co-worker who isn't carrying his or her weight. So now you're mad because that worker gets paid for the same job as you but isn't doing as much. This seems unfair, right?

Thinking like that is going to get you into a heap of trouble. All because you think things should be completely fair—which is an unrealistic expectation, says Kase. When you think like that, you forget the person you're mad at is probably making other contributions. It also focuses your attention on what isn't working instead of what *is* working.

Grudges can develop after someone you work with has betrayed you or you lose a job or get snubbed in a job search. It can be a minor transgression—missing a deadline, being late to a meeting, or not communicating. Or it can be a big deal because someone you trusted or had forged a partnership with saw a better opportunity and took it.

No matter how small, the transgressions become major over time, say Dennis Reina and Michelle Reina, co-authors of *Trust &*

---

*Five months later a new manager came on board, and my client was offered the job.

Betrayal in the Workplace. If you really get raked over the coals, you may say, "I will never trust again," the authors write, or wonder, "How could I be so blind, naive or stupid that I didn't see this coming?" You might even seek revenge.

Grudge holding is a self-protective mechanism, explains psychologist Kase, which could go back to our primal goal of survival of the fittest. Anyone who undermines our survival (and yes, insults and irresponsible people can be seen as threats to your survival) is to be avoided.

But getting beyond a grudge is the goal. The following tactics can help:

- Write a letter to or even call the offending person, asking for what you need—such as an apology. Your goal is not to change how this person feels or to elicit a particular response. It's to be assertive about *your* needs. (This step is not necessarily appropriate for all situations.)
- Write a list of pros and cons for carrying this grudge. You'll probably notice that the cons outweigh the pros.
- Ask yourself what your grudge is helping you avoid.

"I have spent too much time wrestling with this grudge issue in my life. After someone screws you over professionally—or personally—they typically move on with their life. You, on the other hand, are left stewing, hurt and bitter sometimes for years or the rest of your life. The other person hasn't given you a second thought. You allow them to determine your mood and your happiness. You let them play a role in daily decisions such as whether you'll attend a meeting. You wake up hating them and they wake up thinking, 'Corn Flakes or Cheerios?' The only way you can free yourself is to acknowledge this and let go."

—ONE OF MY CLIENTS, a reformed grudge holder

On the bigger transgressions, after you've vented about what happened, think about what led up to the event. What did you learn from it? That may seem like a lame thing to do; the whole thing may have really pissed you off. But you can actually be stronger for it. Because when someone has let you down, you have the chance to build inner strength—which is something you can always count on.

STOP FRETTING ABOUT INCOME EQUALITY

Remember Ben Stein's comment, "There is extreme income inequality in this country"? Economists will tell you that yes, inequality has risen greatly and will continue to do so. But forget for a minute about the fact that some CEOs make more in one day than the average worker earns in a year. And that wages for most everyone else haven't kept up with inflation. His comment is also a cold, hard fact about professions in general.

"You can become indignant and say that it's a violation of American democratic principles," says Stein. "This is a good way to put yourself into a sanctimonious mood" and "offers some psychic satisfaction."

On the other hand, you can decide that you want to learn skills that will help you make money for other people, or go into a field that the market rewards more handsomely. Or you can decide that you're perfectly happy making less money but doing what makes you feel happy.

As Stein puts it, you can have a decent life "if you just stop thinking that everyone is supposed to make the same wage and just feel happy with who you are."

Step 6 covers things you can influence and choices you can make when it comes to earning more money. Right now, let's stay focused on

"The disillusionment of what they cannot do becomes the reality."

—Twenty-five-year-old Bronx native CARINA LOPEZ, speaking for many of her friends and relatives, in *The New York Times*, November 17, 2006 how you view income and how you can keep yourself from getting so mad about things that seem unfair that it makes you miserable.

EXPECT SOME PAIN IF YOU WANT GAIN

A young worker at a television station once grabbed my arm as I was leaving the studio after an interview. She steered me down a hallway, then, looking to her right and then her left to be certain no one was listening, she whispered, "How do I get them to give me a promotion?"

She couldn't understand why management wouldn't let her be a news anchor—her dream job—after two years of working there. They kept telling her, "You have to prove yourself." She kept insisting, "But I know I can do the job."

"Everyone has to prove themselves. Why would you be any different?" I asked her.

She stood speechless for five seconds, looking as if she had just learned The Meaning of Life. Surely, I was not the first to tell her this.

"Wow, I hadn't thought of that," she replied, then headed down the hall to do, I hoped, everything in her power to prove herself.

The entitlement attitude she first displayed "absolutely drives managers (among others) crazy," says Bill Wiersma, author of *The Big AHA!*

This "me-first," self-absorbed worker "wants to maximize pleasure and minimize pain," he says, with their own needs exceeding "the needs of the organization they are a part of."

The generations of workers who experienced either first- or secondhand the no-holds-barred nineties "were indoctrinated with the false impression that as long as you could fog the mirror, you were entitled to equity, stock options and overnight fame and fortune," says John Putzier, author of *Weirdos in the Workplace.*

Younger workers, he says, seek "every and any opportunity to be seen and heard above the crowd, at almost any expense, short of attaining it the old-fashioned way."

On the other hand, some older workers who believe they are entitled to a good job for life may suffer when they don't get that, either. Whether you're younger or more seasoned, if you're only focused on what you'll get out of the deal, you probably won't get what you want, and, yes, you will suffer. To get what you want and be powerful in your career, you have to think about the needs of your organization.

You also have to pay your dues. Writer Don Hauptman told me the story of one Halloween when he was eating dinner at an Indian restaurant in New York City's Upper West Side. "Costumed kids marched in and out endlessly. The staff was aware of this peculiar American custom and was equipped with a large bowl of candy," he said. He asked the waiter if this holiday is celebrated in India. "No," said the waiter. "We have something like it, but you have to sing a song to get a treat. Here they do nothing and still expect a reward."

EXPECT THAT ALL IS FAIR IN LOVE, WAR, AND WHAT YOU POST ON THE INTERNET

Before the Internet, when employers wanted to get the scoop on you, they would ask around. They'd pick up the phone and check in with people who know people who know other people who might know you. I'm not just talking about former employers and those on that tidy list of references you provided. They would talk to people in your industry and community and anyone else who might shed light on what kind of person you were. It was all fair game and added up to what they thought of you.

The Internet just made it easier to find what was once private or harder to dig up and to make it public—any time and to anyone. So why gripe that it is not fair for an employer to use what they find out about you on the Internet or elsewhere? They got the dirt in the past and they will now. Nothing has changed. Except that you might very well be the one who handed them the information by posting comments or photographs on the Internet that could harm your reputation. If that concerns you, well, don't do it. It's that simple.

DON'T LET THE MOVIES FOOL YOU

Even with the best of careers and jobs, you will not love every minute of every day, and there will be things to endure that are not particularly enjoyable. I know the movies portray jobs and careers much differently, but what can I say? This isn't the movies; it's real life.

That is not to say you should join the disillusioned workers who point out that, after all, that's why they call it "work." Work can be

LET'S HEAR IT FOR THE GRAND SCHEME OF THINGS

You will run into little and big issues throughout your career, some of which really won't matter, many of which you cannot change. If you can't distinguish between the issues that don't matter and the ones that do, you will be doomed and caught up in the Pissed-off Vortex. This applies to what happens to you at work and in life in general.

Take the situation that psychologist Carolyn Kaufman witnessed about a year after September 11, 2001, at the airport in Washington, D.C. With national security on high alert, passengers were required to go through security checks at two different points.

The man in line behind her was "flipping out because he was headed out on vacation and was going to miss his golf tee time." Everyone around him "just thought he was nuts. I finally turned around, grabbed him by both shoulders, shook him, and said, 'You are never going to get on *any* plane if you keep acting like this.' After a shocked moment he laughed and chilled out."

Next time you're getting worked up, ask yourself, In the grand scheme of things, does this really matter?

quite enjoyable. But no matter how glamorous your work, you're better off factoring in the not-so-enjoyable tasks.

Even astronauts have to do that. In a 2007 story about work that aired on National Public Radio, the interviewer was talking to astronauts about their jobs. The astronauts said they only spend about one day a week doing what they love—being lowered into a tank of deep water where they practice spacewalking. Most of their time is spent in meetings and doing paperwork.

QUIT WAITING TO HEAR, "SORRY, I SCREWED UP"

If you feel you have been wronged or hurt by someone you work with or have dealt with in a job hunt, welcome to the club. And if you are waiting around for that person to admit their mistakes, take a seat—it could be awhile.

Whether the mistake made was trivial or tragic, most people "find it difficult, if not impossible, to say, 'I was wrong; I made a terrible mistake,'" say Carol Tavris and Elliot Aronson, authors of *Mistakes Were Made (but not by me)*. In fact, they say, the higher the stakes—emotional, financial, or moral—the greater the difficulty.

Whether it's stealing your lunch, your ideas, or your pension, people will come up with reasons for whatever they did. Self-justification "allows people to convince themselves that what they did was the best thing they could have done. In fact, come to think of it, it was the right thing," say Tavris and Aronson.

I once wrote a column in which I asked people why they steal their co-workers' lunches. Some said they're entitled. Others said, "The company owes me because they don't pay me enough anyhow." Still others justified it by saying, "Everybody does it."

It's understandable that people feel the need to justify what they do—even that they avoid taking responsibility for things that, as the authors say, are "harmful, immoral, or stupid." It's also just as hard for people to say, "I was wrong."

Even so, "We want to hear, we *long* to hear, 'I screwed up,'" say Tavris and Aronson. Research shows that doing so can build trust and create forgiveness with the people who feel wronged. And there are benefits for the one doing the admitting: "When we ourselves are forced to face our own mistakes and take responsibility for them, the result can be an exhilarating, liberating experience."

So why aren't more people doing it? Mainly because we may not even notice that we need to, the authors report. Also, people tend to link mistakes with incompetence and stupidity.

So, quit waiting for whoever wronged you to see the light. As the authors put it, you "can't wait around for people to have moral conversions, personality transplants, sudden changes of heart or new insights that will cause them to sit up straight, admit error and do the right thing."

You've got better things to do.

> *"The lighter the load you carry, the farther you can go."*
>
> —FLIP FLIPPEN, author of *The Flip Side*

DROP THE PICTURE-PERFECT PIPE DREAM

Do you think everyone else loves what they do, knows what will make them happy, and has an ideal work situation, or at least one that's better than yours?

I've got news for you: Most people don't. Even someone who has been an accountant for the last 30 years, since the day after college graduation, hasn't necessarily found it ideal or enjoyable. Many if not most people are frustrated with something in their work and career.

There is no perfect job, no one kind of work "you are meant to do" that will make you thoroughly happy, no one perfect company. If you keep demanding that you find it or feel that you should have it because you think others do, you will always feel unfulfilled.

But if you can accept this imperfection, you can stop demanding that you find the perfect job, company, and career. I'm all for finding work that resonates with you and has purpose and meaning. So, yes, absolutely, without question, set goals, explore, and try out new directions. But end the wasteful search for perfection or you will always be searching and disillusioned.

BE OPEN TO SOMETHING OR OTHER INSTEAD OF ALL OR NOTHING

Let's say you've been turned down for an interview four, maybe five times. Or after several job interviews you haven't gotten a bite. If you're just starting your career, are you grumbling, "No one wants me because I have no experience"? Or if you're over 45, are you grousing, "No one wants me because I'm too old"? Or if you're trying to change careers, have you concluded, "It's impossible to change careers after a certain age"?

This is all-or-nothing thinking, or as behaviorists call it, dichotomous thinking. It's an overreaction to a setback. When things aren't going well you simply decide that's it, it's all over, no one will ever want you.

It's a bad habit to interpret every little setback as proof that you're doomed or that fate has it in for you. It's like concluding from one lousy date that no one will ever love you, explains Sharon Begley, author of *Train Your Mind, Change Your Brain.*

If you're looking for simple solutions—and most people are—you will tend to see only the worst-case scenario and focus only on the unpleasant possibilities. But you're not doomed. To change all-or-nothing thinking, consider what other scenarios *could* happen to you. In other words, what's between the two extremes of all or nothing?

For example, if you interview for the types of roles you think you're perfect for but don't get any offers, you might conclude, "This just goes to show that at my age, I'll never get another decent job." Based on these "rejections," you've concluded no one will ever want you. That's the "nothing" part of all-or-nothing thinking.

Here's what the other extreme looks like: Everyone will want me! For every job interview I have, I will get an offer at the salary I want. That's the "all" part of all-or-nothing thinking.

Neither scenario is truly likely. A realistic scenario—and a much better way to look at this that will keep you from giving up—is to be open to what's in between. What are the other, more feasible possibilities? Again, what's between the two extremes of all or nothing?

- You could get two nice offers out of 12 interviews.
- You could get an offer for a job that is not exactly what you had envisioned but is an interesting possibility.
- You could get an offer for a job you'd love, even though the salary is lower than you wanted.
- You could get no offers but four referrals to people in other companies in a market you hadn't previously considered pursuing.
- After six interviews you could learn that if you got a certain type of training, you would be more competitive and more likely to get an offer.

See where I'm going with this? It's not that no one will ever want you. There may be a downside to a situation, but there's a definite upside, too. It's not all or nothing. So if you can stay open to "something" instead of all or nothing, you can end up with possibilities you

WARNING: HOSTILITY IS RISKY TO YOUR HEALTH

First, a quick science lesson. When you are upset about something—from big things like interacting with a customer, your boss, or your co-worker—to small things like not being able to find your glasses—your body automatically goes into fight-or-flight mode. Unfortunately, that's the only way your body knows how to react to stress.

Thousands of years ago, when animal predators like bears and panthers were chasing us, that worked fine. But the reaction your body goes into and prepares you for is overkill for the kinds of dangers you face today. They're much more subtle and sophisticated—and they occur quite frequently.

When predators attacked, our ancestors needed "stress hormones." This increased breathing, heart rate, and blood pressure, which increased oxygenation of the muscles, providing a boost in speed and strength. Along with that, pupils dilated, palms got sweaty, and more hormones were released. All of this made us better fighters. But today, you experience all of this as emotions like anxiety, fear, anger, and exhilaration.

It's OK for your body to go into this state occasionally, but not all the time.

How many times a day does your body go into overdrive? A lot. Think about how many times you feel stress from interacting with someone. Like when someone steals your lunch from the refrigerator. Or cuts you off on the freeway on the way to work. Each of these tiny and not-so-tiny stressors activates the fight-or-flight response and, over time, all those stress hormones, which are bad for your body. That's why over time, all those stress hormones wear your body down and can cause irritability, anxiousness, depression, and physical illness.

> *"It's not reality that matters, but what you're saying to yourself about it."*
>
> —ANTHONY DE MELLO, author of
> *Awareness: The Perils and Opportunities of Reality*

may not have considered—which may be even better than the all-or-nothing options.

So What Will It Be?

To feel powerful about your career, you must first feel powerful about yourself and your choices. Will you choose to be disillusioned and angry? Or will you choose to work with the Naked Truths and the way things are, then cultivate a new way of thinking and acting? Even if circumstances are not ideal, will you choose not to be hopeless? Will you allow your disillusionment to become your reality? Or will you create your reality based on the way things exist right now?

It's really our choice, isn't it? It may be aggravating as all get-out, but, like my parking ticket, it's reality (more on how my ticket story ends later). Here, though, is your chance to start fresh. Let's make it official.

TAKE YOUR FIRST QUIT-BEING-PISSED OATH

I hereby promise myself to quit being pissed off and start being powerful by "thinking about how I think," so I can choose how I might act differently.

SIGN HERE _____

DATE _____

Step 2

Enough Already: Lay Down Your Cell Phones and BlackBerries

Erin's husband and three-year-old son Stevie played in their hotel pool on the third day of the first vacation they'd taken in two years. Erin sat at a table near them under an umbrella in the shade—her third day of being tethered to her BlackBerry.

Her husband was teaching Stevie how to swim. After every successful paddle of more than three feet, Stevie looked over to his mother for approval. But Erin was too busy hashing out a problem taking place two hundred miles away at the office to notice. Delight drained from Stevie's face. Erin's husband was used to this. Erin had missed Stevie's first steps, too.

Finally, Erin set her BlackBerry on the table and stretched. That's when Stevie climbed from the water, ran to Erin's table, grabbed the BlackBerry, and ran for the pool.

"Watch me!" he shouted as Erin gave chase and grabbed her son. "No, Stevie!" Erin yelled. "That's my work!"

"*No! Watch me!*" Stevie shouted again. Then he threw the BlackBerry into five feet of water.

Erin lifted Stevie in the air. "I said *no!*" she shouted. Stevie started to cry.

Erin realized what she was doing and stopped. Time stood still as she watched her BlackBerry sink to the bottom of the pool, her son crying in her arms.

She clutched Stevie to her chest. "Stevie, it's all right. I'm sorry," she muttered.

Erin held her son tight. And for the first time in a long time, Erin started to cry as she realized what she'd driven herself to be.

How did it get to this? How did it get to the point that people are so entangled with and dependent on their phones and electronic connections that they have become so *disconnected*? That they don't even notice what they have become to themselves and the people around them? Well, I can think of at least six ways. We'll get into that in a minute.

First, no doubt about it, some businesses and professions do expect you to stay within reach, even connected 24 hours a day, which can lead to an addictive love affair with your technological gizmos.

There is even talk of employers being liable for technology addiction (a bit more on addiction later). Some people are studying the issue, including Gayle Porter, associate professor of management at Rutgers University, and her colleague, Nada Kakabadse of North-hampton Business School in the United Kingdom, who published a paper on technology addiction to get human resource managers to take the issue seriously.

But that's not the whole story. You've seen the headlines: ONE IN FIVE WORKERS TAKE THE OFFICE WITH THEM ON VACATION. The same survey found that although only 9 percent of workers say their employers expect them to check voice mail or e-mail while on vacation, the workers feel pressured to check anyway.

Remember the other surveys I talked about? Eighty-seven percent of managers stay in touch to some extent when they're supposed to be unwinding. As the surveys say, it's usually the workers who can't let go of the connection.

Are you one of those people? Are you like many of my clients who tell me it is they who put pressure on themselves? Who feel everything rests on their shoulders and won't put away the technology that enables them to stay connected? Who feel they will lose control, won't be needed or important or in the know if they lay down their cell phones and BlackBerries? Or are you one of those people who doesn't even realize you're sitting there sending text messages, but because you get a little bored you do it without thinking?

You may not like this, but until you have one of those epiphany moments like Erin had with her son at the pool, you will continue down your oblivious, perilous path, all the while complaining that you are a slave to your cell phone and e-mail and must submit to their demands.

THE TRUTH IS, AS BRILLIANT AND IMPORTANT AS YOU MAY BE, MOST OFFICES CAN LIVE WITHOUT YOU FOR A DAY, A WEEK, OR EVEN LONGER.

Most of my clients who can't get this through their heads bring this inability to unhook themselves from technology upon themselves. Much of the time they can't see how their need to control or to be needed or important has got them by the throat.

So when people tell me, "I can't escape my work," here's how we figure out where the problem really lies. We hold a conversation that goes like this:

Let's call my client the Constantly Connected Worker, or CCW.

CCW: I never get a break from work.

ME: What makes you say that?

CCW: I'm at my daughter's soccer game and clients call. I'm home eating dinner. Someone calls.

ME: Do you have to answer the phone? Do you even have to keep it on?

CCW: Well, if I don't, it will go to someone else. (Notice she didn't answer my questions.)

ME: So what?

CCW: Then I won't know what's going on.

ME: So what?

CCW: There could be a problem.

ME: So what? What happens if someone else handles it?

CCW: I guess they could . . . but I feel pressure.

ME: From whom?

CCW: Mmmm. Good question.

In this instance, the pressure is self-inflicted. And, more times than not, that's the case.

. . . .

"Is It You or Is It Them?" EXERCISE

If you feel you can't escape your work and are trying to figure out where the problem lies, pretend you and I are talking. I'm asking you the following questions and you respond in the space I provide here.

YOU: I can't get away from my work.

ME: What makes you say that?

YOU: _____

_____

ME: Is someone holding a gun to your head saying you have to do that—or else?

YOU: _____

_____

ME: If no one is threatening you, what makes you [keep your phone on all the time/check e-mail constantly?]

YOU: _____

_____

ME: How is that affecting your life?

YOU: _____

_____

ME: Do you want that to change?

YOU: _____

_____

ME: If the answer is yes, is there someone you need to have a conversation with about what you are and aren't willing to do, or with whom you can arrange an alternative way of handling these situations that impinge on your personal life? If so, who is that? And when are you going to have that conversation? What else do you need to do?

YOU: _____

_____

_____

_____

_____

_____

_____

_____

_____

_____

How do you know if it's you or them?

- If no one is saying, "You must be on call 24/7," then it's you.
- If no one is saying, "If you're not available 24/7, it will cost you your job/you won't advance/it will severely affect your career," then it's you.
- If there is not a company policy that everyone must be on call, then it's you.

If someone *is* saying these things, or you feel you really don't have a choice, and it's affecting your health, relationships, or life in a detrimental way, please think about whether this is how you want to work and the type of environment you want to be in. The choice is *yours* to make.

. . . .

How I didn't enjoy my summer vacation

My clients who work in information technology used to be the ones who had the hardest time letting go of this connection. Nowadays I see it in all professions—from health-care administrators, project managers, lawyers, and entrepreneurs to accountants, advertising executives, and architects.

Others—even though they bellyache about the constant barrage—get a rush out of always being on top of the issue or the one to save the day (I get into thrill-seeking types later). Or they think they are the only one who knows how to solve the problem at hand. But in enough pain, even they have learned to turn off phones and log out of e-mail.

Some companies realize the potential negative impact and are trying to wean employees off cell phones, fining them five dollars (which gets donated to charity) each time their cell phone rings and interrupts a meeting.

But certain workers can't seem to help themselves no matter what the consequences. David nearly lost his family because he was so afraid to miss a call or not be there at the very moment someone wanted him. What began as a work habit became an obsession. He started taking his phone to the beach at family vacations. Then he moved to the hotel room, where—except for an occasional ten-minute walk on the beach—he holed up pretty much the entire vacation. Eventually, he sent his family on trips to Florida without him. When his boss learned what he was doing—and that his wife was going to leave him—he instructed David to go on vacation with strict orders for the receptionist not to take his calls when he tried to check in.

Alan, another client, called me on a Monday morning, on the verge of a breakdown. "I can't do this anymore," he said, his voice shaking. "On the one day I have off to be with my children, my cell phone rang over and over again with one problem after another." Why not just turn it off? He was afraid he'd look like he was dropping the ball. He couldn't bring himself to turn off his phone even for four hours on a Sunday.

Now let's talk about those six factors that contribute to that need you feel to be constantly connected and available at the expense of your life and, maybe, your loved ones—all enabled by technology.

1. The "I Just Have One More Call to Make" Fallacy

At 8:00 p.m. Eastern time on April 17, 2007, over 5 million BlackBerry users in the United States could not get wireless e-mail. BlackBerry withdrawal could be heard across the world.

The wireless handheld device, which is a mobile telephone that also offers text-messaging, Internet faxing, and Web browsing, was on the blink for ten hours. In those anxious hours many people had a technology meltdown. In a *New York Times* article, Stuart Gold said he started taking his BlackBerry apart, cleaning the battery on his shirt and running around his hotel "like a freak." One woman, who had quit smoking nearly 30 years before, said that experience was easier than being without her BlackBerry.

Officially psychologists have classified technology addiction as an "impulse disorder." They also refer to it as "compulsive overuse." There are computer-addiction services and support groups for this type of thing. Although the American Psychiatric Association said it "does not consider 'video game addiction' to be a mental disorder at this time" (nor similar addictions to technology), "if the science warrants it, this proposed disorder will be considered for inclusion" in the next edition of their *Diagnostic and Statistical Manual of Mental Disorders.* For the record, they're open to suggestions from the medical community as well as the public while they sort this out between now and 2012, when the next edition comes out.

The South Korean government has built a network of 140 Internet-addiction counseling centers, plus treatment programs at hospitals and Internet rescue schools for young people who they believe are addicted to cyberspace. In September 2007, South Korea held the first international symposium on Internet addiction.

Whether or not it is identified as a disorder, something's going on, or so many people wouldn't be discussing it.

OK, OK, you may be saying, now that you mention it, I do check e-mail and respond to calls a lot of the time. Come to think of it, I do it *most* of the time. In fact, I wouldn't be caught dead without my cell phone turned on. But it's just easier to deal with it as it comes up. It's more stressful to have to face it the next day or after I get back from vacation. Or, if you are like nearly half of the Americans who were surveyed by Yahoo Hot Jobs about their vacation days in 2006, you didn't even take vacation, because you had too much work to do. Or, perhaps, like many workers, you didn't take your allotted days because you felt guilty about taking time off. Did you know there's even insurance you can purchase now in case you need to cancel your vacation due to work?

Remember my client the poster child for the Worker Who Has No Life? He traveled three weeks a month and took calls from clients and managers six to seven days a week until 1:00 a.m. He couldn't sleep and complained of his heart pounding so fast that sometimes he couldn't catch his breath. He too felt it would be more stressful to have to return to the phone calls and e-mails that would await him. The phone calls and e-mails never ended. But his life nearly did.

Yes, he's an extreme case. But he and his extreme-worker peers are a growing breed (more on that coming up). Even if you're not that hooked, you may suffer from techno stress. Which is not exactly a picnic in the park, either.

According to Dr. Kimberly Young, director of the Center for Internet Addiction Recovery, signs of techno stress include feeling:

- like personal and work boundaries are blurred
- anxious if you haven't checked voice mail or e-mail in the last 12 hours
- as if your perception of time has altered—that is, what you feel can be accomplished in a day has sped up
- like no matter how much you do, you should still be doing so much more

If your employer does *not* require you to be hooked into the business 24/7, yet you complain, "I have no balance . . . I can't get away from work . . . I'm always connected and cannot drag myself away from it," then you probably have a problem. Please check to see whether you have these signs. It's not making you anything but more powerless.

And as I said in the "Is It You or Is It Them?" exercise, if someone is actually saying you *must* be available 24/7, or you feel you really don't have a choice and you've checked this out to be accurate (you're not just assuming it), you also need to think about whether you want to be in that job.

To sum it up, let me ask you this: Are you waiting for a time when there's nothing to respond to—no calls or e-mails? That'll be the day. You and I both know there will always be one more call you can make. There's always, always going to be one more e-mail to delete or respond to. It's endless, until *you* decide to end it and go have dinner in peace. With the cell phone turned off and the IGNORE button on your BlackBerry turned on.

2. The Busy-bee Addiction

People think being busy is a really good thing. Watch the next time someone asks you how you are. If you say, "Busy," nine times out of ten they'll say, "Wow, that's great!" or "Good!" And it's not just a polite, neutral "good." They're excited. Sometimes their response is tinged with envy. Or just notice how many times someone greets you and their first question is "So, are you busy?"—as if that is what constitutes a worthwhile life.

But don't most people want to be *less* busy? Have you ever heard someone say, "Gee, I don't have enough to do?" Nearly half of working moms would take a pay cut to spend more time with their kids. According to *every* survey I read and nearly every worker I talk to, the majority of people feel overwhelmed with work and say they'd rather *not* be so busy. Yet they seem to think everyone else is lucky if they *are*.

The "it's-great-you're-busy" reaction perpetuates the belief that being busy is a *good* thing. That you're successful and well-thought-of, and that you must be in demand and make lots of money. Your ringing phone gets others thinking "Gee, she must be important." But as you and I know, that is not necessarily so. Even if it is, perhaps you'd like to be less important.

Having less work and more life is a priority for most everyone. Most people refer to this as "balance." More than 90 percent of workers aged 25 to 64 said this is an issue for them in Work+Life Fit Reality Check research. But more than half said they have not discussed how to achieve more balance with their supervisors.

Why, if this is what they all want, won't they have a sit-down with the boss? Well, 45 percent said if they did have more flexibility they might make less money; 32 percent said the boss will say no; 32 percent said even if the company has flexible work programs, taking advantage of them really isn't OK; 29 percent said others will think they don't work as hard; 29 percent said they might lose their jobs.

OK, assuming you're like those surveyed, let's look at this. Why do you think you'd make less money or lose your job? What exactly would the boss be saying no to? What makes you think the company doesn't truly believe in flexible work programs? Why would others think you don't work as hard and why would it matter? Are they—or you—jumping to conclusions? You may have more influence than you think (more on that in Step 6).

I know, I know—in the real world, bosses, clients and co-workers expect you to be there when they need you. Everything is about size, speed, cycle time, bits of data per second, and nonstop, lickety-split decisions. And you know what? To make things faster, bigger, better, and cheaper, there will always be more to do. Others will keep you as busy as you *let* them.

Many of my clients also complain they're just as busy in their personal lives and can't do things they really *want* to do. Work and personal life are one big blur. This makes them resent work even more. When I ask them what they're involved in that they don't want to do anymore, they'll tell me the following:

- "I don't want to be scoutmaster of my son's scout troop anymore."
- "After four years of being in charge of my family reunion, I want out."
- "I've been on the board of our church for ten years. Someone else should do it now."

So why not quit? "I can't," they say. "Who else would do it?" Or "I don't want to upset anyone." "Besides," they add, "I can do some of the work that's involved on my cell phone while I'm driving or on my computer at home." Aha! And how do my clients feel about that? You guessed it: pissed—and as if they can never get away from technology.

So now that they see how their life is one astronomical technology blur and they don't want to be so busy, they are considering alternatives. If they decide to do anything about it, it's usually a simple fix. They approach the people involved with whatever it is they don't want to be involved in anymore, and tell them they want out, and, voilà, they figure out another arrangement. My clients now have 12 to 20 more hours per week all to themselves to do what they *want* to do. In addition, their *work* doesn't seem so oppressive.

Some people just seem to be obsessed with getting things done. They will only sleep four to five hours—a badge of honor to them. "Why waste time sleeping when I could be on the computer?" I heard one of these get-more-done-in-less-time types say.

Just because you're surrounded by technology and can talk to anybody anywhere, anytime does not mean you forfeit your right to peace and quiet or somehow sidestep your body's need to sleep. If you want to stop being addicted to being busy in *and* outside of work—both of which can affect how stressed you feel *at* work—you have to take time to figure out what kind of work and life you really want. Then you'll need to rearrange a few things.

But you'll have to stop being so busy and pay it some mind. Here's my "Do Nothing but This for 5 Minutes" exercise to get you started.

"Do Nothing but This for 5 Minutes" EXERCISE

Sit down in a quiet room and write down the answers to these questions:

1. What do I do all day—at work and outside of work—that keeps me so ridiculously busy?
(Write specific activities you try to fit into 24 hours each day of the week.)

_____

_____

_____

_____

2. How much of that gets done because I'm on my cell phone or computer outside of work?

_____

_____

_____

_____

3. What do I get out of being so busy?
(Does it make you feel important? Are you putting off something you'd rather not do or deal with? Are you trying to control everything?)

_____

_____

4. What does it cost me?
(Relationships? Other commitments? Peace of mind? Regret?)

_____

_____

_____

5. Is being so busy worth it?

_____

_____

6. What activities do I not want to do anymore? What can I do less of to replenish my juices and feel less pressured all the time? What activity can I delete, do less of, or ask someone else to take over?

_____

_____

_____

ALTERNATIVE:
If you have trouble answering these questions, simply make a list prioritizing your activities, then try not doing the activities at the bottom of your list for one week, or ask someone else to do them.

. . . .

3. The "I Can Do 4 Things at Once" Myth

A lot of people boast about the ability to multitask. Yes, they proudly proclaim, they can listen to what someone is saying, read and respond to e-mail, delete old messages on their cell phone, file papers on their desk—all at once. Right.

Their e-mail responses will be peppered with errors, unknowingly curt in tone, and perhaps unclear. Ask them what the person in front of them just said and they can't tell you. Just as important, ask the person doing the talking how they felt while the other person was doing three other things while "listening" to them. They'll say, "I felt invisible, that the person didn't give two hoots about me." This leads to another set of problems—but that's a separate story.

Or how about the mom who drove out to the ball field to cheer her kid on at a softball game but instead sat in the stands on her cell phone talking to a client? These are the people who complain the loudest about how everything is a whirl of activities and how unsatisfied they feel about their lives.

It's like watching the Bloomberg TV channel. I'm sure it's very helpful, but it's got up to six different running displays on the screen at one time: stock prices and lists of companies for the Dow and NASDAQ, NYSE losers and movers; market data concerning mutual funds, the S&P 500, and futures; *plus* a person talking. I want to listen to what the person is saying, but I keep getting distracted by the stuff on the screen. Bottom line: If you're trying to do two things at once (let alone five or six), both will suffer.

Walk and chew gum at the same time? That I'll give you. But even with your brain's 100 billion neurons processing information at a rate of up to a thousand times per second, you simply cannot effectively do two tasks at the same time, say Vanderbilt University neuroscientists Paul E. Dux and René Marois.

For quite some time researchers have believed a central "bottleneck" exists in the brain that prevents us from doing two things at once, according to an article in *ScienceDaily*. But Dux and Marois have identified the regions of the brain responsible for the bottleneck. Not to get all scientific, but their research offers neurological evidence that your brain can't effectively do two things at once because the bottleneck is caused by "the inability of the lateral frontal and prefrontal cortex and the superior frontal cortex to process two tasks at once." This is one reason the two neuroscientists also say they don't use their cell phones while driving. You simply can't do both well. And, apparently, they value their lives.

But enough with the science. It's just plain not doable, smart, or, in the end, truly productive. And it's just plain common sense that when you try to be two places at once you end up being nowhere at all. But, you say, "My boss (or client) *expects* me to multitask." Or, "I'm constantly being pulled in ten different directions, so I have to do ten things at once. They don't give me the option. So I can't get away from my computer (or phone)."

Remember Naked Truth #12: People rarely act the way you want them to act. So, first you have to decide that this way of working isn't working—no matter how others act. Of course your particular situation, role, and company culture will affect this. But in the end, you may decide that you'll have to seek a workplace, career, or culture more conducive to meeting *your* wants (more on this in Step 5). First, consider what you *do* want. Then come up with alternatives. Here is how three other people looked at their workplace, how they or others acted—which in turn affected them—and what they decided to change.

The "I hate my phone" woman

I have a client who hated her phone but always answered it. No one told her she had to answer it whenever it rang. It was her idea. When the phone rang she became a crazy person. She screamed at it—"Shut up!"—before answering it because it was pulling her away from the project in front of her. It wasn't the fault of the people calling. They didn't know she was busy. She was the one who let it control her. Half the time it was a friend or relative who wanted to talk about personal problems. She'd talk and talk and end up staying until 2:00 a.m. to get her work done.

We discussed this and she made a decision: She would not answer the phone when working on a project that required concentration. She'd just let it ring and go to voice mail. When the time was right for her to set aside her other work, she would check messages and respond. She also asked friends and family not to call her at work.

No big deal, right? Then why was it so hard to do? It was not a pretty picture the first day she tried it. The phone would ring, and she'd scream, and her fingers would automatically grip the headset. Then she'd stop herself. She survived, and so did the people calling. This simple choice changed everything. Instead of always being annoyed about interruptions and trying to do two things at once, she stayed focused on her work and called people back when she could give them her full attention. She's no longer a lunatic, and she doesn't scream in her office anymore. And most of all, she feels good about her work.

The no-calls-no-computer-for-an-hour administrative assistant

An administrative assistant in New Mexico told me she used to be frustrated all the time because she never had time to reflect, plan, and organize—tasks she enjoyed and that enabled her to be effective at her job. She'd start, then get interrupted by people wanting her to do things, or by phone calls or e-mails. One day she decided to make a concerted effort to focus solely on these things that gave her great satisfaction for an allotted amount of time. Instead of treating them as if-I-can-get-to-them items, she made a point to get them on her schedule and do nothing else.

She put a sign on her desk saying I'M IN THE TOMB, meaning the library. Anyone who came looking for her knew she was in organizing mode for the next hour. If they really needed her, they knew where to find her. But no one has ever hunted her down since she started this ritual. As a result she gets all her work done and takes time to focus solely on these tasks, making her one happy camper.

If your employer does expect you to do two things at once—or won't allow you to give a task the focus and time it requires to be done right—and it's affecting your ability to do the quality work you expect of yourself, you may decide this company is not a place you want to be.

On the other hand, sometimes it's a matter of picking and sticking to your priorities or finding a way to operate that works for others as well as for you.

The "be here now or not" exec

A senior executive I work with told me he noticed his staff members weren't fully participating in meetings when they called in via speaker phone. "I knew what they were up to—checking messages and answering e-mail instead of focusing on the meeting," he said. As a result, people weren't contributing their all, and he felt *he* wasn't doing his best work since his staff wasn't really "there." So he began requiring face-to-face attendance at his meetings. People showed up but brought laptops and BlackBerries and messed with those. So he banned the electronics, saying, "You're either here or you're not."

This same executive told his administrative assistant to stop forwarding calls to his cell phone when he was driving into the office in the morning. "I don't want to be disturbed and dealing with issues while I'm driving. It can wait until I get there."

Let me add that this executive, who works for an international company and has thousands of employees, working in six time zones, is one of the most productive people I've ever seen and extremely well liked and trusted. He rarely if ever is angry about, frustrated by, or overwhelmed by his work.

You're the Decider

There will always be distractions, new priorities, phone calls, and e-mail to pull you away from what you're doing. But at any given moment, *you are the one* who gets to decide how you're going to deal with whatever comes at you. Very few people have a job where they do only one thing. But you can create more satisfaction in your work and make a conscious decision to not let technology and others run you. How? By managing the technology and your response to those who think you can do three things at once. Ways to do this include:

- reading and responding to e-mail at two or three set times a day instead of while you're on the phone or while someone is in your office
- asking someone if it's OK to get back to them when you've completed the thing you're working on
- staying focused on something until it's done or at a good stopping point
- setting boundaries about how and when you talk to others

You may be busy, but you're still the decider.

3 MORE REASONS TRYING TO DO 4 THINGS AT ONCE ISN'T GOOD FOR YOU

1. Constantly switching gears causes stress. You make mistakes, lose your perspective, and don't perform well at the things that you normally would.

2. Trying to do several things at once reinforces the feeling that you're just existing to get something done. There's not much satisfaction in that.

3. Being constantly distracted makes it hard to be creative and engaged.

"So You Think You Can Multitask"

This test requires two other people and you. Go find these two people and take a seat. Ask person A to tell you about his or her day. As person A is speaking, you and person B are going to talk about how you each slept last night. So, you're going to listen to person A talk about his or her day while holding a conversation with person B about last night's sleep. Do this now for two minutes.

How did it go? What did you learn about person A's day? What about person B's sleep? What did you conclude about how effective you are when doing more than one thing at a time?

4. The Thrill-of-it-all Addiction

I felt like I needed a vacation after I'd meet with Jonathon, a fortyish senior executive who got a rush from the intense challenges he faced every day as CFO of a growing international company. He made great money, worked with smart people, and got a kick out of zipping through phone messages on his 5:00 a.m. drive to the office, then whipping the butts of everyone who worked for him for the next twelve hours. The people around him were dizzy with things to do and problems to resolve and had orders to be more efficient while they were at it. I was exhausted just listening to him talk about it.

In his hyper, fast speech, he'd complain to me about his crazy life. "I'm flying to Chicago at 3:00 today to see my son for a day, then back to Tennessee tomorrow for meetings with operations. In two weeks I fly back to pick up my son to be together for two days. I've got to prepare for the annual meeting and the sales convention in the meantime." Then he'd laugh.

"You sound like you like it," I said, to which he replied, "I guess I do get a thrill out of it all."

He is part of a new extreme ethos that has taken over the workforce. The report "Seduction and Risk: The Emergence of Extreme Jobs," by the Center for Work-Life Policy, describes the new breed as workers who give huge amounts of their hearts and brains to the job. There are 1.7 million of them, the organization claims, driven by global operations, modern communication technology, a client-is-king culture, and gargantuan rewards at the top. We have created "a new cadre of superworkers grappling with an American Dream on steroids," the center adds.

Many—like my client—are hooked. "They love the thrill, the meaning, the challenge, the oversized compensation packages and the brilliant colleagues. They are not only productive; they are devoted," says the report. And the majority surveyed "are exhilarated by their jobs and feel the oversized burdens are freely chosen or self-inflicted." Their companies love them, too, these engines of "innovation, productivity and profit."

But just as the report goes on to describe, my client was exhausted and teetering on the edge of a cliff. That's where I came in. His boss was worried about him, and the people who reported to Jonathon who were dropping like flies.

His type, says the report, "are losing sleep and suffering anxiety-related disorders. They have deeply compromised their personal lives" and suffer from "brown out (a decline in productivity due to overload) and burn out," two things that the center's research shows compromise these workers' value and squelch innovation. Yes, that was Jonathon.

Jonathon kept telling me he'd only live like this another two years—then he could quit. Maybe. While the research does show that the majority of "extreme" professionals may want to quit, it also shows that older males are more likely to hold an extreme job. (The last I heard Jonathon had taken another job. His other company had gone out of business.)

The research also shows that while women do hold these extreme jobs, at a time when the demands of parenting and caregiving have also become more extreme, they simply can't—or choose not to—work these 70-hour weeks.

I am not saying that working hard and being continually plugged in is necessarily dangerous for everyone—although it might be for those *around* them. Some people won't suffer physically and emotionally. But it sure takes its toll on the people *I've* seen who work at this pace consistently. It's also been extremely difficult to make headway with Jonathon types. It wasn't until some of them lost key relationships, went through a first or second divorce, or developed health issues that they paid attention to how their work affected them. By then they were really pissed—at their companies and at themselves.

If you are seduced and preoccupied by the thrill of it all and feel anxious and/or your relationships are suffering, answer these questions to see whether it's worth it:

Is Teetering on the Edge of a Cliff Worth It?

- What do you get out of it? (Power and status? Safety? Money? Do people like you?)
- What do you risk?
- Is it worth it?

Who doesn't want recognition, status, and love? But are you paying too high a price to get it? Are you paying attention to the effects on your body and life? In a 2007 interview on National Public Radio, the Rock and Roll Hall of Famer Bo Diddly said, "We're a nation of slow understanders." If you think you qualify as a superworker, what will it take for you to understand what you're doing to yourself and the people around you?

5. The Rush-to-do-whatever Addiction

Whether you get a kick out of zooming through the fast lane or not, like everyone else you probably complain about how rushed you feel to get things done. OK, I exaggerate. Not everyone. But *a lot* of people.

I don't know which came first—the mad rush to get things done or the tools (including the technology we just talked about) that were intended to help you get things done faster. I suspect it's both. There's pressure to speed things up. And the tools enable you to speed up,

> "In America, only monks possess a firm sense of 'enough.'"
> —NELSON ALDRICH, *The New York Times Magazine*

DO YOU HAVE WORKER FATIGUE?

Fatigued workers cost employers $136.4 billion each year in health-related lost productivity—$101 billion more than nonfatigued workers, a study in a 2007 issue of the *Journal of Occupations and Environmental Medicine* revealed.

Researchers for the study defined fatigue as "a feeling of weariness, tiredness or lack of energy." Symptoms include weepiness, irritability, reduced alertness, lack of concentration and memory, lack of motivation, increased susceptibility to illness, depression, headaches, giddiness, loss of appetite, and digestive problems.

feeding the urge to move faster. Whichever came first, everything has become a race, and most everyone has turned into a mad-rush fiend.

States race to hold the first political primary, retailers bring out Christmas earlier every year, and schools ask 13-year-olds to declare college majors. People talk so fast you can't understand them. They rush to get to the end of whatever they're doing so they can rush out to do whatever they think they'd rather be doing so they can rush through that. In the book *Travels with Alice*, author Calvin Trillin describes American travel this way: "Americans drive across the country as if someone's chasing them." That seems to describe just about *everything* people do.

There's also the rush to get to the next level of your career. To get to the American Dream—something people used to work toward steadily over many years. The path to that dream has shifted from creating a "vision for the future that includes time, sweat and ultimate success" to seeking the shortcut to wealth, says Matthew Warshauer, professor of history at Central Connecticut State University. In his article in *American Studies Today*, he says the dream "has become more of an entitlement than something to work towards."

Along with that comes the rush to get rich. For many that turns into the rush to have more than the next guy. They then become the wealthy who *don't* feel wealthy and are perpetually stressed, striving for more.

A 2007 *New York Times* article headlined, in part, MILLIONAIRES WHO DON'T FEEL RICH focused on anxious Silicon Valley workers who have banked more than $2 million and don't feel particularly fortunate, partly because they're surrounded by people with a lot more wealth.

The rush to get rich takes its toll on "useful work"

More and more people are latching onto opportunities either within their fields or in different fields that offer significantly higher incomes, said a 2006 *New York Times* article about the quest to become abundantly wealthy.

They are moving from academia to Wall Street, for example. And "business-school graduates [are shunning] careers as experts in, say, manufacturing or consumer products for much higher pay on Wall Street," says the article.

The American Bar Foundation found in its surveys that "fewer law school graduates are going into public-interest law or government jobs and filling all the openings is becoming harder," the article reports.

Young doctors often bypass lower-paying fields. "The Medical Group Management Associations, for example, says the nation lacks enough doctors in family practice, where the median income last year was $161,000," according to the *Times*.

The net result? As New York University economist Edward N. Wolff is quoted as saying, it's "draining people away from more useful work."

Forty-three-year-old Gary Kremen, founder of Match.com, estimates his net worth at $10 million. He works 60- to 80-hour weeks because he doesn't think he has enough money to ease up. Celeste Baranski, another working-class millionaire of Silicon Valley who is anxious about her financial future, founded a software company. The article describes her as "resigned to the sleepless nights and other stresses that await her."

6. The Quest-for-balance Fallacy

This is going to be brief, because my point is simple: It's not that the idea of "work/life balance" is a bad thing; it just *isn't* a thing. The whole notion of "work/life balance" implies that it's something "out there" that you can strive for and get. That if you spend less time connected to work, you'll have "it." That's not how it works.

Here's where you find balance: in knowing what *matters* to you. If you know what matters most to you in life, then you live your life accordingly and won't need to seek "work/life balance." And that means you will have one less thing to be busy trying to do. Here's a simple exercise to help you:

"Balancing Act" EXERCISE

1. Turn off your cell phone, computer, and any other gadget that buzzes, beeps, or interrupts you.

2. Ask yourself, What do I want from my time?

Is it learning something? If so, what?

_____

_____

Is it getting to know someone? If so, whom?

_____

_____

Is it supporting someone or taking care of something or someone? If so, whom or what?

_____

_____

Is it improving, changing, creating, building, enjoying, or experiencing something? If so, what?

_____

_____

3. Now that you know what matters to you, you can make room for the activities and interests that support that. So now, ask yourself:

What activities are those?

_____

_____

What kind of limits do you need to set on the time-sucking stuff that can wait until later and that might distract you from those activities?

_____

_____

_____

Who do you need to say no to—nicely—who could otherwise keep you from what matters most?

_____

_____

_____

What else do you need to change or do so you're not angry that something is keeping you from what matters most?

_____

_____

_____

. . . .

THE DISTURBERS OF YOUR HARMONY

Thomas Jefferson referred to the English as "the disturbers of our harmony." Today the disturbers of your harmony can be your cell phone, e-mail, and other things that go hand in hand—anxious competitiveness, measuring your life against others', the push to get things done, believing you can accomplish more in a day if you can speed up what you do, and the rush to get rich.

Time Flies When You're on the Phone

Technology is not a bad thing. I'm not against it. I've worked on a computer since 1985 and had a cell phone since I can't remember when. But technology can become an all-devouring thing. Of course dealing with it is part of doing your job. But sometimes it needs to be put to bed. At

---

Make friends with people, not just technology

If you have at least three close friends at work you're 46 percent more likely to be extremely satisfied with your job. This is one finding from the Gallup Organization based on interviews with over 5 million people and research compiled by Tom Rath, author of *Vital Friends*.

When you've got a best friend at work, you are seven times more likely to be engaged in your job, meaning you are eager to work with passion and creativity. You also have fewer accidents, are more engaged with customers, and are more likely to be innovative and share ideas, according to the research.

Friends, scientists have found, are "catalysts for high points in any given day," says Rath. The "dreaded commute to work is tolerable" and the "most tedious work activities enjoyable" with the presence of a friend. Look around at the other people you work with and consider the benefits of making a new best friend—or two or three. Because those surveyed who had at least three very close friends at work were not only more likely to feel better about their work, but they were 85 percent more likely to be satisfied with their lives.

And while we're on the subject, next time you get ready to send an e-mail, think about whether a phone call or face-to-face conversation might be a better way to connect—not to mention a more satisfying one.

---

a certain moment you must say to yourself, "Just because I can do this [something on your electronic gizmo], should I? Must I?" If you don't, you will be at the mercy of it, pissed off about your work and life.

Before you know it, you'll look back at the week and say, where did the week go? Then a month and another year will pass, and before you know it, you'll look back at a lifetime and say, where did it go? Where did that time with my family and friends go?

Before it gets to that, take the time to notice how often you spend your days constantly twirling, reacting, and juggling, fueled by your cell phone, computer, BlackBerry, and other electronic gadgets just doing their jobs.

TAKE YOUR SECOND QUIT-BEING-PISSED OATH

I hereby promise myself to quit being pissed off and start being powerful by noticing how much my computer, cell phone, and other electronic gizmos run me and by turning them off when they interfere with what matters to me most.

SIGN HERE _____

DATE _____

Step 3

Have a Brush with Greatness (Even If No One Notices)

Marty sat squeezed between the CEO and senior vice president of operations. The boardroom was somber as the executives took turns around the massive slab-of-wood conference table explaining what should be done since their biggest client was about to jump ship. Millions of dollars were at stake. Marty had just been named to the troubled account and had met with the client, read all the back-and-forth e-mails, and knew better than anyone what had gone wrong.

"I can't speak up and say what I think to the CEO's face. I'll be dead meat. My career will be over," he thought to himself. Except for a few "Yes, I agrees," he zipped his lips, keeping to himself what he knew should be voiced but might be politically dumb to divulge.

"I felt like crap," he told me. "I hated myself for not saying anything. I let down the company. I let down the client. But it was just too risky. Most of all I let myself down."

I don't know anyone who gets up and goes to work determined to do a rotten, stinking job. People just don't head out the door saying to themselves, "Today I'm going to have the crappiest call with my sales team I can possibly have and leave everyone feeling despondent." Or "Today, I'm going to do everything in my power to louse up our system so software goes haywire and shuts down all 12 call centers around the world so no customers can get through!"

Most people take enormous pride in their work and want to do their damnedest. I'm certain you are one of them. You wouldn't be reading this if you weren't.

Not only that, if you're like most people, you want to know that the good work you do *counts*. That you're a part of something. That you help improve human existence, materials, objects, processes, or techniques. And that the success of that something—whether it's manufacturing medical equipment that saves lives, writing ads that entice parents to take their kids to an aquarium, or designing aesthetically pleasing buildings for people to live and work in—depends, in part, on you and your abilities. That feels pretty darn good, right?

But maybe, because of your boss, who you think is a numbskull, or of the productivity-obsessed, eye-on-the-bottom-line culture of your company, you feel that what you do or say doesn't matter, never has and never will. Or that you can't make a difference or count because no one will listen to your ideas. Or that you can't speak up because you don't want to rock the boat or be seen as someone who hampers progress or slows things down. Mind you, no one has told you *not* to speak up, but you've decided it's best not to if you want to survive.

And since you think it's best *not* to contribute your ideas, you don't feel like you can do good work. Any of that sound familiar?

So, why are you letting others decide the quality of your work and career?

It's no wonder you're pissed. Here's another thing I'm certain of: *If you don't do the best work you know you're capable of, you will feel like crap. And if you feel like crap, you're not doing your best work.*

You're not going to like this but, if you're not doing the best work you're capable of because you're afraid of what might happen or what others will think, that's *your* choice. It's not the company's fault. No one else can make you do bad work.

You may think there are consequences to doing or saying something others won't like. There just might be. But unless someone is holding a gun to your head, and you think they'll shoot if you speak up or do or say what needs to be said or done, you have the choice of whether or not to offer your insight.

So I contend that part of why you might be pissed is because *you're* not doing the greatest work you're capable of. It goes back to what I just said. Who doesn't like to feel good about their work? To know that their efforts are worthwhile and to be recognized for it? But that requires *doing* great work. If you're not doing great work, you won't feel your efforts are worthwhile. And no one will give you recognition. And that also makes you unhappy.

Remember the vicious Pissed-off Vortex from Step 1? Here it is again. Only this time your pissed-offness is getting in the way of your doing work you feel proud of, work that's challenging and makes you feel you've made a difference.

This reminds me of George Orwell's 1946 essay "Politics and the English Language," in which he describes how the effect of one thing can become a cause, which reinforces the original cause and produces the same effect in an intensified form. He writes: "A man may take to drink because he feels himself to be a failure, and then fail all the more completely because he drinks."

You probably don't even know how you're getting yourself caught up in this kind of tizzy. So let's look at how you may be contributing to the problem.

The I'm Afraid, You're Afraid Tizzy

I can hear you protesting, "It's not that simple. You don't know what it's like at my company."

For the record, I'm not talking about situations where you're afraid to speak up because you're being bullied by a supervisor. That's different. Those are hostile environments where bullying ranges from humiliation and screaming to throwing things and physical assault. Those call for a different approach.

I am, however, talking about a workplace where:
- you feel pressure to keep your mouth shut
- you feel pressure to not do what needs to be done
- you feel uncomfortable asking questions that need to be asked because:
- you don't want to look bad
- you think no one will pay attention
- you think it might upset the apple cart
- for whatever reason, you just don't feel comfortable speaking up or doing what it takes to do quality work

Believe me, I am very aware of this ongoing tension you feel to conform to the status quo or do the right thing. Pretty much everyone (from those who work for companies to those who have their own businesses with clients to answer to) feels this way—afraid, nervous, and uncertain about what to say or do. So stay with me here so we can focus on the only thing you control: you and your choices.

Now I won't be covering every predicament you might find yourself in that inclines you to hold back your greatness. But based on my clients' experiences in small, medium, and large companies, and in their own businesses and your letters, here are the most common predicaments. These can apply in meetings or conversations with co-workers, staff, managers, clients, or customers—even job interviews.

Check any that apply:

☐ **You don't share brilliant or innovative ideas that occur to you.**

What's behind it: When you get a brilliant idea, do you twiddle your pen or pick at your fingernails and think, "If I suggest [fill in the blank], they'll think I'm a fool? They'll stop inviting me to lunch and strategy meetings (or whatever it is that keeps you in the know). It's not politically smart."

What you're really doing: You're frittering away your creative input—things that make for greatness. Not sharing your brash and bold ideas also makes you feel undervalued, unappreciated, and like you're not making a difference. This leads to—guess what?—being pissed off.

☐ **You don't challenge the status quo or speak up when you know the direction a project is headed in is wrong.**

What's behind it: When you know a project is doomed or can see it going in the wrong direction, do you keep your lips zipped because you figure no one will listen anyway? Or it's not your place to speak up? Or it wouldn't be smart to rock the boat with an unpopular opinion? Or because the last time you spoke up you felt scorned and mocked?

What you're really doing: When you stay mum you're keeping your great insight inside, throwing away the chance to save the day and get the recognition you deserve for being smart, confident, and committed to doing the right thing. This is what not only gets you noticed but also makes for greatness and feelings of satisfaction. But when you keep your valuable contributions to yourself, how does that leave you? Pretty pissed.

☐ **You only do what's expected of you to get by and nothing more, or you hesitate to try new things that are a little risky.**

What's behind it: You would like to try a new role or help out in a different department that could use your expertise, but you figure, "Hey, I've kept my job this long, why do more? Besides, my manager is on the insecure side." Or "He seems happy enough with my work. I wouldn't want him to feel threatened." Or, when it comes to trying out a new way of doing something, do you think, "My company expects me to be perfect, and if I make a mistake, it could be curtains. So it's best to keep my head down rather than getting smacked for trying something new"?

What you're really doing: You're making yourself invisible. No one will notice you and it will be hard to move up, take on more responsibility, or increase your salary. You may feel comforted thinking, "At least I'm secure." But that may not be the case. Besides, you leave yourself feeling empty and unchallenged and undoubtedly pissed that you have such a boring job where you're just biding time—not to mention how soul-sapping that is.

☐ **You silently sizzle or complain to others when someone really ticks you off instead of confronting that person.**

What's behind it: When it comes to confronting a feckless nincompoop or anyone who has it coming, do you figure it's probably best to let sleeping dogs lie? You don't want to create problems. Besides, you might make things worse. Even if your co-worker is taking credit for your idea or saying something really stupid to the customer, ruining a relationship that took years to build, you don't think you should say anything. You don't want to upset the person you have to work with. Or hurt her feelings—what if she cries?

What you're really doing: You're keeping your observations and frustrated feelings to yourself and letting them build up inside you. This almost always makes the issue and the relationship worse. You probably make subtle hints or crack snide, sarcastic remarks to the person you're annoyed with. One day you may just explode. As a result, you feel like crap now and will feel even worse if do you lose it in a moment of pent-up anger. It's anyone's guess what that could lead to.

Un-great-like Behavior All Over the Place

Many of my clients do these exact things. They don't realize it until they're telling me about a meeting or a conversation and I say, "Wait, let's talk about that. What stopped you from telling everyone that the project was about to fall flat on its face?" Or "What made you not spell out clearly what you needed to make the project successful?" Or for clients who are job hunting, "What stopped you from asking about the company values or exactly what's entailed and expected in this position?" (More details on this last one in Step 5.)

I tell them, like I'm telling you now, if you don't want to feel like crap, and if you don't want to miss out on the chance to do great work, you'd better pay closer attention to what's going on in your head and how you're reacting so you *can* make different choices. Only then will you be able to:

- Speak your piece
- Open up to share your valuable advice and brilliant insights
- Take a position that challenges the conventional wisdom
- Say what needs to be said
- Do work that's beyond your job description
- Stick to your principles
- Use your good judgment
- Ask questions that need asking

All of this is what a good company is paying you for, and it's what makes for satisfying work. (Research also shows that people who say what needs to be said are the most successful and well liked in a company.) "There is something within us that responds deeply to people who level with us . . . who describe reality so simply and compellingly that the truth seems inevitable, and we cannot help but recognize it," says Susan Scott, author of *Fierce Conversations*. Doing these things will also help you identify a good job match when you're at an interview, plus differentiate you from everyone else.

If you don't work in a culture that values employees who want to contribute and be partners, not just "yes" people, or if you have customers who, as one of my clients puts it, "treat us like drywall contractors," get pickier. Find a company or customer who appreciates what you have to offer (more on this in Step 5).

If you want to start having better days at work and a more satisfying career, you need to know if you're exhibiting un-great-like behavior. Let's start by examining four reasons you might be acting that way in the first place and how to change.

4 REASONS YOU MIGHT BE ACTING THAT WAY

1. You've lost that sharing feeling.

I know the pressure is there to keep your trap shut and get things done. Most everything that goes on in business is about getting it done quicker and cheaper, and you don't want to be seen as an obstacle.

Then there's social pressure. If one person in a group says something, you tend to go along—especially when there is a lot of pressure. Under pressure, a group starts to act like an individual under stress, according to a *New York Times* article referring to the committee that worked on the design for the new Freedom Tower in New York. Under pressure, groups "become committed to bad decisions, to save face or to protect themselves against criticism."

Sarah was a client who held her tongue in meetings because the culture she grew up in didn't encourage speaking up. It was considered rude. Many of my female clients feel uncomfortable expressing their thoughts when surrounded by men in meetings.

Some clients tell me they used to speak up, or have tried, but no one wanted to hear it, so they gave up. Surveys back this up. Research conducted by Crucial Conversations Training found that more than 90 percent of employees said they know early on when projects are likely to fall short; 71 percent who said they try to speak up don't feel they are heard.

I have also had clients who, when faced with the choice between saying or doing what they thought was right and what they called "the politically smart thing to do," chose the latter. As one woman told me, "It was between my personal integrity and keeping my job." For the record, she had no evidence to support this; it's just what she believed would happen. And after we explored what might happen if she broke her silence, she tried it. She was lauded for having the nerve to bring up an unpopular opinion that ended up saving a major account. She even got *promoted.*

Those who do speak up sometimes wonder if it is worth it. Janice, who worked for a radio station, told me in an e-mail how she piped up at a meeting among her peers and boss—who had recently delivered bad news to the staff. Apparently, people were grumbling, and this manager "gathered us all together in a huff and told us to get over it," she wrote. No one in the room spoke. "I felt like an explanation was owed for all, so I spoke up and said that people felt unappreciated and like second-class citizens. He got pretty PO'd, and only one other person in the group supported what I was saying. My relationship was never the same with my boss. I have mixed feelings about whether I'd do it again if given the chance, but tend to think no, because it really didn't do any good."

It would be terrific if you were in the ideal business culture, where speaking up and challenging the status quo *is* valued. The culture might be like the one Charles Nagele, president of the Art Institute of California–San Francisco described when I wrote about this issue in a column. He encourages his teams to "tear apart a proposal, shoot holes

"Some people throw their weight around with those they perceive to be below them. Cowering is the wrong thing to do. Just like running from a lion is the wrong thing to do. It makes the lion attack. If you stand very still and stare the lion down, there's a good chance it will go away. Likewise, telling a blustery boss confidently and clearly what you think, and having alternative ideas, you are likely to earn their respect."

—A successful and confident woman I know

in a plan and challenge the assumptions of an idea." His attitude is that it's better to do that on the front end than to have the marketplace do it. A lot of managers could learn from him, don't you think?

In his world, he encourages people to attack issues, plans, and assumptions, not each other. Are you willing to do that? If you're not sure, here's an exercise to help you work through it.

. . . .

"Looking Back at Monday" EXERCISE

For the next two weeks, at the end of each day or week, answer these questions. Have your daily calendar nearby to remind you of what meetings you were in and where these situations took place. These questions can also apply to you if you're a job hunter. Look at your various interactions and interviews and think of the work you do as a job hunter.

Looking back at _____ (the day) or _____ (the week), what did I want to say but didn't?

_____

_____

_____

What stopped me?

_____

_____

_____

What's the worst thing that could happen if I do speak up?

_____

_____

_____

What good can occur if I speak up?

_____

_____

_____

How will I feel if I don't speak up?

_____

_____

_____

What do I need to say about this to feel I've done my greatest work?

_____

_____

_____

How can I say it in the most appropriate and effective way?

_____

_____

_____

What will I do about this tomorrow?

_____

_____

_____

. . . .

2. There's a whole lotta mediocrity goin' on.

What about the tendency to just do what's expected of you to get by or to not try something new and a little risky for fear of making a mistake? Or to not go beyond your job description? You've probably noticed that mediocrity rules many workplaces—perhaps the one you work in. Research shows that about 75 percent of workers in many companies only do the basics, says Susan David, a psychologist in the Department of Psychology at Yale University.

It wouldn't surprise me if your manager condones mediocrity. Some put up with it because they're threatened by stupendous performance. If it's any consolation, if your manager seems threatened by you, it could be because it's actually a primal urge to "defend, display or increase their status and to keep people and ideas who threaten that hierarchy down," explains David L. Weiner, author of *Reality Check: What Your Mind Knows but Isn't Telling You.*

Mediocrity is even rewarded. And in many cultures it doesn't pay to try something new, because, as I pointed out before, you might get smacked in the head. Are you willing to look at this tendency towards mediocrity? Here are two exercises to help.

. . . .

"Half-ass Job" EXERCISE

For the next two weeks, at the end of each day or week, answer these questions. If you're a job hunter, look at your various interactions and interviews and how you might have done a half-ass job.

What did I do a half-ass job on today or this week?

_____

_____

_____

What stopped me from doing more?

_____

_____

_____

How could I have done more?

_____

_____

_____

How could I have helped the company and others by doing that?

_____

_____

_____

How would I feel if I did that?

_____

_____

_____

What do I risk by not doing more?

_____

_____

_____

What do I gain by doing more?

_____

_____

_____

What will I do about this tomorrow?

_____

_____

_____

"Are You Acting Like a Wimp?" EXERCISE

For the next two weeks, at the end of each day or week, answer these questions. If you're job hunting, look at your various interactions and interviews and think of how you might have acted like a wimp.

What was I afraid to try today or this week because I was afraid I'd make a mistake?

_____

_____

What would happen if I made a mistake?

_____

_____

What would happen if what I did worked?

_____

_____

_____

How would that help the company and others?

_____

_____

_____

What do I gain by trying this?

_____

_____

_____

How would this affect how others see me?

_____

_____

_____

What will I do about this tomorrow?

_____

_____

_____

. . . .

WHERE DOES ALL THE GREATNESS GO?

Nicholas D. Kristof wrote in a *New York Times* op-ed article about the trajectory that occurs when a new political party takes over, saying, "At first, it brims with ideals. Then it makes compromises to stay in power. Finally it becomes devoted simply to staying in office."

This is similar to what happens when people take a new job. At first, they brim with ideals. Then they begin to make compromises to stay in power (or to keep their job) by giving up their ideals, keeping their heads down, holding back ideas, and not challenging the status quo. Eventually, they do what they have to just to keep their job. Before you know it, they've given up their greatness. The same goes for job hunters. At first they may be all gung ho and clear on what they want, but as they are rejected or get nowhere in their search, they start lowering their standards and not asking difficult questions, and may eventually take any job, even a bad one.

3. You avoid and suffer.

Have you ever noticed how people do all kinds of things to get along or get others to agree with them? There's little stuff like laughing at a joke that isn't funny. (In fact, researchers recently concluded that laughter is an instinctual survival tool for social animals, not an intellectual response to wit, according to a story in *The New York Times*. "It's not about getting the joke. It's about getting along.")

Then there are big things like when people ignore what's bothering them, hoping it will go away. Take yourself. How comfortable are you confronting someone who missed a major deadline or is constantly late? No way, you say? You're not alone. Say the word "confront" and most of my clients change the subject quicker than you can say "can we talk?" The mere suggestion that they initiate a discussion about their peer's chronic lateness is met with a laundry list of reasons why they can't. It might turn into a *confrontation* where people grit their teeth, spit, and raise their voices above proper cubicle-decibel etiquette until someone storms off to the bathroom. So, hoping the problem will go away if they ignore it, they give it the silent treatment.

Yes, most people will go to football-field lengths to avoid conversations in which they think someone will get upset or not like what they have to say—and then they suffer as a result of keeping quiet. Case in point, one Boston-based condominium owner wrote advice columnist Randy Cohen of *The New York Times Magazine* saying his downstairs neighbor's snoring is so loud, the entire bedroom shakes. He debated approaching his neighbor, but doubted "any solution [would] arise through confrontation." So he and his wife are debating whether to *sell* their condo. In his response, Cohen expressed surprise that the man would regard selling his apartment and moving "as a more appealing solution than simply talking to your neighbor."

I have a client so fearful of being seen as a "cranky witch" that instead of talking to people about problems, she laughs, hems and haws, then complains that none of her staff get anything done. She is constantly pissed off. No wonder people *do* think she's a cranky witch.

It's scary not knowing what will happen if you initiate one of these conversations. But the silent treatment only makes matters worse; your resentment builds like a "savings account collecting compound daily interest until it explodes into a needless fight," says Aaron Nurick, professor of management and psychology at Bentley College in Waltham, Massachusetts. Not to mention how angry you walk around feeling.

JUST TALK TO ME

It's all in the approach, which should not involve flinging down the gauntlet and taking up arms or becoming a belligerent meathead. Instead, keep your cool and have a calm, direct conversation with the person you're at odds with. I was struck by something movie director Judd Apatow (*The 40-Year-Old Virgin*) said in a *New York Times Magazine* article. After having combative relationships earlier in his career, he said, "I finally learned something maybe most people learn as a kid. If you want someone to come around to your point of view, it's not wise to curse and then tell them they're idiots." If he can do it, so can you.

To help a person at least *hear* your point of view, you need to do the following:

- Plan your words carefully.
- Approach the conversation with the goal of getting your point across *and* preserving the relationship.
- Make sure the moment is right. (In the case of Janice, whom I mentioned earlier, who spoke up at a meeting among her peers and boss, the intent was good, but the timing was off. Managers don't like to be embarrassed. Challenging her boss in front of everyone probably ticked him off. She would have been better off talking to him one-on-one.)
- If appropriate, tell the person what's getting in the way, how that feels to you and how that affects the project you're working on—or whatever it is that happened that's creating a problem.

I DON'T HAVE TIME FOR THAT TOUCHY-FEELY STUFF

Many people (usually men, but not always) tell me they don't have time for all that, which mostly means taking people's feelings into consideration.

What some of these people do instead is start a shouting match behind closed doors. Then they come out smiling, patting the other person on the back, and believing everyone is reassured that "it's business; it's not personal."

What a load of crap.

Do you really think after you've trashed the project someone poured their heart and soul into that they're fine and dandy? Even if you didn't exactly trash it, if you didn't think through your words it probably felt that way to the other person. When it comes to work, *everything* is personal. Work is too big a part of how most of us define ourselves for it not to be.

Sticking with "it's business; it's not personal" is a rationalization that only makes things worse. People who feel disregarded disengage from work, even sabotage projects, spending more time complaining and commiserating. It keeps getting *more* personal. And that can make you more pissed off.

If you take time to think through your approach, you'll have a productive, adult conversation. And if you really think about where you want to be when the conversation is over, you'll know, more or less, what to say. Many of my clients ask me for the "right words." If you know what you want out of the conversation, the words will come. But here are three steps and some wording to keep in your hip pocket when you're about to say something that may conflict with someone's point of view:

Mr./Ms. Sensitive Approach

Before you utter a word, ask yourself:

1. Why is this person taking this position? Are they trying to protect something or someone? Are they afraid of how they might look?
2. Knowing that, how is what I'm about to say going to affect them?
3. Considering their position and feelings, what do I need to say to be diplomatic and move us to the next step?

The first words out of your mouth are important. You can set the stage with something like this:

"I appreciate what you're saying and . . ."
"I've had time to think about this . . ."
"I understand why you're concerned. Maybe there's another way to go about it . . ."

Every time you're about to have a conversation with someone—difficult or not—think about:

- What do I want this conversation to lead to?
- What am I worried might happen or what should I anticipate?
- How can I set the stage so they don't feel belittled or disregarded but, instead, like part of the solution?
- When is the right time to bring this up?

With practice I think you'll find it works. As one client who took a stab at it told me, "Hey, this touchy-feely stuff really works." It's not really touchy or feely, just sensible. And if you can see it in that light, you don't have to be afraid of it.

But there will always be *touchy* stuff to address and people who disagree with you over this and that. If you're job hunting, there will be times when you may need to call up someone who didn't hire you and ask, "What could I have done better?" Or there might be questions you hesitate to ask in an interview, but need to in order to assess if a company fits you (more on this in Step 5).

You may have to have a heart-to-heart with a former supervisor who may be talking trash to potential employers. If you're resigning, you'll need to face your manager and explain your decision. (I know a woman who was so afraid to do this she left a note taped to the front door of the building where she worked, saying, "Dear Owner: I quit.")

Unless you sit in a room with your dog all day and never interact with humans, whether you're in a two-person office or a mega corporation, you will run into conflict. People you're counting on will not get back to you in a timely fashion—if ever—which will put other people off and make projects late. People will do and say stupid things and put projects in jeopardy. You will make comments that upset others. Co-workers will make mistakes. You will make unpopular decisions that will lead others to want to get back at you. Some clients will make unreasonable requests. Others will hate your ideas. Your boss will annoy you. Projects will run over budget.

So you might as well learn how to deal with people who have different viewpoints in a direct yet sensitive manner. Knowing how will come in handy about 95 times a day. You'll pave the way for future conversations. Just remember: *A misunderstanding may at first break you apart, but your conversations can bring you together.*

LET'S TRY THIS AGAIN

Although Janice (the woman who spoke up at the radio station's employee meeting) is gun-shy now, she has a new opportunity to approach her boss about the misunderstanding after her first attempt at speaking up. And if you've found yourself in a similar situation, so do you.

Here's how. Remember the points I talked about: Plan your words carefully. Approach the conversation with the goal of preserving the relationship while getting your point across. Make sure the moment is right. If appropriate, tell the person what's getting in the way, how that feels to you, and how that affects the project you're working on— or whatever it is that happened that's creating a problem.

Let's figure Janice has set up a time to talk to her manager in his office. Here's how the conversation might go:

"I've been thinking about that meeting in which I stood up and explained how people felt unappreciated. I've been feeling uncomfortable ever since and get the sense that things aren't the same between

Playing well with others

In his book *The World Is Flat*, Thomas L. Friedman talks about one very important ability: playing well with others. "Although having good people skills has always been an asset in the working world, it will be even more so in a flat world," he says, referring to the concept of his book—competing on a level playing field in the twenty-first century.

"There are going to be a whole slew of new middle jobs that involve personalized, high-touch interactions with other human beings," he says, "because it is precisely those personalized high-touch interactions that can never be outsourced or automated and are almost always necessary at some point in the value chain." He goes on to quote lunar and planetary scientist Alan Binder: "Perhaps, contrary to what we have come to believe in recent years, people skills will become more valuable than computer skills. The geeks may not inherit the earth after all."

He adds, "I am not sure how you teach that as part of a class-room curriculum, but someone had better figure it out."

I say that treating people as what they are—creatures with emotions—is a start.

us. First, I want to apologize if I said something to upset you. I probably should have picked a different time to say what I said. I'd like the opportunity to explain it better. May I share that?" (Unless he's a bumptious jerk, he would want to hear more.)

Then she would explain how the new policy has affected morale, how she knew others would be hesitant to share this, and how that's affecting their work. She would also say she realizes he might not have control over all of management's decisions, but more than anything, she thought people needed a chance to ask questions and better understand the new policy.

Not all managers, co-workers, clients, and peers are going to be open to having these conversations. But don't assume someone won't. If you're thinking about whether it's a good idea or not, bounce it off someone wise in these matters.

By the way, it's best to have these conversations in person. If that's not possible, pick up the phone. But *do not* have difficult "conversations" via e-mail. Ever. Even if someone initiates it. In a 2007 Attitudes in the American Workplace poll conducted by Harris Interactive, 17 percent of workers said their boss used e-mails to avoid difficult face-to-face conversations. I'm surprised the numbers aren't higher. But that's still 17 percent too many.

You're probably thinking (as most of my clients who resist this approach at first do), "But it takes so much time to do all of that." Yes, conversations take thought and time. But when you realize how many screwups were made on a project, how many feelings got bruised, and

But she's crying

Leslie, hardworking and dedicated, worked for Howard, a no-nonsense executive who liked to get to the point and not "dillydally around with emotions," as he put it. He and Leslie were at a standstill after he shared her performance review. She was so hurt that he had not rated her more highly that she cried during the conversation. Howard "couldn't handle it," he told me. "After I sent her to the bathroom, I ended the meeting." As for Leslie, she swore she'd never work for him again, and began looking for a new job.

After I had separate conversations with Leslie and Howard, they came back together and talked. She didn't cry, and he didn't just get to the point. She told him what bothered her, and he listened. It opened up a new level in their relationship. Leslie worked for Howard another four years. And when he moved to another company, she followed him.

how much business was lost, you'll see how *not* taking the time to have appropriate conversations wastes a lot *more* time and creates more trouble down the line. The time those conversations take will be a minor investment compared to the potential risk.

. . . .

"Fraidy Cat" EXERCISE

To see how nervous you are about confronting others or saying what needs to be said, answer these questions each day for two weeks.

Who did I need to confront or have a conversation with today but didn't?

_____

_____

What stopped me from doing that?

_____

_____

_____

What's the worst thing that could happen if I do?

_____

_____

What good can occur if I do?

_____

_____

What will get worse if I don't?

_____

_____

What do I need to have or know to be able to talk to them?

_____

_____

_____

What do I need to say or do so they don't get really upset?

_____

_____

_____

How will I feel if I don't talk to them?

_____

_____

How would this affect our relationship?

_____

_____

Frank Lloyd Wright on speaking out

Susan Stamberg of National Public Radio once interviewed the granddaughter of architect Frank Lloyd Wright. She recalled sitting around with her family listening to a particular piece of music. After it played once, there was a pause, and her grandfather said he'd like to hear it again. They played the music again. Wright said he'd like to hear it once again. This went on three or four times. Finally Wright's wife said she just couldn't listen to it again. Wright laughed and said, "If you do not speak out, you cannot change anything."

> **"I decided if I want it to change I have to be willing to do something about it."**

When my client said those words, I was as proud as any career consultant can be. The "something" she was referring to was her boss's behavior, which was making her angry.

Her boss was constantly scheduling meetings after 9:00 p.m. without asking my client if it was OK. She was just expected to show up whether she had plans to be with her family or was in bed. One day during a staff meeting her boss asked everyone to share their pet peeve. The boss's habit of setting meetings at night without asking was hers.

"At that moment I decided if I want it to change I have to be willing to do something about it. She had asked for the feedback, so I said to myself, 'This is your moment.' I took a deep breath and went for it. She listened. And she never again has scheduled a meeting at night without asking me first."

How would it help me?

_____

_____

Who else would it benefit?

_____

_____

What will I do about this tomorrow?

_____

_____

4. You can't change what you don't notice.

One of the biggest obstacles to your doing your greatest work is not even being aware of what you're doing to stop it. But you *will* notice something if you keep putting it in front of your face. Take the jumbo box of triple-chocolate-chunk brownie mix I bought at one of those stores that sell large quantities of products stacked on rows of warehouse shelves. Every time I open my kitchen pantry I see this oversize box with its photograph of chocolate kisses and semisweet chocolate chunks, and I think about those brownies. If I didn't see the box, I wouldn't think of the brownies.

I'm not a brain expert. But based on this brownie-mix experience, it seems to me that whatever is in front of you is uppermost in your mind. So if you want to start noticing what you do that might stop you from doing great work, you need to stick reminders of what you want to think about smack-dab in front of your face.

IN-YOUR-FACE

For instance, if you want to work on speaking up, ask yourself how often you stuff a brilliant idea away. Don't know? Well, stick reminders in front of your face that *make* you stop and notice. It could be a Post-it note that you stick on the calendar you carry with you, or your electronic gizmo that you set in front of you at all times. The Post-it might read BRILLIANT IDEAS? or SAY IT or !!!—some code that reminds you of what you want to watch for.

At the end of the day evaluate how well you noticed your thoughts and behavior. You'll probably need another Post-it note on the dashboard of your car to remind you. This one could say HOW'D I DO?

One of my clients wanted to be more aware of how he didn't speak up at meetings even though he had valuable opinions. He told me, "I leave these meetings feeling disappointed in myself and come home wondering what opinions everyone is forming about my abilities as a strategic thinker." So he programmed his reminder word as his password on his BlackBerry. Every time he turned it on, he got the reminder. After three months, though, he had to change it because he got used to it and didn't notice it anymore.

Of course he and I had talked about what might be stopping him from speaking up. His awareness of that, together with this technique, spelled results that were something to brag about.

"I was in a management meeting yesterday and people were jumping to conclusions and solutions about a problem," he told me. "This time I said to myself, 'OK, dummy you've got something to say, say it.' And I said, 'It seems to me that the problem is . . .' and people didn't blow it off. I had something useful to say! We got to the real issues. My boss noticed and asked me to be on a task force. I felt more involved and engaged than ever before. Everything had more meaning."

So create your own "in-your-face" system to develop habits that inspire great work by *noticing* whenever you do the following:

1. You stuff a brilliant idea away.
2. You hold back your insights.
3. You just do what's expected.
4. You're annoyed with someone and not telling them why.

Start with daily reminders. As you improve and notice your behavior changing, you can use the reminders less frequently. Mark your calendar so that at the end of each month you review how the month went. See how that works?

RELIGHT YOUR FIRE

All of these un-great-like behaviors actually put you in a very vulnerable position. Because if you:

- can't offer creative, innovative solutions
- aren't confident enough to say what needs to be said
- aren't willing to go beyond your job description
- don't know how to deal with conflict and communicate
  effectively
- aren't willing to take a risk

. . . who needs you? You simply won't be seen as particularly valuable. That can also be the case in a job interview. In either scenario you won't be viewed as being what some corporations call "high potentials"—folks they invest in and want to develop because they see them as able to move up, handle more responsibility, and offer the type of skills and thinking the company needs to be competitive.

To be competitive, companies will depend on "a deep vein of creativity that is constantly renewing itself and on a myriad of people who can imagine how people can use things that have never been available before," states the report by the New Commission on the Skills of the American Workforce.

How can you see opportunities for developing innovative products and services if you keep your head down and your thoughts to yourself, stuck in your fearful world of how things will look if you step outside your comfort zone?

"The best employers the world over will be looking for the most competent, most creative, the most innovative people on the face of the earth and will be willing to pay them top dollar for their services," says the report. "This will be true not just for the top professionals and managers, but up and down the length and breadth of the workforce."

Do you want to be one of these people? Then do great work for yourself. Depending on where you work now, no one may even notice any new behavior on your part—yet. But *you* will. It won't be comfortable or easy. That's not why you're doing it. You're noticing and changing your behavior because it will help you get what *you* want: to be engaged in your work and challenged, to make a difference, and to be a part of something that is better because of you. To be part of a work world that is very, very different from the one you may be used to or are just entering—one that needs people who are itching to offer the greatness they have to give.

STOP ACTING LIKE A POTTED PLANT

While houseplants do important things like emit oxygen into the atmosphere and look nice, they basically just sit there. They wait and rely on others to make sure they grow and thrive by checking on them and giving them water when they need it. Stop conducting your career the same way. That includes no longer waiting for someone else to come around to your desk and tell you what problems need to be solved and how to do it, and no longer waiting to be asked what needs to be done.

It's natural to want to hold on to and defend what you have now (in some cases, what you perceive as the security of your job). But where's that at? Besides, what kind of joy can you get from your work when you're scared to make mistakes and not challenged to do your best? What kind of satisfaction will you ever take home at the end of the day if you don't feel you've made a difference?

If you want to grow and be challenged, stop sitting passively at your desk doing what's expected. Yes, acting differently and taking risks will be uncomfortable at first. But most successful, powerful people didn't get there feeling comfortable. As Dr. Susan David of Yale says, excellence is yours to give—not the organization's to take.

> *"Great work is done by people who are not afraid to be great."*
>
> —FERNANDO FLORES, philosopher, former Chilean minister of finance, and political prisoner under Augusto Pinochet

The Price Tag for Being Great

It takes nerve (and a little sacrifice)

You have the right to do good work. When I wrote a column on this once, a retired government worker in Michigan responded, "Oftentimes there is a cost to wanting to perform at one's maximum potential. Doing excellent work usually takes more time than doing a mediocre job, so my supervisors were always pressuring me to have my employees do just what was required to get by. I refused to ask my people to generate a product they could not be proud of, but that decision put an end to all further promotions in my career.

"However, I am satisfied with my choice, because I know I have given the taxpayers full measure for their dollar, and my standards for high quality were not compromised in the process."

The people in your work world are going to do what they are going to do. If you can—like the man in Michigan—find a way to do excellent work despite them and accept the cost that may come with that, you will also find satisfaction in upholding your standards. If you cannot do that in the environment you work in, find a place where you can (more on this in Step 5).

How do you get to Carnegie Hall? Practice.

"The best people in any field are those who devote the most hours to what the researchers call 'deliberate practice,'" said an article in *Fortune* magazine on the exploration of what it takes to be great. *Deliberate practice* is defined as activity "that's explicitly intended to improve performance, that reaches for objectives just beyond one's level of competence, provides feedback on results and involves high levels of repetition."

> *"Whatever you are, be a good one."*
>
> —ABRAHAM LINCOLN

One way to begin your own deliberate practice is to go at tasks with a new goal. "Instead of merely trying to get it done, you aim to get better at it." This applies both to work you do and to how you conduct a job search.

Greatness also requires particular attributes, skills, and attitudes, including:

- Being a contrarian, or someone who takes a position different from others'.
- Evaluating yourself independent of the world's evaluation of you.
- Being capable of enduring and thinking under pressure.

No putting off today what you otherwise may never get to

My lawyer client came to me with a list of issues he wanted to work on to improve his performance and the likelihood he'd make partner at his firm.

"I'm willing to do whatever it takes," he promised. After a few weeks of working together, however, I noticed he always had an excuse for not doing his homework. He "got busy," then kept rescheduling and canceling meetings.

Then there's the woman from the South who wrote, "I've been dreaming, hoping, wishing, longing to move west for six years." She said she had bought my book on how to find a new job in a different city but never finished it, assuring me, "Please don't take that personally, I never, ever finish anything."

Not completing something is a form of procrastination, says John Seeley, author of *Get UnStuck!* Procrastination often has to do with perfectionism. You feel you have to do everything perfectly, he says, and put off something until you can do it just right.

Another woman wrote saying she wanted to start her own newlywed magazine because when she got married three years ago, "There was nothing else out there for this readership."

But she didn't follow through. Then she read an article about a similar magazine being launched. "I'm so disappointed I didn't follow through with my instincts and goals a year ago!"

People get in the way of themselves, says psychologist Patricia Farrell. They fear failure and usually attribute their failure to finish something to forces that are outside their control. Or they can't handle success. "Success means you'll have to keep on producing, and if you can't, then it's better not to put yourself in harm's way," she says.

Have you ever plunked down money for a class, tapes, or consulting, and then failed to do anything with it? Is all the tedious preliminary work you did on a project gathering dust while the idea hovers and guilt builds? Did you decide to investigate a new career or job and never follow through? Part of doing good work and feeling personal satisfaction is deciding how much time you're willing to invest in something and following through on what you wanted in the first place. Here are two exercises to help you put the lid on what you start.

. . . .

"Be a Terminator" EXERCISES

EXERCISE 1:

Think of something you started that you haven't completed and write it here:

_____

_____

_____

Now answer these questions:

What would happen if I completed this?

_____

_____

What am I losing out on by not finishing this?

_____

_____

How would I feel if I finished it?

_____

_____

_____

What fears do I have about what will happen if I do finish this?

_____

_____

_____

What can I do to overcome those fears?

_____

_____

_____

How would that help my career, the company, and/or others?

_____

_____

_____

How would this affect how others see me?

_____

_____

_____

How would this affect how I see myself?

_____

_____

_____

Thinking of the same or a different thing you started and didn't complete, answer these questions:

What circumstances need to exist to do something with this?

_____

_____

_____

_____

What do I need to do to make those circumstances possible?

_____

_____

_____

_____

Will those circumstances ever be perfect?

_____

_____

_____

_____

If it's unlikely those circumstances will ever be perfect, am I willing to go forward anyway?

_____

_____

_____

_____

. . . .

No short cuts

Eric is a client who is hardworking and bright and was gung ho about finally getting serious and making a better career choice. He told me he was tired of going to a job where he was "always waiting for the day to be over." But he couldn't wait for us to get through the steps to define his likes and dislikes. And even though he swore, "I'm tired of picking jobs without thinking them through and holding on to this miserable job," when he got a call about an opening, he decided it was perfect. He was so eager to be offered the job, he was ready to take a fifteen-thousand-dollar pay cut. He not only told the interviewer what he was making, but that he'd take less. Ouch.

When he told me about this perfect job he interviewed for, I tried to get him to slow down, quizzing him on what he knew about the company. Did it fit the environment and culture he wanted? He wasn't sure because he hadn't asked enough questions. When I asked about job expectations and how his performance would be evaluated, he didn't have a clue. He was annoyed with me for raising these points, saying, "Can't I just be happy for a day?"

Nothing in our culture encourages delayed gratification or long-term thinking, says sociologist BJ Gallagher. That desire to "have it now" can lead to making snap decisions you might regret. Like Eric, you might want something so badly that you take shortcuts.

Wanting a job too badly can lead to taking another kind of short-cut—lying. This is a route that has cost some people dearly. You may remember hearing about the dean of admissions at the Massachusetts Institute of Technology (MIT), who in 2007 admitted that in 1979 she had claimed to have degrees from three institutions when she had never received them. As a result, she was fired.

Out of nearly five hundred thousand reference verifications that ADP Screening and Selection Services did in 2006, 41 percent showed some type of discrepancy between actual employment, education, or credentials and information provided by applicants. That's a lot of potential lying.

And where does it get you if you're caught? Possibly fired and, depending on who you are, into the news. *The Wall Street Journal* cited several such high-profile professionals who, when found out, resigned, got kicked off boards, or got suspended. They included David Edmondson, who resigned in 2006 as chief executive of RadioShack after lying about having a college degree, and motivational speaker Denis Waitley, who was forced off the board of Usana Health Sciences after it was discovered that he hadn't received a degree as he had claimed.

It's no different than athletes who shoot themselves up with steroids because they feel the pressure to compete. Many of them end up remorseful and begging for forgiveness.

Most of all, short cuts that add up to lying and cheating can kill your reputation—no matter how good you do your job. People loved the MIT dean for her good work. But as the school's chancellor Phillip Clay said, "We take integrity very seriously . . . We dismissed her even though she has done a great job."

Take your integrity as seriously as others do. Take to heart the words the former and fired MIT dean posted on the school's Web site after the incident: "I did not have the courage to correct my resume when I applied for my current job or at any time since. I am deeply sorry for this and for disappointing so many in the MIT community and beyond who supported me, believed in me, and who have given me extraordinary opportunities."

Slow down. Stop letting the pressure to achieve and produce drive you. Without patience, you're in store for a short-term fix. Remember, you are looking for *more* than just one day of happiness.

"Make haste slowly."
—CHINESE PROVERB

BE HERE NOW, PLEASE

A couple of years ago I was sitting in an audience in Cincinnati listening to a conceptual artist from San Francisco respond to questions from his interviewer. I can't recall the question the interviewer had just asked him, but I remember the artist's response. He just sat there and didn't say anything for about ten awkward seconds. Then he explained that he hadn't heard the question. He said he was worrying about the fact that his wife, who was in the front row of the audience and taping the interview on a handheld camera, was going to use up the battery on the camera. "Could you repeat the question?" he asked.

It was a perfect example of how easy it is to not "be there." To the man's credit, he noticed and admitted it. Who knows, in those ten awkward seconds of silence it may have crossed his mind that he'd look silly admitting this, but even sillier trying to answer a question he hadn't heard. But I didn't get that feeling. He hadn't come all the way from San Francisco to sit on this stage and not share the insight we were all waiting for, nor to create an all-around empty experience. The man seemed to have made a conscious decision to "be there."

There is nothing more rewarding than to really, really *be there* in mind, body, and spirit when you're solving a problem or talking to someone—on the phone, in an official meeting, or during a chance passing in the hallway. You could be talking to them about their or your performance, how they spent their summer vacation, what they had for breakfast, how to rewrite a sentence in a proposal, or how to handle a client problem. But you're really, really *there*—meaning you're paying attention to them and nothing else. Sensing their mood and even acknowledging it. Listening to their every word and responding to them, even though you have twelve other pressing issues going on. I realize this may sound out there, but it's actually the most down-to-earth thing and the most meaningful brush with greatness you can have.

It's hard to explain what this feels like. Can you think of a moment when you were totally absorbed, engrossed, or focused on something, and you can't remember hearing or seeing anything else around you? When your attention was right there in front of you and nowhere else? I once heard the playwright Steven Dietz talk about this issue in relation to how an artist must work. He said that an artist's attention is required to be right here and now. How do you make art for the present moment? he asked. You have to be there—even when everything around you demands that you be somewhere else.

Likewise, how do you do great work—whatever your specialty? You have to be there. It seems so obvious when you think about it. But whether you're writing a play, being creative in another way (something many people say they want in their work), or responding to someone sitting across from you, you have to be there.

If I can go out on another limb here, I'd say this is that fundamental "being present in the moment" thing that people talk about, and which seems so unattainable. Yet these opportunities present themselves every time you interact with someone at work or in a job interview or when you're involved in a project.

One of my clients found his mind constantly "being invaded by thoughts when I'm doing something. It feels like someone barging into my house," he told me. He added, "I noticed that I don't remember the experience I'm having, because I don't focus on it. That's disturbing."

It's easy to miss the opportunity if you haven't developed the attention necessary to "being there." It whizzes right by when you're absentmindedly e-mailing someone while talking to someone else on the phone. Or thinking about how you're going to respond to what the other person is saying *while* they're talking. Or fretting about how you may look ridiculous if you speak up. When you do that your mind has gone away from the moment at hand and is instead obsessing about getting one more thing done, or showing someone how much you know, or worrying about how you'll look. Now you've missed out on contributing what you have to share, which can help lead you to what you really want.

GREATNESS IS LOOKING YOUR OWN DISCONTENT IN THE EYE

If you're in a job or career that's not what you signed up for, it will be terribly inconvenient and take great courage to look your discontent in the eye.

After a long day at work, when you'd rather be watching *I Love Lucy* reruns on cable, the last thing you may feel like doing is spending soul-searching hours answering questions like: What do I like to do, and why? Why am I unhappy? What would make me happy? What would I do if I wasn't worried about money? But you must.

You also need to:

- Accept that there are no guarantees. And that even though you're worried you might fail, you're going to take a chance and explore the possibilities anyway.
- Get over the "what will others think?" hump.
- Accept that everything has a price. And that to explore or change for the better you will have to rearrange the details of your life and maybe give up time, money, and vacations to get there.

Your great deed will pay off in the form of getting up every day to do work that doesn't feel like a burden—even work so enjoyable you don't want to put it down. The kind of work that movie director Stanley Kubrick once described when someone asked him if he ever took a vacation: "A vacation from what?"

How can you come close to knowing, let alone sharing, your best judgment or insight when you're busy trying to check another thing off your to-do list or being scared?

It's Not Me, It's You

A satisfying and lasting brush with greatness doesn't come from me or someone else telling you how great you are or what a fabulous job you're doing. It comes at the very moment you are paying full attention to the problem you are grappling with or the personal interaction you are having. It comes when you forget about what you're afraid of—the past you cannot change and the future that isn't yet here—and you become part of what's happening at that very moment. A moment when you can give it your best and touch others with the greatness you have to give. That, dear worker, is what feels truly great. And any given moment, you have the choice to let it pass or to seize it.

TAKE YOUR THIRD QUIT-BEING-PISSED OATH

I hereby promise myself to quit being pissed off and start being powerful by becoming aware of my un-great-like behavior and the opportunity I have to turn any given moment into a great moment.

SIGN HERE _____

DATE _____

Step 4

Prepare for Hurricanes, Sinkholes, and Mañana

You probably don't lose sleep over being hit by a hurricane, tornado, earthquake, tsunami, volcanic eruption, or meteor, or worry much about coming into contact with an avalanche or landslide or stumbling into a sinkhole. This is reasonable—depending, of course, on where you live.

It's another story if you're one of the more than 34.6 million people who live in the higher-risk coastal hurricane zones from the Carolinas to Texas. You *should* be concerned about hurricanes. But seven months after the devastation of Hurricane Katrina in 2005, half the coastal residents in 12 Atlantic and Gulf states surveyed didn't feel vulnerable to hurricanes, and three out of five had no family disaster plan.[*] People who have been hit by hurricanes still tend to chalk it up to bad luck or a fluke, says Max Mayfield, director of the National Hurricane Center.

Sounds like how most people view their careers. Lose my job? Something go wrong with my company or industry or my work relationships that puts my career at risk? Won't happen to me! Even if it is in the back of your mind as a remote possibility (in the stumbling-into-a-sinkhole category) odds are, like so many of those folks in the hurricane zone, you're not prepared in case disaster does strike. And that, I'm here to tell you, increases the chance that if something does happen to threaten your security, you'll suffer a lot more than you need to. So we need to work on that.

For the record, you have lots of company. I have met and heard from thousands of panicked people who lose their jobs, get fired, or for some reason cannot work in their field and have not prepared for this possibility. But misery loving company is not an excuse. Unless, of course, you love being miserable.

I'm not saying you can plan for everything. But there are some scenarios to consider and backup plans to have in waiting. Before we get to the latter, consider these scenarios:

---

[*] According to a poll conducted by Mason-Dixon Polling & Research and released by the National Hurricane Survival Institute.

- Your career seems hunky-dory on Friday, but new management takes over on Monday, which, yes, could mean your job.
- Your company merges, is bought, or closes your division.
- Your industry goes kaput.
- New technology makes your work obsolete.
- A terrorist attack occurs, affecting your way of doing business or your job. (Many New Yorkers wrote to me about how the events of 9/11 devastated their careers.)
- Your body breaks down.
- You can't take it anymore—and work is literally making you sick.
- Your boss has it in for you.
- You slip up big-time and lose your job or your best client and are out on the street in 24 hours.
- Your trusted partner betrays you.

All of these things have been known to happen. If for some reason you are currently without a job, you already know what this kind of uncertainty feels like.

Still think it won't happen to you? So did the workers at Topps Meat Company. Who would have thought that the largest U.S. manufacturer of frozen hamburgers, founded in 1940, would be at the top of its game one day and closing its doors the next? But on October 5, 2007, CEO Anthony D'Urso announced the company was unable to withstand the financial burden of the previous month's recall of 21.7 million pounds of ground-beef product. After management told them the news, workers streamed out of the plant, stunned.

And don't forget Naked Truth #6: Technology, a machine, or someone overseas may replace you or affect your wages. Like it or not, technology and machines have made it possible for companies to eliminate jobs people do. Like it or not, the world has a lot of highly educated workers who will work for lower wages.

On the brighter side, your industry, profession, or company might be heading in a new, challenging direction that will call for enhanced skills and knowledge that could take you with it—*if* you're prepared.

Who knows what could happen? You could attend a cookout or art opening and meet the CEO of a startup who's looking for someone just like you. Your company could buy another company and need someone who knows operations (or is willing to learn) and the latest technology related to the new firm's products or services.

The point is, things are always changing. And a change doesn't have to turn into a cataclysmically negative event—not if you are prepared for it. When you're prepared you can also jump at an opportunity when it presents itself. Obviously you don't control all situations. And if something bad were to negatively affect your status and career, you probably wouldn't be jumping for joy, even if you *were* prepared. But you'll be back on your feet faster or at the front of the line when opportunities come knocking, and you'll feel a whole lot more powerful if you've done everything you can to prepare for such unpredictable events.

So let's talk about how to do that. Think of what we're going to cover here as your career survival kit—tips, strategies, and tools you don't want to be without. As Kay Wilkins, CEO of the Red Cross's Southeast Louisiana Chapter, said as the first storm of the 2007 hurricane season was forming, everyone can do three simple things: make a plan, build an emergency preparedness kit, and stay informed.

You're doing that for your career because nobody—not your manager, human resource department, career coach, or mentor—is going to rescue you, make a plan for you, prepare you for emergencies, or keep you informed. You never know what opportunities could arise or what you may decide to change. You may decide you've had enough of your current job and want to shop around. You may want to have an intelligent conversation with a recruiter or someone else you meet. You may decide you want to make a career change. Out of the blue, you may be asked to throw your hat into the ring for a new, challenging role at your company or elsewhere, and you will have to explain why you're the best of the breed—or know whether it's a good fit.

. . . which brings me to my "Who Knew?" strategy.

My "Who Knew?" Strategy

This strategy is based on the fact that you never know what can happen. Then, looking back, you say, who knew things would go kaflooey? Who knew you'd get tendonitis and not be able to write anymore?

Who knew the company would merge and you'd be next in line for a shot at the vice president position? Who knew a recruiter would call and ask you to interview you for the job you've always dreamed of? Who knew your wonderful boss would leave and be replaced by a borderline lunatic? Who knew the market would crash or the mortgage industry would tank with so many thousands of jobs lost? No one, of course! (Actually, there were plenty of warnings about the mortgage industry, but few people were listening.) My point is that even though you never know what could happen, there are three things you can *do* to be prepared if and when they do.

Let's start with the first item in my "Who Knew?" strategy, which consists of three things you need to *know* so you will be ready for whatever comes your way.

First Item in My "Who Knew?" Strategy: 3 THINGS TO KNOW

1. Know why you matter.
Or, what have you done for them lately? What about tomorrow?

If new managers walked in the door of your organization today, you'd probably be shaking in your boots. After all, they have the pick of the lot and the power to decide whether to keep you around. Would they? It depends on how much you matter.

"Of course I matter," you're thinking. "Why, if it weren't for me they wouldn't be able to . . . well, let's see, I have to think about that."

If you can't explain exactly why they would fight tooth and nail to keep you on the payroll, you'd better figure it out. Because, as I've already said, you never know what could change tomorrow. Your division could be sold, and new senior managers would want to know why you take up space. Or someone who does know his worth could be having lunch with your boss right now and persuading her over a Cobb salad that he has gobs more to offer than you. Or you might decide you want to follow up on an opportunity you got wind of. To be prepared for any such scenarios, you need to know why you matter.

When the *Business 2.0* magazine staff was compiling its 2006 list of the 50 people who matter, they emphasized two questions: What have you done for us lately? And, What will you do for us tomorrow?

Those are the same two questions you need to answer to know how much you matter to your company. If you're job hunting, you'll have to explain what you did for your last employer and what you will do for the new firm if they hire you. You also need to answer the question: Would my company rehire me today, and if so, why? Even if you're changing careers, you want to know why you matter, because your value is transferable.

To help you get to the crux of whether you'd pass muster, here's an exercise. As with most of my exercises, give yourself plenty of time and find a quiet place to work. (Yes, turn off your cell phone.)

. . . .

"Why Do I Matter?" EXERCISE

Answer these questions:

How does what you do everyday translate into something that matters to your company? If you're unemployed, how does what you used to do every day translate into something that matters to a new company? Does it help the company reach customers twice as fast, increase Internet traffic to its site, or train new employees in half the time? Why does that matter to your company (or to a new one)?

_____

_____

_____

_____

Another way to look at this question is to ask yourself, What are the overall goals of your company (or the one you're interviewing with) and how do you (or will you) help the company meet those?

_____

_____

_____

What knowledge do you have that the company depends on?

_____

_____

What skills do you have that the company relies on?

_____

_____

What relationships do you have that are key to the company?

_____

_____

How do you keep your knowledge up to date?

_____

_____

What have you done to keep your skills fine-tuned?

_____

_____

What have you done in the last three months to demonstrate that your skills and knowledge made a difference to your company (or the one you used to work for)?

_____

_____

_____

How have you gone beyond what's expected in the last six months and made a difference?

_____

_____

What have you done to help others get something accomplished?

_____

_____

_____

_____

What issues, problems, and trends face your particular line of work, and what are you doing to figure out how to be more effective?

_____

_____

_____

_____

If you're employed now, what will you do in the next six months to help your company stay competitive and be more valuable to its customers or clients? If you're job hunting, what would you do in the next six months to help the company you're interviewing with stay competitive and be more valuable to its customers or clients?

_____

_____

_____

_____

What are you doing to reshape the future of your industry and the company you work for (or would like to work for)?

_____

_____

_____

_____

In a sentence, how would you describe "the essence of what makes you unique," identifiable among your peers, and someone a company wants to have around?

Here are a couple of examples of what I mean by "the essence of what makes you unique" as described in a *Business 2.0* magazine article: Media mogul Rupert Murdoch is someone with a "flair for bombastic populism." Genentech's president of product development, Susan Desmond-Hellman, is "focused on creating drugs that make the difference between life and death," contributing to the company's positioning as a pioneer.

You may not be helping turn cancer into a manageable disease. But what you do matters, and you better know what that is. Completing this "Why Do I Matter?" exercise will not only put you in a stronger position if something changes, but it will also do the following:

- renew your belief in your talents, which we all need from time to time
- build confidence, which you'll need if you're defending your job, making a case for a new position, or job hunting
- make you feel more powerful, whether you're job hunting or gainfully employed
- help you figure out what to do to be prepared for new, challenging opportunities that could come your way, whether or not you've been looking for them.

2. Know where things stand . . .

Let's say you just entered a working relationship or business arrangement all smiles. But who knew the business plan would go haywire, world events would change, your closest ally would die, one of the associates would get mad or offended, someone would have a change of heart, or someone would fall in or out of love? Any of these unforeseen circumstances could affect you adversely if you haven't spelled out where things stand. This applies to any and every work relationship or business arrangement. So whether you're taking a new job, changing your present arrangement, joining forces with a partner, or forging a new business relationship, spell out who does what and how, where, and for whom, and plan for contingencies in case things don't work out or change.

One of my clients began working for a man who ran his own small business. Every time my client and I met, I'd ask him whether he had finalized an agreement with the man on how he'd be compensated for bringing in new business. My client kept saying he trusted the man, who assured him, "We'll figure out a way to do that." They got very busy delivering the work he sold, and when it came down to it, he didn't want to press the issue or get it in writing for fear of seeming too pushy. After six months, he still had no agreement. When my client finally asserted himself, the man claimed the new business developments had been a joint effort and that he didn't owe my client any more money. My client lost out on thousands of dollars. He was mad, and his wife was furious.

Most people don't like to deal with or pay attention to the nitty-gritty details that apply to contracts, verbal agreements, and work relationships. And it almost always comes back to haunt them. They not only lose money, but they get angry at themselves for not handling the situation better.

"I didn't know I couldn't work for a competitor." "I didn't know I'd have to travel three weeks out of the month." "I didn't know I'd be working for *him*." These are not good spots to find yourself in. Or take the man who invested two years of his life in a project that could reap big financial rewards and a promising new career. He had forged a partnership with people he trusted to make the project happen. But he hadn't spelled out all the details of how that would work. "I trusted them. I thought they had my best interest at heart," he told me.

He and his partners had their first success, and everyone was celebrating. But behind closed doors his partners were conspiring, deciding they could make more money with this man out of the picture. So they cut him out cold.

It was a gut-wrenching shock to his system. How could they do this after all they had been through together? Easily, apparently.

Emotions get in the way. A change of heart can be about money, power, sex, or revenge. You may be leery of discussing business issues—ranging from salary, benefits, and work arrangements to work environment and job expectations—because you're afraid it will create conflict. But you risk everything when you're so focused on playing nice-nice.

It's the biggest reason partnerships between two business owners break down, says Joy Butler, a business and entertainment attorney in Washington, D.C., who consults with people after business partnerships implode.

Whether you're entering a working relationship with a small or large business or an individual or individuals, know where things stand by candidly discussing expectations and roles. Then put agreements in writing.

ON THE PERSONAL FRONT.
Remember in Step 1 I talked about Naked Truth #9—business *is* personal—and the fact that how people decide whether they want to hire, fire, or do business with you is based in part on how they feel about you? Well, if your company is going through change and looking to cut bodies, if you're up for a promotion, if you're being considered for a board or committee in or outside of work, or if you're job hunting and companies will be snooping around about your past, it would be smart to know how your present employer and others feel about you. That is, what's your reputation?

Most of us don't have a clue as to how others see us. We tend to view ourselves much more glowingly than they do.

Dr. Miguel A. Quinones, business professor at Southern Methodist University, concurs, saying evidence shows most people in organizations rate themselves higher than those who work with them.

When some of my clients get feedback that sizes them up critically, they can't believe it. "They just don't know me," one man insisted, after hearing that co-workers described him as abrasive, insincere, and manipulative. But how can six people hold similar views and there be nothing to it? And what happens if you ignore such feedback?

You could end up extremely pissed off. That was the case with a client of mine who refused to hear that others think she's pushy. She lost out on a promotion she felt she deserved. And it could have been prevented if she'd only listened when others told her how she was doing.

When my clients have been open to hearing how others see them and have adjusted their behavior as a result, they have gotten promotions, raises, more responsibility, and access to key decision makers in and outside their companies. Some learned that they needed to listen more. Others learned they needed to take a firm stance instead of asking opinions, show more interest when someone is talking, or stop getting bogged down in details.

The only way any of us will really know how others see us is to do what former New York City mayor Ed Koch used to do: go around asking people, "How'm I doin'?"

So figure out your own way to discover how *you're* doin'. Maybe that means getting a coach or a mentor who will be brutally frank with you. When a former boss told Bill Treasurer of Giant Leap Consulting that he was a brownnoser, it made all the difference in his career.

"I had moved into a new role, and sucking up to the executives I was coaching wouldn't serve them or me well," says Treasurer. His boss's words "showed me how brownnosing is really manipulative and dishonest." Ultimately, the revelation helped Treasurer, in his words, "learn to rely on my own ideas. Today, I like to think I am more honest." The fact that he even shared that and let me write about it tells you a lot about him—and the reputation he surely creates by being open and willing to share, so that others can learn.

Knowing where you stand helps you change or deal with it. You may even need to develop a strategy to overcome or counter a perception. For example, if you're job hunting and discover a former boss is bad-mouthing you, you'll want to nip that in the bud by talking to the former boss or human resource department. What if you discover your good name is listed in news reports or blog postings in a damaging way, and the information isn't accurate? There are companies that claim to help you "search and destroy" negative information about you on the Internet. But they can't wipe everything off the Internet. Their efforts can even backfire, generating unwanted attention. There's no perfect solution, so think long and hard about the pros and cons of doing this.

When it comes to your reputation, it's best to clear up these kinds of issues before they become big trouble.

> "We need the power to see ourselves
> as the world sees us."
>
> — JAMES FULBRIGHT, senator from Arkansas

3. Know the gist of you.

You want to know not only *why* you matter, but also what you *possess* that makes you matter. In my first point (know why you matter), we touched on this. You wrote out the knowledge and skills that make you valuable to your company or to a new one—that is, what they depend on you for. Now I want you to think more broadly. Think about the skills and knowledge that your company or former employer appreciates. But also think about what other skills, knowledge, and data make up who you are.

You absolutely must know this information, because, as I've already said, disaster could strike with no warning and you may *need* to go out and look for a new job. But also because you may want to initiate a change or respond to an opportunity.

To be ready, be crystal clear about five things that more or less are the gist of you:

WHAT YOU'RE DARN GOOD AT — YOUR STRENGTHS

Your strengths (I also refer to these as your most joyful skills) are concrete, basic skills you perform well and enjoy doing—not your job title or things like "revenue and market-share growth," "client relations," or "new market development." Those are not basic skills. Strengths are simple verbs that describe the actions you perform well and enjoy, such as "organize," "research," "conceive," "lead," "advise," "persuade," "present," "teach," "plan," "problem solve," "write," "analyze." *You can discover these by doing two things:*

▶ Look at situations or activities at work that you consider achievements, then identify what you did well and enjoyed doing most when you were involved in those activities.

For example, if you're an administrative assistant, after analyzing activities you've enjoyed most, you may discover that your strengths include the ability to organize, coordinate, handle details, and systemize. If you're an executive, after analyzing what you've enjoyed doing most, you may discover that your strengths include the ability to envision, lead, motivate, inspire, and develop strategic plans.

▶ Look at situations or activities in *other* areas of your life that you consider achievements and liked doing, then identify what you did well and enjoyed most when you were involved in those activities.

For example, one of my clients loved to create elaborate, six-course meals and entertain his friends. But his most joyful skills, which he used to do this, did not come up when he talked about his "day job." Some of the things he loves to do, which can go on his list, include his ability to organize, plan, and coordinate these elaborate meals, research menus, and whip up these feasts that his friends savor. So when I say think more broadly about your skills, that's partly what I mean. This was helpful for him to know because he was looking to make a career change.

Even if you're not doing that, look at other areas of your life to help you discover your strengths—or, as I refer to them, your most joyful skills. The same strengths may show up at work and in your personal life. These words may seem basic, but if you do need to market yourself due to an unpredictable event or want to change career directions at some point, you'd better understand what those basic skills are so that you can build on them. You'll also need to leverage them and explain to others what you can do well—especially if a job is called by a different name than what you've always done. You are not your title. I don't care what list of titles you've held. You are a body of fundamental skills that you can pack up and take with you. Know them intimately.

What you know — your body of knowledge

This is all that stuff you've accumulated in your head and you use in your work every day (or have in the past) to one degree or another. It can be an understanding of particular processes, concepts, procedures, policies, theories, and other information. Depending on your profession or background it might be tax law, media relations, certain equipment and materials, construction methods, safety prevention techniques, training, educational methods, staffing and hiring, Spanish, alternative medicine, budgets, logistics, operations. If you've worked for a period of time, your list will be long.

Again, look at *other* areas of your life. When my client who liked to entertain did this exercise, he realized how much he knew about wine, gourmet ingredients, family traditions, and culture. This helped him understand how he might capitalize on this knowledge and tie it together with his work experience to market himself to a new employer or start a small business.

Trust me, this will come in very handy if you need to market yourself because you're suddenly available, or *you* want to test the waters or change career directions. The people you're talking to will want to know what you *know* that makes you an expert or can translate into another field. Best of all, when you sit down to write a list of everything you know, you'll surprise yourself with your depth of knowledge. Like knowing why you matter, this builds confidence, helps you explore new career directions, and prepares you to talk about yourself and create marketing tools with detail and pizzazz—especially compared to the drivel that most people write.

What you care about and how you want your work to make a difference

Being suddenly thrust into a job search can be hard enough. But believe me, you will be more excited about the search and your work if what you're looking for revolves around issues or things you care about. Knowing what you care about can also help you build your career around that. This is especially useful if you're exploring a career change and don't have experience but do have excitement.

Whether it is behavior, nutrition, children, the elderly, women's issues, personal finances, real estate, world affairs, ecology, energy, the environment, film, art, religion, or couture, knowing what you care about will open up your mind to ideas and help you explain to others why you're so interested in a particular area.

If you do find yourself suddenly needing to market yourself, and you're excited about what you do and can explain *why* you do it, you'll be a more passionate marketer. So ask yourself, What issues, trends, institutions, causes, or problems do I care most about? And how will this make a difference? Is it making the world a safer place? Is it saving the earth? Is it helping people have more fulfilling relationships or healthier lives?

HOW YOU TEND TO ACT — YOUR PERSONAL CHARACTERISTICS, STYLE, AND PERSONALITY TRAITS THAT AFFECT HOW YOU DO YOUR WORK

Here you're looking for words that describe *who* you are and the way you do things. They can describe what you're known for—seeing a project through from start to finish, for instance, or assessing situations with objectivity and reason. Examples include the following: "precise," "disciplined," "articulate," "tactful," "mature," "consistent," "fair," "thorough," "ambitious," "orderly," "diplomatic," and/or "good in crisis," and "take charge." As you can see, these aren't things you do (like your strengths); they describe the way you apply those strengths.

If disaster strikes, with this information on hand you will know what type of environment, culture, and kind of work suits you best for your next position. It also gives you language to jazz up your resume and other marketing tools, which, again, will be a refreshing change from the typical wishy-washy business blabber most people use.

WHAT CHALLENGES YOU

What is it that keeps you interested and stimulated? Is it learning new ideas and techniques, changing an opinion, experimenting, designing, or discovering something new?

Knowing this will help you seek out experiences, companies, jobs, and cultures that suit you, whether you're trying to cope with unexpected job loss, wanting to change directions, or trying to figure out if a particular job you're considering is a good fit.

Now that you know why you matter, where things stand, and the gist of you, it's time to put it all together. So let's move on to the second item in my "Who Knew?" strategy.

Second Item in My "Who Knew?" Strategy:
EXPLAIN IT TO MY MOTHER

Nothing would be more frustrating than having the 15-second chance of a lifetime to tell someone about yourself and your career and blowing it because you can't get the words out. You just never know when that will be. It might be a shot you get to introduce yourself at a meeting or with someone you've just met waiting in line at the post office. Or perhaps it will be a more focused, involved conversation, like an informational or job interview or impromptu conversation with someone you meet in an airport lounge. Not being prepared for that opportunity would be a shame.

In my previous books, dealing with everything from job hunting in a new city to changing careers, I've called this little verbal presentation a Stump Speech, a Move Mantra, or a 15-second, 30-second, or 3-minute commercial.* It doesn't matter what you call it, just make it simple, meaty, and real, and connect with the live human in front of your face.

Also keep in mind that at any time you could be talking about yourself and your career to two distinct audiences. You might be chatting with someone in your field who will understand what you've done or where you want to go. Or you could be addressing someone like my mother (who wouldn't necessarily understand your line of work but is a good person to know anyway).

You've already got the high points to create a concise overview of your career that you can whip out when the moment is ripe. We just reviewed them in two places:

▶ In "Know the gist of you," where we covered your strengths, your knowledge, what you care about and why, your personal characteristics, and what challenges you

---

*See how I help Patrick develop his 3-minute commercial in my podcast Episode #22. Go to iTunes and search for Career Whisperer Andrea Kay, or my Web site, AndreaKay.com, which links to my podcasts.

▶ In "The essence of you," where you described why you matter. (This is that one sentence that explains what makes you unique, identifiable among your peers, and someone a company wants to have around.)

Again, the content depends on the circumstance and who's asking you to talk. But now you've got the words to play with.

You may not be describing any of this to anyone today. But it can't hurt to create the outline of your personal "commercial" to have when you need it, which could be tomorrow or in two months—whenever you might stumble into a sinkhole.

When you're talking to people in your field, you can be technical but real. Don't go into too much detail too fast or use a lot of jargon and gibberish. Let's spend some time on this, because it really is important. After all, if no one understands you, you defeat the purpose of talking. What I'm going to cover applies to the spoken and written word (as in your resume). Because when speaking *or* writing, most people are tempted to use lazy, vague, and stale words that are not well chosen but are more like "phrases tacked together like the sections of a prefabricated hen-house," as author and critic George Orwell stated so well in his 1946 essay "Politics and the English Language." You're not going to sound real and sincere or connect with the live human in front of you when you use worn-out, bloated, imprecise mumbo jumbo. Even if you hear others who you think *know* what they're talking about throw around this type of talk, don't do it! Just because they describe themselves as "person-centered change agents who drive results through innovative human resource solutions and learning frameworks that deliver maximum value" does not mean you should. Do not talk like this—ever.

First, because, well, it's a bunch of useless nonsense. Second, after you've uttered all that useless nonsense, what will you say next, when someone says, "What do you mean?" And they will, because they won't understand. Or they'll just politely walk away.

You can prevent this ugly recitation by being on constant guard and making a conscious effort not to surrender to "sheer cloudy vagueness," says Orwell. When developing what you might say, be like a scrupulous writer, who in every sentence would ask himself these questions Orwell poses:

- "maximum value"
- "change agent"
- "person-centered approach"
- "real time [fill in the blank]"
- "expectation clarification"
- "culture of deliverability"
- "mutual interdependence"
- "theoretical underpinnings"
- "actionable"
- "drive results"
- "conductor of human development in action"
- "change leadership practices"
- "systems theory"
- "learning framework"
- "systems" following any noun
- "solutions" following any noun
- "pursuant to" used in any way

1. "What am I trying to say?"
2. "What words will express it?"
3. "What image or idiom will make it clearer?"
4. "Is this image fresh enough to have an effect?"
5. "Could I put it more shortly?"
6. "Have I said anything that is avoidably ugly?"

When you're talking to someone who *wouldn't* understand your line of work, or you're trying to help them see how your background transfers to another environment or field, visualize yourself talking to my mother. So, of course, no mumbo jumbo or snoozer words with this audience either. Keep it short and sweet and use real words that people can relate to.

Naked Truth #12 back to haunt you

In 2007 I wrote a column aimed at the many young servicemen and women returning home to start new jobs and careers. You've got tons to offer the civilian workforce, I told them, but the hard part will be explaining what that is to the nonmilitary audience you want to work for.

I quoted a story from CBS News in which Major General William H. Wade II, referring to these soldiers, said, "They learn unique skills—communications, technology, managerial, logistics. Employers need to understand how to translate those skills to the civilian sector."

Yes, employers do need to understand that. But, it doesn't matter who you are, or how great or noble the work you've done is. It is not up to the *employer* to figure out how to translate your skills into their business. It is up to *you*. This is especially important for those in the military or any profession where titles don't easily translate.

If you have been in the military, you have skills and knowledge as managers, communicators, leaders, technicians, logistics and procurement experts, and much more. Not to mention personal attributes like commitment and dedication. All of these skills can translate into civilian businesses. But you won't get the chance to prove it if you don't explain how.

So cut the jargon. Saying "I enjoy MOS" "served as an 18D" "with SOMEDD" "experience as M2 gunner (50-CAL)" won't help civilian employers understand what you can do in private industry. Most won't even know what these words mean. What skills and knowledge did you develop, and how do they relate to the civilian world? Explain *this*.

Some people don't want to hear this. John, a returning veteran, wrote to me saying he ran into people who didn't understand how what he did translated into the civilian workplace. Finally, he wrote, "I said 'Screw them. I understand their language, why am I making excuses for them not understanding mine?' So when someone says to me, 'Give me an example of being a team player' in an interview, I say, 'I carried extra ammunition for the 60mm mortar and M-60 ammo for the support guns. And then stood watch at midnight so the patrol could get some rest. And if you don't understand that, then that is your problem, not mine. Because we are in a war and you should understand it.'"

Mmmm. He sounds a little angry, which brings me back to Naked Truth #12: People hardly ever act the way you want them to act. In this case, John may think people *should* understand what he did, but most people won't. And you'll cut down on your suffering if you can accept that. Make it your responsibility to help them understand. Be ready to explain that incredible set of skills you bring to the civilian table, along with the dedication and commitment you demonstrated with your last employer, a grateful nation—and that will need a little more explanation.

Please do not write out on paper what you might say like it's something you're going to memorize. When I get to this exercise with clients, many times they do just that—even though I tell them not to. Then they e-mail it to me, saying, "I'm sending this ahead of our meeting so you can review it and see what you think." I never read it when they do this. For the same reason I never read it when we're meeting in person and they hand me a piece of paper with their spiel written out word for word. I hand the paper right back and say, "Are you going to hand a piece of paper to the person you're talking to?" "Of course not," they say, "I'll be saying it." "So, say it to me so I can hear what you sound like."

Saying it and practicing it out loud are totally different from reading it. You need to see how it rolls off your tongue. What it feels like. Where you get stuck, which you will. What sounds idiotic and forced, which it will at first. What sounds brilliant, which will also happen after a lot of editing and practice. You're not delivering a memorized speech here. It's a conversation starter. Yes, spend lots of time fiddling with and crafting your words based on what we've talked about here. But speak it; don't read it.

Create an outline using the various elements we just covered. Write out phrases, and figure out how they fit together and tell a logical story. Then practice it out loud at your kitchen table. Speak it out loud in the shower. In the car. Again. And again. One more time until you're sick of hearing yourself. Create 15- and 30-second versions, and longer renditions with more detail. Even though this takes time to craft and is not easy to do right, you will thank me for it. Especially if you unexpectedly find yourself out on the street one day.

> *"You've got a great future, kid. But remember—talk low, talk slow and don't talk too much."*
>
> —JOHN WAYNE's advice to fellow actor Michael Caine

Now that you've figured out the language you'll use to talk about yourself, you're ready for the third part of my "Who Knew?" strategy.

Third Item in My "Who Knew?" Strategy: GET IT ON PAPER

Whether a good opportunity pops up or a disaster strikes, somebody somewhere is going to ask for your resume. So you need one. You may even want to create a portfolio that demonstrates your work and achievements. Maybe an electronic portfolio. Perhaps a Web site or another marketing tool appropriate for your profession and updated and ready to go. But a resume for sure.

You don't need to go hog wild and spend a load of time and money making fancy-shmancy electronic marketing tools. It depends on you, the way you want to manage your career and job search, your profession, how you like to communicate, and your technology know-how. What matters is that you have an appropriate format in which to tell your story and a way to track, update, and tweak content through-out your career.

So please keep a folder, notebook, or electronic file in which you add your achievements as they occur, including continuing education and any other relevant information. It's a pain in the rear to have to start from scratch when you sit down to write your resume. Especially when you're already freaked out because something unexpected happened in your career. If you don't have a current resume, get on it.

Not exactly branding, but . . .

Whether you're starting from scratch or updating your old resume, the same rules we've discussed in talking about yourself apply here. Before you write a word, look at why you are memorable and distinctive. Go back and see what you wrote in the statement that describes "the essence of what makes you unique."

Come up with a list of attributes, beliefs, perspectives, and experiences that make you different from others. If it feels like a colossal struggle, try this:

Just think about how you want to be seen. This is what's called "positioning," a term Jack Trout wrote about in 1969 in his book *The New Positioning*.

People's "minds are limited," wrote Trout. They can't cope with the mountains of information. Plus, "minds hate confusion." So you need to "oversimplify your message." You do it by figuring out your positioning, or as Trout puts it, what you want to "do to the mind." The purpose of this resume is also to explain who and what you are and then prove it. So first figure out how you want your audience to see you.* Then you can demonstrate that with the right written words and examples.

Instead of writing a document—as most people do—focusing on "what they want to know" (all those people "out there" who may read your resume), write a document that positions you the way you want them to see you and tells them what they'll need to know, so that you are indeed seen that way.

---

*See how I help Kathy do this in my podcast Episodes #34 and #35. Go to iTunes and search for Career Whisperer Andrea Kay, or my Web site, AndreaKay.com, which links to my podcasts.

"Not Exactly Branding" EXERCISE:

How do you want to be seen?

EXAMPLES:

I want to be seen as:

- the authority on helping women overcome personal crises.
- the one who can fix any problem on a Macintosh computer.

_____

_____

_____

_____

> *"What's the old thing they say? 'Luck is basically preparation plus opportunity.'"*
>
> —CHARLES GIBSON in *The New York Times*, May 2007, after being passed over for the prestigious anchor job of the ABC evening news, then getting the job after all

Another Tool for Your Survival Kit: Keep a Watch Over You

Everyone else is probably too busy with their own problems to worry about your career. Even if you have a mentor or coach whose role it is to advise you every step of the way, it's pretty much up to you (more on this in Step 6).

Depending on your company and supervisor, you might get career planning at your job. The company may pay for training and education, and it may not. But even companies that pay for training may leave it up to you to figure out what you need. Since you don't get to dictate what kind of career-development program a company has, or since you may be self-employed or in between jobs or careers, this career-planning issue is your baby and a crucial tool for your career survival kit. I've got six suggestions for staying on top of it.

1. CHART THESE MUNDANE BUT NECESSARY ISSUES

You'll want to create a notebook or some way of capturing any notable insight you have about your career. But before you do that, start by writing answers to these more mundane, but important, questions:

- What am I working toward in my career?
- What knowledge am I lacking to do well at my job—or the job I want?
- In what areas do I need to excel or gain more expertise to move up ?
- What do I need to learn or master to feel I am the best I can be?
- What specific knowledge do I need to progress?
- What classes, experiences, or professional assistance would help me achieve what I listed?

Check in with yourself on these issues from time to time, since things change. Do it every six months or so, before you got to bed. You might get some ideas in your dreams.

2. YEARN TO LEARN

Little did many of us know that earning a degree was just the beginning of our education. To be taken seriously and really get anywhere today and to make yourself more valuable when change is in the air, a yearning for learning is a must.

If you aren't already, you need to be racking up continuing education classes and learning new information on everything from communications to the latest data in your field.

As the experts who are looking at a major overhaul of the U.S. education system put it in their report for the National Center on Education and the Economy, "This is a world in which a very high level of preparation in reading, writing, speaking, mathematics, science, literature, history and the arts will be an indispensable foundation for everything that comes after for most members of the workforce."

Your passport to a good job will also include being comfortable with ideas and abstractions, because "creativity and innovation are the key to the good life, in which high levels of education—a different kind of education than most of us have had—are going to be the only security there is," according to the report.

You'll also need to demonstrate your *desire* to learn and keep up on issues that affect your field to be considered the best in that field and when job hunting.

For example, look at someone who wants to get into pharmaceutical sales. Pharmaceutical-sales jobs reward for assertiveness, persistence and knowledge, explains *The Princeton Review*. If you're a pharmaceutical-sales job seeker, you will be rewarded for the same things. Since education is imperative in this job, you'll want to make sure prospective employers are aware of not just what you know now, but how you'll stay updated on health issues and the problems your target audience faces. This goes for just about any profession nowadays.

3. Take their problem-solving breath away

Kenneth Cole relates on his Web site how he began his business when he had just completed the design of his shoe collection. His limited funds kept him from doing what big companies do next—getting a fancy showroom to sell their wares. So he decided to borrow a truck and park it in midtown Manhattan. But he needed a permit, which the city only granted to utility companies and movie crews. He changed his firm's name to Kenneth Cole Productions, Inc., and applied for a permit to shoot the film *The Birth of a Shoe Company*. When his team parked on Sixth Avenue complete with a director, models as actresses, and (sometimes) film in the camera, they sold forty thousand pairs of shoes in two and a half days.

He could have let many things get in his way. Resourcefulness and problem solving won the day, and he built a successful fashion footwear, apparel, and accessory company.

So consider that as you think about and write answers to the following questions:

- How do I demonstrate my resourcefulness and problem-solving skills in the job I have now? Or how did I do that in previous roles?
- How can I do this better?
  If you're job hunting:
- How can I be more resourceful in this process?
- What examples of innovative problem solving can I share with interviewers?

4. KEEP UP TO STAY UP

Staying clued in to what's happening in the world will help you be prepared in case disaster strikes. You'll know where you can fit in next as the world changes, what education you might need to stay relevant, where your particular field is headed, how changes might affect your field (or one you're considering), and how to stay valuable and employable.

So read reputable news publications, keep up with the news, and talk to people. Check out the U.S. Department of Labor's Web site, www.bls.gov, to learn of jobs and careers in higher demand. Take note of what other people discuss and seem to consistently need or complain about. And while you're at it, here are some questions to keep you in the know and on your toes (this too, can go in the career development journal I just talked about):

- How will my line of work be affected by such trends as the green movement, population growth, longer life spans, the loss of traditional culture, and the overall decline of the environment?
- What needs or problems have I heard about that potentially affect my field or industry but that no one is doing anything about, that aren't being handled, and that will probably grow?
- What needs or problems have I heard about that affect another industry or market but that no one is doing anything about?

- Is there something I can do to add value in this area for my customers, company, or peers?
- How will my profession or line of work be affected by technology?
- How might a news item potentially trickle down and affect my industry or work? (Example: The fall of the mortgage industry affects the lumber industry.)

5. Keep turning out your greatest hits

When songwriter John Mellencamp licensed "Our Country" to Chevrolet to use as the theme for a commercial for the Silverado truck, people accused him of selling out. His response? "I'm a songwriter and I want people to hear my songs. This is just what I did this time to reinvent myself and stay in business," he told *The New York Times* in 2007. I say good for him. He was open to letting his music be used in a way it wasn't originally intended to be, and as a result, we still know Mellencamp and his music.

The longer you're in a career, the more you have to stay on the lookout for new ways to stay valuable in your line of work—so others *know* you and *want* you. Some musicians do it by remaking classic songs. Ron Isley, Barry Manilow, Rod Stewart, Boz Skaggs, Willie Nelson, Linda Ronstadt, and Bette Midler: they've all done it. Others, like Deborah Harry, co-founder of the group Blondie in the late seventies, have created new music. In 2007, she released *Necessary Evil*, her first solo album in 14 years.

I've known artists who became representatives for paint manufacturers, radio executives who became music producers, commercial radio newscasters and disc jockeys who moved to public or Internet radio, dancers who became teachers. So figure out a way to keep turning out hits to stay employable and valued. Sometimes the move will be based on the past. Other times it will be a totally new direction.

Whether it's due to the marketplace or your body not letting you do the same work anymore, things change. But most people still resist this. They write to me all the time saying, "I'd like to find a place where I can be for the next 15 years." Wouldn't that be nice? It's possible, but it's asking for trouble. Because what this person is really saying is, "I'd like to find a nice, secure job where I don't have to worry

PEOPLE WILL PAY YOU IF . . .

Not all jobs are in traditional corporations or small businesses. There are problems to be solved everywhere. Just keep this in mind: People will pay you to do something if you add value to their lives. Today there are all kinds of ways to add value that didn't exist in the past. To get your creative juices flowing, consider three questions:

1. **What task might someone pay me to do that they can't do because they're too busy working? (Watching kids, walking dogs, cleaning houses, or making meals.)**

2. **What task might someone pay me to do that they don't *want* to do because it's too gross, too complex, or not how they want to spend their time? (Picking up dog droppings in their yard, snatching head lice from their kids' hair, or wading through health insurance and medical bills.)**

3. **What task might a rich person pay me to do because they are, well, busy doing things rich people do? (Providing medical concierge services that feature hotel-room or at-home visits 24/7, or high-end household services like caring for art collections and wine cellars.)**

about anything changing, or about having to change myself. I'd like to be able to go home every day and have a few weeks of vacation every year, knowing I can retire in 15 years." Highly unlikely.

If you just focus on staying secure you won't be thinking about how to stay valuable. Best be ready for the urge to move on or the need to adapt at *any* point. Who knows—a career itch could set in after two or twenty years. The risks of staying put in what seems like a secure role, company, or industry could outweigh the benefits. To get a handle on this, do the following exercise.

"The Risk of Staying Put" EXERCISE

What do I need to do to stay relevant in my field? Does that require me to go to a new company, go out on my own, get more education, or what?

_____

_____

_____

_____

What do I risk if I stay at this company or in this career?

_____

_____

_____

Just because my industry is doing OK today, is it headed in a different direction that I should be preparing for? What direction is that? If I'm not sure, what do I need to do to figure it out?

_____

_____

_____

What if I am not physically able do this work in five or ten years? What should I be doing to prepare?

_____

_____

_____

_____

6. Know people who know people who know people

One thing that hasn't changed is that people are still your ticket to a robust career. It's very simple: People do the hiring. People know other people. People like to help people they know, like, and trust. People hire people they know, like, and trust. So it makes sense to get to know people and develop relationships so they'll know, like, and trust you and want to help you in your career.

But don't just do it for what they can do for you. That plan will backfire. When I say get to know people, I mean *really* get to know people and have meaningful relationships with them. Because most of all, it's very fulfilling when you know people you can trust and who trust you and whom *you* can help in return.

But I don't know anybody . . .

I hear this constantly. "Of course you know people!" I always insist when someone says this. And, of course, they do. They just haven't been taking time to talk to any of them. These people live around you. They are the other professionals you go to for services. They are former co-workers and professors.

One of my clients was a 50-year-old woman who, until the day she lost her job in broadcasting, was happy and completely focused on her job. She never got around to meeting up with friends, colleagues, or others in her community, or volunteering. When new owners took over and cleaned house at the station where she worked, she was a goner, out on the street with no one to turn to for support. The notion of "keeping in contact" and "building relationships" was not in her vocabulary. Who has time?

Things were bleak. She was very angry about what had happened and even angrier that she had let her network deteriorate. One day she told me that a man she had been getting to know and wooing for a position at a broadcast company was taking a job in another city. My client told me, "All the goodwill I built up in him is down the drain." And boy, was she pissed *again*.

"Pleeeze," I said to her. "Haven't I taught you anything?" It's true, all the goodwill you've built will go down the drain if you see people as only a means to your end—to help you with your career now.

But this is a short-sighted strategy, and, I might add, not very personally fulfilling. If you treat people like that, they'll sniff it out and you'll be networkless. It's just an out-and-out dumb way to run a career.

The encounter she had with this man was just the beginning of their relationship. It doesn't end because the guy was moving to another city and she didn't get what she wanted from him. I suggested she write the man a note congratulating him on his new position and to keep in contact. That's how you build long-term, meaningful relationships with people.

Here are some examples of how people *have* developed meaningful relationships with others that made a difference when the right time came in their careers.

Claudia has pals all over New York

Claudia's last day at her job of ten years was on a Friday, as most last days on a job go. But before she packed up her desk, she already had offers to work at two other companies.

As a supervisor at a New York firm that sells Broadway theater tickets, Claudia found that her job was eliminated after the company acquired another firm. When her departure was announced to clients, she got an e-mail from one of them saying, "Sorry to hear you're leaving; would you like to work for us?" Her clients knew her because she had been developing relationships with them for years.

"I guess after ten years they felt as if they had come to know me," she says. Not only had she proven herself to be "a dependable, reliable worker" but she had also, in her own words, "remembered birthdays and new babies. I arranged for small gifts to be sent . . . and if someone mentioned leaving early one day for their kid's school piano recital, I wrote it down on my calendar so I would remember to inquire afterwards."

She also had an informational interview with an Off-Broadway theater company that began with, "We have nothing now," she relates. "But after about an hour, it ended with 'Hmm, let me think on this. Maybe I can come up with something.'"

Mike knows his competitors' kids' names

When word got out that Mike, a sales representative for a California company, was leaving his job, he got calls from his company's competitors saying, "Come work for us, we'd love to have you." They knew him because over the years he had made it a point to meet them and show he cared.

He'd start conversations with them at trade shows. He'd sit next to them at association meetings. He had lunches with them. He knew their kids' names and when their father or mother was having surgery. He set his butt down in front of people, and they talked about life and work and what mattered to them. They got to know him, and he got to know them.

That's how people like Claudia and Mike get jobs, build their careers, and add one more tool to their emergency preparedness kit. Which means you have to stop sitting in front of your computer in your pajamas sending your resume off to job sites. Instead, put on your Sunday best and set *your* butt down in front of people.

By the way, my client who was so pissed off because of first losing her job in broadcasting and letting her relationships fall apart pulled herself up from her depressing, poor-pitiful-me state. She talked and talked and talked to people until she was hoarse. That was a humbling year for her. Eventually—eight months later—after holding conversations, following up, and getting to know four different people at one broadcasting station, she was offered a new position.

Sometimes a simple conversation will do

Russ Berger, president of the Russ Berger Design Group in Addison, Texas, learned that conversations "can have some unexpected business or personal consequences that are downright karmic," he said in *The New York Times* segment Frequent Flyer.

About 20 years ago, he was flying back to Dallas from New York. Seated next to him was a tall, long-haired guy who said he was a musician and songwriter and that his first breakthrough album would be released soon. Berger told him he designed recording studios and broadcast facilities and that he'd look for his record. The musician said he'd try to record in one of Berger's studios.

Four years later, Berger heard from a recording engineer who worked for this musician: Grammy Award–winning Michael Bolton. "They wanted me to help with the design of a recording and mix studio at his residence." When they met, Berger recounted their meeting from four years earlier. They went on to work together on another project, and, as Berger said, "A simple plane ride home turned into something of an extended adventure. All because I took the time to talk."

Take advantage of the moment you have when strangers park themselves next to you at a meeting or on a plane. And if you don't get out much, make a point of creating these face-to-face opportunities that could lead to your next career adventure. You just never know where a simple conversation can take you.

. . . .

"As I Think of People" EXERCISE

It's hard to think of people at the precise moment you are wondering, "Who do I know?" So keep a piece of paper called your "As I Think of People" list close by and jot down their names as you run into them or they pop into your head. Then, when someone like me says, "So, who do you know?" you can tick them off and get to work on building those relationships.

. . . .

When the Tornado Warnings Go Off

When the civil defense sirens go off warning of a possible tornado—typically in the middle of the night—the last thing I feel like doing is jumping out of bed, scooping up the weather radio and cat, nudging the dog out of his snoring slumber, and scrambling to the designated safe room of our house. But I do it since it's a small price to pay for so much at risk.

After a long day of work, when, as I mentioned in the last step, you'd probably rather be lying on the couch watching *I Love Lucy* reruns, the last thing you may feel like doing is everything I just covered in this step. You don't have to build your career survival kit in a day. Take a few hours every week—doing these exercises, updating your resume, or talking to people. I realize it's work. But it's work you're doing for *you* that will make you more powerful. These are steps you're taking to protect your present and secure your future and to lessen your suffering when things don't work out as planned. These common-sense tactics will prepare you for unforeseeable predicaments and possibilities that can sneak up with no warning.

No one knows what lies ahead. That's why doing these steps is a small price to pay for so much at risk.

TAKE YOUR FOURTH QUIT-BEING-PISSED OATH

I hereby promise myself to quit being pissed off and start being powerful by putting together my "Who Knew?" strategy so I'm prepared for unpredictable events and ready when opportunity knocks.

SIGN HERE _____

DATE _____

Step 5

Develop a
Sixth Sense

Mark was flattered when the president of a small start-up where he had been a part-time consultant asked him to come on board. "I remember the day he made the offer," he says. Mark was sitting on his couch in the living room of his town house and got a sudden, sharp pang in his gut.

"I took a few days to think the decision over," he says. He stewed. He paced the halls. He made a pros-and-cons list at his dining room table. On the third day he made the decision to take the offer. "I ignored my gut because I saw the promise of stock options. I would later regret the decision."

Thomas also wished he had listened to his instinct and the sage advice of others. He left a good career in higher education to manage a business for a celebrity, a job that seemed to fit, in his words, "my dream since childhood to work in the entertainment industry." Even though something kept telling him "to be cautious and watch out for myself, I didn't listen. I think I knew at a gut level right from the start that it would not be a smooth working relationship." Although others warned him the situation was destined to end badly, he left his job and took the celebrity's offer. After he spent "a considerable sum of my money keeping things running while I wasn't receiving compensation for my work," he quit.

Latisha, on the other hand, did heed a warning she got from the very person interviewing her for the job of personal assistant to a well-known and apparently ridiculously demanding individual. "Don't take the job," the interviewer told her. "You're too nice a person."

How do you know if a particular job, career, or company is right for you? Does anybody really know before they jump in? How do you smoke out bad companies or decipher if they are who they say they are? How do you find out if they're the upright corporate citizens they profess to be on their Web site and in their press releases? How do you know that they're not just about profit, but care about people, and if they really are flexible about work hours? You don't, for sure.

But whether you're job hunting, considering a promotion or

other role in your present company or making a career change, if you don't do more digging, like Mark and Thomas and thousands of others, you might very well end up pissed that you didn't, with a severe case of "I should haves."

If you're job hunting, deeper digging will give you a feel for the players in an industry or a company and their modus operandi and history. You can also learn what an industry or company is like and if they match up to your ideal. If you're considering a new position in your company, going below the surface can help you decide whether the move is a plus or a huge blunder.

But digging up the dirt is only part of the picture. There are subtle and not-so-subtle clues you can pick up about management and culture. There are questions you can ask, policies and day-to-day practices to root out, behavior you can observe, and gut reactions to heed—all which will add up to your sixth sense about whether or not a place or particular career is the right one to park yourself for a while.

We're going to cover that in detail. But first, and most important, you need to know what precisely you are looking for. What matters to you most. What the ideal work and career situation—or close to it—looks like for *you*. That way you'll know *what* to look for, what questions to ask, what areas to probe, and how to recognize the right situation when you *do* see it. If you're like 99 percent of the people I talk to, you haven't done a good job defining that. So we're going to walk through that now.

What Fits You Like a Glove?

You actually know a lot of this information already. Now it's a matter of putting it all into a new context.

Remember in Step 4 when you wrote "The Gist of You," so you could talk about yourself at any given moment? That information described the following:

1. What you do best
2. What you know about (or want to know about if making a career change)

3. What you care about and how you'll make a difference
4. How you tend to act
5. What challenges you

All of that is also part of what constitutes your ideal or best work and career situation. To complete that picture, we need three more pieces of data:

6. What kind of environment and culture you thrive in (One that's informal and flexible? Hands-off management? Management that communicates and invites feedback or management that provides a lot of direction and rules?)
7. What kind of manager you work best for and how this person thinks and acts
8. What kind of work arrangement fits you (Part time? Working from home? Job sharing?)

The question you're trying to answer now is, *At this point in my career, considering who I am and what I want, what does the ideal situation look like? Specifically, what would I be doing, who would I be doing it with, and in what type of environment and working arrangement?* Here's an exercise to figure that out.

. . . .

"What Fits You Like a Glove?" EXERCISE

Write here what your ideal would look like using the answers you wrote to the first five elements (see Step 4, Know the Gist of You) and the data you just came up with for numbers 6 through 8:

At this point in my career, the ideal situation is one where I:

1. Do what I do best (my strengths):

_____

_____

_____

_____

2. Apply what I know about or want to want to know about, if making a career change (my body of knowledge):

_____

_____

_____

3. Can work with this product, service, or cause that I care about:

_____

4. Can make this kind of difference:

_____

_____

5. Can be who I am, which is (how you tend to act):

_____

_____

6. Can be challenged by:

_____

_____

7. Can be in this type of environment and culture:

_____

_____

8. Have this kind of manager:

_____

9. Have this kind of work arrangement:

_____

. . . .

Now that you know what your ideal situation looks like and specifically what you'd be doing, who you would be doing it with, and in what type of environment and working arrangement, let's talk about how you sniff out whether a place has it. Remember, this is your *ideal*. You may not get 100 percent of what you've defined. And you may get a greater degree of one thing than another. Like most things, you may have to compromise. But to get close we need to start somewhere.

How to Find Out What You Want to Know

WATCH AND LEARN

You can shed light on the unwritten rules of how people act, treat each other, and communicate at a company with first- and secondhand observation. All of these elements add up to culture—probably one of the most crucial components of a happy union. Here's what to look for.

1. How does the front desk treat you?

I'm talking about how companies respond—or not—when you contact them online or on the phone. If you're thinking, "Are you kidding? You

---

**The first time ever you see its face,
does a company pass these two tests?**

Pay close attention to all your encounters with a company—from the first interaction on the phone to correspondence and follow-up. When you do get an interview, note what you see and sense, keeping these two questions in the forefront of your mind:

▶ How do I feel about the company now that we're eyeball-to-eyeball?

▶ Is the company who and what they say they are? (Do their public relations match the experience I'm having from the time I walk in the door and with all the encounters I've had?)

---

can't get through to anyone!" that tells you something right there. And if a company greets you with a barbed-wire-laden phone tree, well, that tells you something, too.

If you do stumble upon a live person who wears you down with officialese and red tape and seems more interested in getting you out of their hair than helping, that's also telling.

To test this, I called two behemoth companies—Procter & Gamble and Microsoft—about whom many people would think, "I'd like to work there." At Microsoft, if you're lucky enough to bypass their "auto attendant" and find an operator, good luck trying to get to a live human. It seems to be part of the culture, which you'll discover if you dig around more.

On the other hand, at Procter & Gamble you get a real person, who, with a few relevant questions, connects you to a department where there are actual people or you can leave a message.

2. What's in the news?

Let's stick with Microsoft. If you snoop around, you'll find news articles and analysis that can give you insight into such a company's culture. One *Wall Street Journal* article, by Robert Guth, discussed the company's plan to bring in outside talent, saying Microsoft's insular culture has made "integrating new executives a lingering problem" and that throughout the company's history, "decisive and aggressive outsiders have been worn down by the second-guessing of Microsoft veterans before stepping down to less prominent roles or leaving altogether."

3. What do others—besides reporters and commentators—say?

There are two sources to look for: company insiders and outside observers. Not to pick on Microsoft, but I'll use them as an example again. When computer scientist Kai-Fu Lee left Microsoft for Google, and Microsoft sued him to stop him from going to Google, he painted a "distinctly unflattering picture of the company's inner workings" in his testimony, according to a *BusinessWeek* article.

The article cited criticism from dozens of former and current employees in court testimony and personal blogs on how the company operates internally. Readers' comments on the magazine's site are telling, too.

As for how people communicate there, a contractor for Microsoft said in a 2005 *Seattle Post-Intelligencer* article, "All of the communication is done via (instant message) and e-mail. So if people start ignoring your electronic communication, it gets very frustrating, very quickly."

You can also talk to people you know who have worked for a company or had relatives who worked there, as well as those who have done business there.

Recruiters can also offer perspective on company culture and where a company stands in the marketplace. Take Simon Francis, partner at CTPartners, an executive search firm in Menlo Park, California, for whom Microsoft is a source of talent. He describes Microsoft as "a culture characterized by corporate arrogance," an "aging tech giant fighting for dominance in new markets" against a "hot-shot young company (Google) with tremendous valuation and brand."

People talk about companies all over the Internet. You need to take what you read with a grain of salt, of course. But when you see an overwhelming number of comments saying the same thing, it does make you wonder.

4. How do they treat you in the interview?

How do you feel in the process and with the people you meet along the way? Do they respect your time by being on time? Do they treat you professionally? How do they treat others? Can you envision your-self working side by side by with them every day and in the way they operate? How does it *feel?*

I once had an interview with a man who propped his feet up on his desk (so that I was talking to the soles of his shoes), smoked a cigar, took phone calls, and opened mail the entire time we conversed. I felt demeaned, and figured, if this is how he treats me in the interview, I can't imagine how he would be if I worked for him. I was very clear that I would never work for that man or that company.

Get "picky picky"

To learn about who companies really are, including their finances, see the following sources:

- ▶ CorporateInformation.com
- ▶ Search engines such as Hotbot.com, Northernlight.com, and Google.com
- ▶ EuroMonitor.com, which sells information on 350 international consumer goods and services companies
- ▶ Hoovers.com
- ▶ Finance.Yahoo.com
- ▶ Research.Thomsonib.com

ASK AND LEARN MORE

Remember the elements we covered to define your ideal situation? That's what you use to develop the questions you're going to ask to learn more about a company and a job. The questions themselves and where you are in the process will determine when and where you ask them—on the phone; with a human resource professional, a recruiter, or a hiring manager; or in a first, second, or third interview. Consider how much rapport you've developed, how well you've gotten to know the person, and how bright things are looking before you pose a question.

To get a better sense of:

Whether you'd be using your greatest strengths and doing work you enjoy and applying your knowledge, you could ask:

- What are the responsibilities of this role?
- What types of issues would I face?
- What's a typical day or week like?
- What are the expectations of the position?
- What does it take to be successful in this role?

Whether and how you can make a difference, you could ask:

- How does the position contribute to the company's goals, productivity, or profits?

Whether your personality, style, and attitudes fit the company and the role, you could ask:

- What personal characteristics and style fit best in this role and at your company?

Whether you will be challenged, you could ask:

- How important is learning, experimenting, coming up with new techniques to this position?

What the environment and culture are like, you could ask:

- What's your customer service philosophy?
- What's the company's leadership style, and what's it based on?
- How are employees recognized for their contributions?
- How does management communicate with employees?
- How do employees develop and learn?
- How do you evaluate performance?
- Do you encourage creative input from your employees?
- What does it take to be successful here?

What kind of manager you'd be working for, you could ask:

- What's your management style?

MIND YOUR GUT

It's a pang you might get in your gut. Or it's a little voice in the back of your head. It's like an immediate flash of truth. But as I pointed out at the beginning of this step, people ignore their intuition much of the time.

In part, that's because intuition isn't logical. We're taught critical thinking, which requires you to back up any conclusions with logical evidence, says psychologist Carolyn Kaufman. How do you explain a weird tingly feeling you get in your body?

Microexpressions are one way to explain that intuitive sense, she says. These are superfast expressions that show you how another person really feels. For example, if you ask an interviewer if she believes in career development, she may smile and say yes, but you have the feeling she is annoyed. You don't know why, and since she's smiling it seems illogical, but you just have that feeling.

She may have sighed or made a facial expression so quickly that neither of you realized she did it. But your brain is quick enough to pick it up. And what you get is a "gut feeling" that she's annoyed. It's the subconscious processing of information that the conscious is not aware of. It's like the fine print—often where the most important information is hidden, says Kaufman.

Where do you feel it? Most people experience intuition as emotion, and most people do experience emotion physically. When I work with clients who are trying to learn to tap into their intuition, I always ask them: Where do you get that feeling in your body? That's what you want to pay attention to.

Lynn Robinson, author of *Trust Your Gut,* says the ancient Chinese believed wisdom resides in the stomach. But you also might "break into a sweat when faced with a choice you know isn't right," or you might "feel a tingly zing" up your spine, she says.

To get more in tune with it, Carolyn Kaufman encourages people to talk back and forth with their intuition. Imagine the part of you that believes, feels, or is saying (fill in the blank) is sitting in a chair across from you. If it could talk, what would it say? Ask it questions. For example, why might it be a bad idea to accept this job offer? How do you know? See this as a fact-finding expedition or an interview, not an interrogation.

So if you are interviewing for a job or have the chance to move into a new position with your company, and you're trying to decide if it's a good decision, you can try a similar exercise. Looking back at the offer, conversations you've had, and things you've observed in the interview process, ask yourself the following questions:

- What did you feel or sense? If that voice in the back of your head was sitting in a chair across from you, what did it believe or feel or say to you?
- What worries you about that?

I Met Him/Her on a Monday Form

Use this form right after an interview to capture how it went. Since you're probably a busy person who can't remember what you did five minutes ago, trust me, this will come in handy.

Fill in the blanks:

I met him/her on (whatever day your meeting took place), and upon our first meeting, thought: (this guy is nuts . . . this woman is psycho . . . this guy is kind . . . she is really sharp and I like her)

_____

_____

_____

_____

_____

When we were talking about (whatever stands out as a moment you got great insight into the person, the company, or the job), I discovered: (this job would be the kiss of death . . . working for this man would be like working for a sociopath . . . this company is run by religious zealots, and it's not a place for me . . . this woman is the kind of person I'd love to work for)

_____

_____

_____

_____

_____

When he/she said (whatever it was that gave you a twinge in your gut or somewhere in your body), I got a weird feeling that told me: (he wasn't being truthful . . . she was not sure if she believed what she was saying . . . he had another agenda)

_____

_____

_____

_____

_____

GIVE ME A CREATIVE CHANCE

Most workers put a high premium on creativity at work, says a 2007 survey commissioned by the Fairfax County Economic Development Authority. Yet the survey points to a possible "creativity gap" in the American workplace.

While 88 percent of those surveyed consider themselves creative, only 63 percent said their jobs were creative, and only 61 percent thought the company they worked for was creative. Twenty-one percent said they would change jobs even if it meant earning less money to be more creative at work. Twenty-nine percent said they'd move to be part of a more creative community—especially those ages 18 to 34.

Nearly every worker in another survey, the Emerging Workforce Study, conducted by Harris Interactive, said they preferred roles that allowed them to think creatively.

Having said that, what's stopping you from being creative in how you think, attack problems, or create opportunities? Why do you need someone to *allow* you to think creatively? If you're creative, be creative.

The Bird's-eye View of What to Look For

A company's size and type can determine its daily practices, policies, initiatives, work arrangements, benefits, and resources. A larger company might offer resources that just aren't feasible for a small company. On the other hand, some small companies offer better pay and benefits than some large ones. It all depends on the senior managers' philosophy.

What matters to one senior manager or company owner (the person who sets the tone for the culture of a company or division or who has great influence) may not be important to another. A COO of one company told me he was a big believer in keeping stress to a minimum. He had firsthand experience with that, as he tried to raise a family, go to school, and move up in his career. So he offers all types of optional work arrangements for his workers.

Another executive, Kory Kolligian, COO of Continuum, a design studio in West Newton, Massachusetts, developed his philosophy of how to treat people when he was just seven:

"When I was out for dinner with my family I would always ask my parents if I could say hi to people at other tables (in most cases they were eating alone). I have always viewed the world through a very empathetic lens. There is nothing more important to me than to know as much as I can about who people are . . . what motivates, frustrates, and energizes them."

As a result, Kolligian has an "open-air policy." He has no office and sits out among his 140 employees, which "ensures that you never lose touch with the vibe of who we are individually and as a company."

Some practices and policies will matter more to *you* than others—depending of course, on your ideal. Some things may be important to you but don't influence whether you'd take a job at a place. For example, according to a 2007 Hudson survey, 75 percent of U.S. workers think companies have responsibilities to the community, but 70 percent don't consider a prospective employer's corporate responsibility program very important when it comes to evaluating a job offer.

Here is a list of those things you can think about when rooting around a company's Web site, observing, or asking questions. Remember, not everything I list here may matter to you. Most people don't know *what* to look for. This list will help you sort it out.

Keep your eye on these:

- How transparent are people in the interview process? Do they make it easy for you to learn about how things work? Do they let you talk to other employees?
- Do they seek and value employee feedback? If so, what do they do with it?
- Do they promote diversity? What holidays are celebrated?
- Do they have a mentoring program?
- Do they conduct performance reviews?
- Do they offer in-house training? Do they help employees get continuing education through tuition reimbursement or student loans?
- Do they offer family-caregiving assistance?
- What is their overall guiding principle, philosophy, or code of conduct?
- How do they communicate? Does the CEO get around and talk to people?
- Is the company involved in the community?
- Do they have green business practices that help them clean up how they do business or support the environment?
- Do they offer such resources as legal or financial services, career transition programs, counseling, or wellness programs?
- Do they offer bonuses based on performance?
- Do they offer alternative and flexible-work arrangements?
- Do they do cross-training?
- What do they and others say about sexual harassment, discrimination, communication, results, integrity, and accountability?
- How do employees get recognized?
- Does the staff of the department you'd work in meet regularly?
- How does the company help employees develop professionally?
- What does the company do to stay competitive in the marketplace?

One value that's popping up as a criterion for consumers and some workers is that a company incorporate green values into its business. This can cover the following things:

- selling environmentally friendly or recyclable products
- emphasizing green operations, including reducing energy in how they make or distribute products
- increasing the use of solar and wind energy
- fuel-efficient fleets
- turning waste into fuel
- reducing carbon emissions and using materials that have a low carbon impact
- doing business with more energy-conscious suppliers

If these things are important to you, ask around, check out a company's Web site, and watch the news for information on how the company treats these issues.

Shower the People with Decency

Hearing from as many upset, angry, and frustrated workers as I do, I often get asked, "Are there *any* decent leaders and companies?" "Yes, you just don't work for one," I say. But they're out there.

Decent leaders run small, medium, and large companies. But it's interesting that people surveyed in a 2007 Harris Poll said they had the most confidence in leaders of small businesses. Next came leaders in the military. Then came leaders of major and medical educational institutions—these tied for third place. Then came organized religion, the U.S. Supreme Court, public schools, the White House, the courts and justice system, television news, Wall Street, major companies, and organized labor. Congress was last. Overall, people don't seem to have much confidence in our large institutions.

When I asked for feedback from workers and leaders on how they create great workplaces, I was bombarded with e-mails. These examples of what decent leaders in companies of all sizes are doing might help you form a better picture of what you're looking for.

James Parker, former CEO of Southwest Airlines and author of the book *Do the Right Thing*, told me, "Personal interaction with customers and employees was a big part of our culture." He said he helped flight attendants hand out peanuts on flights "fairly often," although sometimes they "preferred to let me just pick up the trash from customers, which I was happy to do." All of the company's officers tried to show up in unexpected places, loading bags onto an airplane or checking customers in at the ticket counter.

They also work hard to take care of the company financially. "We tried to protect the jobs of our people by protecting the profitability of the company," says Parker. "After 9/11, we were the only major airline that decided not to furlough any of our employees or demand major pay cuts. The only people who gave up their paychecks were the board of directors and executive officers of the company."

Instead of dictating employee conduct with a "bunch of rules, regulations and policies," Parker liked creating a workforce of people who understood the mission of his company. He then sought to "encourage them to use their energy and intelligence to make decisions that will help you achieve your mission." Sometimes they will make mistakes, he says, and you just have to accept that.

According to James Buckmaster, CEO of Craigslist, a classifieds Web site that serves 450 cities in 50 countries with the help of about 25 employees, "Our primary goals are about making a positive difference in the world and absolutely not about trying to maximize our financial performance."

"We go to great lengths to find talented and self-motivated employees, do what we can to make them happy, and leave them be to do great things," says Buckmaster.

They do that by compensating workers at or above market levels; giving superior benefits; having a "laid-back, progressive, quirky, brainy, goofy, fun" culture with flexible hours, lots of telecommuting, and matching charitable contributions; and by holding "almost no meetings or dreary corporate rah-rah motivational stuff or 'team building,'" he explains.

James Sinegal, president and CEO of Costco Wholesale Corporation, answers his own phone, and when someone comes to visit him at company headquarters in Issaquah, Washington, he walks down to the lobby to escort his guest to his fourth-floor office, according to *BusinessWeek*. It seems to be a part of his overall philosophy of keeping things simple and being involved in the details.

How much of a peek can you get?

When Scott was trying to decide whether to become a part of the company Nerds On Site,* he not only did a thorough job of investigating them, but the company made it easy for him to understand their business model and how others felt about the operation.

They were very open, holding a meeting where applicants from around the globe gathered by telephone, and then allowing participants to ask questions. The way they let "prospective Nerds" and "real-life Nerds" talk to one another—with an emphasis on listening, not preaching—"showed their commitment to open communication and the sharing of ideas," he told me.

"The transparency allowed me to get to know many of the players and see that their values were compatible with mine. An organization that opens itself up immediately conveys the message that they have nothing to hide."

But, he points out, transparency is not an end in and of itself—it's just a means to find out more. "I'm sure there are cases where one could say, 'I found out a lot about that company and based on that, I'm confident I don't want to work there.'"

---

* You can learn more about how Scott made this decision in my podcast Episode #29. Go to iTunes and search for Career Whisperer Andrea Kay, or my Web site, AndreaKay.com, which links to my podcasts.

"While I was at Southwest Airlines, we were sometimes asked who we put first: shareholders, customers, or employees. We always answered without hesitation that we put employees first. We believed that if we created a workplace where our employees loved our company . . . they would share their passion with customers, creating a culture of great customer service . . . Happy employees create happy customers, and happy customers usually create happy shareholders. This is not a matter of policies or mission statements. It is just a matter of building a culture in which people respect each other and share a passion for a common mission."

—JAMES PARKER, former CEO of Southwest Airlines

When it comes to employees, his philosophy is "pay good wages and you'll get good people and good productivity," he said in a *USA Today* article. He is fond of saying that good business comes down to "doing the right thing."

How Are Those Ethics?

Just because something is in writing doesn't make it so. But when a company goes to the trouble to create and post a code of conduct on its Web site and other conspicuous places, it's a good start. For one thing, "building an enterprise-wide ethical culture reduces misconduct by as much as 75 percent," says Dr. Patricia J. Harned, president of the Ethics Resource Center in Arlington, Virginia. If a company has a decent ethics and compliance program that is well implemented, it nearly doubles employee reporting of misconduct, she says. Less misconduct takes place, and when it does, management is more likely to know about it.

So when you're scoping companies out, see if they have such a code. It should identify a set of values that guide the operations, she says. In general, Harned suggests getting a sense of the ethical culture of the organization, how things get done, and who gets rewarded. Is it the person who gets ahead by any means necessary, or the one who is successful while upholding a high standard of integrity? In an interview, notice how the interviewer refers to these standards. Is emphasis placed on whether they are taken seriously by employees?

Specifically, Harned suggests asking:

- Is there an ethics office or program?
- Are employees trained on the ethics and compliance regulations that relate to their job?
- Is there a way for employees to make management aware if they think there are ethics violations taking place?

Depending on the situation and who you're talking to, these additional questions can be trickier to pose: Do employees ever feel pressured to cut corners to get their jobs done? When was the last time you remember anyone in management talking about ethics at work?

Talk About Culture Shock

These are the stories of Howard and Barbara. Their experiences make a strong case for asking lots of questions about culture, minding your gut, and being aware of your own biases before you take a job.

A CUBE FARM WITH A CEO WHO ONLY SHOWED HIS FACE AT CIGARETTE BREAKS

Howard had a job where everyone loved their product as well as their customers (who loved their products as much as the employees) and a CEO who believed in being open, having fun, and letting people make mistakes.

"When a decision needed to be made, it wasn't, 'Let me ask my manager,'" he explains. "We were all about taking great care of customers, training, and helping others and living it every day."

YOU DON'T HAVE TO MAKE UP FICTITIOUS DENTIST APPOINTMENTS HERE

To help new employees get to know who they are, the Los Angeles advertising agency Ignited hands out "The Guide to Self-Actualization," which, among other things, encourages open communication. Here's an excerpt:

"We interview a lot of people. Most of them are employed somewhere else at the time of the interview. None of them tell their employer they are interviewing with us. We find that odd. If and when the time comes that you have an interview, we encourage you to tell your manager. He or she will grant you the time off, and you won't have the guilty conscience associated with a fictitious dentist appointment.

"All we ask is that you allow your manager to help you make the right decision. Ignited is a great place to work. But it isn't the right place for everyone. If you'd be happier working somewhere else, we don't want to stop you. That said, we don't want to let great talent get away without at least having a conversation. Regardless of the outcome, everyone can walk away feeling good about the honesty of the process."

But Howard was ready to do a different type of work. So when he heard of an opening in a publishing house, where he could be around people who created and loved books, he jumped on it.

"At the interview, I asked, 'Does the company have a corporate culture?' and the human resource person said, 'Why yes, we do.' I wished I had phrased it differently. I took the job and soon discovered the emphasis was on 'corporate.' It was a big cube farm, buttoned down, everything in order. It was so quiet, if you wanted to talk you had to whisper. They had a white-noise machine with a low hum going. And if you laughed out loud you could hear it across the place. People didn't seem excited about what they did. It was kind of like a hive with a buzz of drone-like activity. There was also a lot of whispering of rumors. Turns out they weren't people who loved books, they just worked on books."

What mattered most to the company? "The CEO lived and died by sales numbers. The 'suits' were upstairs and God knows what went on up there, because they never told us or came down among the lower life-forms. I only ran into the CEO because we both smoked and I saw him outside.

"After two years I was dragging my ass to work every day. I couldn't wait for those five days to burn through and get to the weekend. I don't know if I ever got properly depressed, but it sure wore me down."

BARBARA WONDERED: IS THE ABUSE NORMAL? AM I TOO SENSITIVE?

Barbara is an information technology project manager. When her company went through a series of layoffs she took her time looking for her next position. "I wanted to be passionate about work—my job and the company. I thought that if the company was contributing to space science, then I could really take a sincere interest in it. I'm an amateur astronomer and have a degree in physics." So she went to work for a firm that serves government and military contracts related to aerospace.

"Things were not right from the very start," she says. In fact, it began in the interview. In her telephone screening interview, one person yelled "when he didn't like my answers. I thought it was some kind of test because one of the things he asked was, 'Are you thick-skinned?' I thought I was; I've worked with many tough engineers with many personality quirks. The manager actually laughed at me when I asked if there were bonuses or stock options."

It got worse when she came on board. "The first week was awful because of the verbal abuse. Mistakes made (real or imagined) were brought up in public. When you went on break or to meet with a client, people immediately asked where you are. Not working overtime was seen as bad behavior. The office was drab army brown, with no decorations allowed. My co-workers thought I was a rebel because I had 5 x 7 pictures of my family on the desk. We weren't allowed to know what the products were, due to the security levels."

Every day, she says, she "struggled to understand if this was normal. Was I being oversensitive? Did I need to develop a thicker skin and just get through this for some reward on the other side? After three months I decided, no. It was all wrong for me. I love to learn and teach. I want to be respected and manage my own time. They didn't want a creative person, but a time-tracking machine."

Looking back, she says, "My gut really was blinded by the illusion that the interview was a test. And I really felt this was exactly what I wanted to do and where I wanted to do it. I justified the lumps and bumps at first, thinking it was part of adjusting. I thought I might have to prove myself before they accepted me."

The experience has her worried about whether she'll ever find the right culture, so now she's "looking for 'incrementally better.'" She is questioning whether she should even change careers. Her passion for information technology "hasn't been beat out of me yet," she says, but the last experience "was like being spun in a circle and when I stopped to look for a new job I felt dizzy and uncertain of my judgment."

"No Thanks" to Bad Politics

Workers tell me all the time that they'd do a job they didn't want if they were making big bucks or it gave them exposure to important people. But even a "good job" can spell disaster for your career if you don't consider the whole picture. Besides the type of work you'd be doing and the physical *and* emotional environment you'd be in, you need to consider your ability to be successful in light of the politics and current events.

Here are two examples of people who did consider that and, as a result, turned down the jobs.

When FEMA was trying to find a new director after the Hurricane Katrina disaster, *The New York Times* reported that the response from the country's most seasoned disaster-response experts to the job of a lifetime had been the same again and again, "No thanks." One candidate who did not want to be considered for the FEMA director job or another top FEMA post, Ellen M. Gordon, said that she declined because there hadn't been a proven commitment "that whoever takes the job is going to have 100 percent support."

> Develop a sixth sense about *yourself*: Are you seeing the company and job as they truly are or how you *want* them to be?

My client, an executive at a midsize corporation, was asked by the senior vice president at her company if she'd consider a role in another subsidiary that was in big trouble. She'd report to an executive with a bad reputation who was dealing with a do-or-die situation. "What if it doesn't work out?" she said. "I'd be reporting to a nut who has gotten the company into a jam that may not be able to be fixed. They couldn't care less what happens to me. They'll use me, chew me up, and spit me out." Which is exactly what happened to the person who did take the job after my client declined.

You need to ask yourself:

- How could this job affect my reputation and future?
- How are current events shaping the job and my ability to do it?
- Even if it pays well, is it worth it?

So You Got an Offer; Time for Comparison Shopping

If you've been offered a different position in your company or have discovered or been offered a position while job hunting, it's time to decide whether it's right for you.

You've done all your digging, observing, and asking of questions. But before you decide, do some comparison shopping between what you want and the situation at hand. Find a quiet, comfortable place to situate yourself, and let's sort out all the data.

Looking back at what you wrote in the "What Fits You Like a Glove" exercise, see how the position matches up by answering the following questions about the company, the manager, and the role:

- Will I be able to use my best strengths?
- Will I be able to contribute my knowledge?

- Will I be doing work I care about and that makes the kind of difference I want to make?
- Will I be able to be "me"?
- Will this work and environment challenge me?
- Will I be able to have an impact in this work and at this place?
- Will I have the chance to contribute what I do best and am most valued for?
- Will I have the opportunity to do what makes me unique and identifiable among my peers?
- Is this a place that values what I value?
- Will these people appreciate and respect me?
- Do I feel good about the people?
- Do I feel good about the product and service?
- Will I thrive in the culture and environment?
- Will I have the type of work arrangement I need?
- Will I grow and develop professionally?
- Will I be creative?
- Is the company innovative and growing?
- What does my gut say about the offer?
- What am I willing to compromise?

. . . and now that you have an offer, you also can weigh this:

- Are the pay and benefits what I want?

A WORD ABOUT PAY AND BENEFITS

You may have noticed that we haven't talked about financial compensation and benefits in terms of what to ask to get a feel for the company. There's good reason.

While how well a company pays and what types of benefits it offers are certainly part of company culture and overall philosophy, you don't want to be asking about it *before* you get an offer. I realize that pay (and most likely benefits) are part of what matter to you when going to work someplace new or taking on a new role in your company. So it should come into your thinking.

But it's not the most important thing to most people. I have seen this over and over again. I've had clients making six figures who left

Google: Loosey-goosier than most.
Is it for everyone?

Google gets over three thousand job applications a day, so a lot of people are itching to be a part of the 16,000-person workforce that stretches around the globe. It's a company that prides itself on living up to its philosophy, "Don't be evil," by "always doing the right thing for the world and the company and how we treat each other," Stacy Sullivan, chief culture officer and director of human resources, told me.

It sure looks like a fun place by the photos on its corporate Web site. Googlers lounge around on exercise balls and play what looks like hockey in an outdoor area. People share spaces with couches and dogs, which, they say, "improves information flow and saves on heating bills."

The company has the reputation of giving people the freedom to be as creative and innovative as they can, as well as the freedom to fail. "The essence of our culture is one that promotes a non-hierarchical, collaborative environment where the best and brightest can work closely with other colleagues," explains Sullivan.

Its Web site says the founders "built a company around the idea that work should be challenging and the challenge should be fun" and that the company "puts employees first when it comes to daily life in all of our offices." Emphasis is on "team achievements and pride in individual accomplishments . . . Ideas are traded, tested and put into practice . . . Meetings that would take hours elsewhere are frequently little more than a conversation in line for lunch." Sounds like what a lot of workers want.

But not all. People who haven't succeeded or enjoyed the place usually leave within six months, says Sullivan. The lack of structure and "getting something done right the first time is more of what these employees wanted," she explains. "We expect people to try things and see what sticks."

It's an ambiguous work environment. "You may know generally what you're supposed to accomplish," she says, but you might be on your own. "The most successful people shape and define their role and reach out and connect to others. It's a company that's all about relationships."

If someone has something to gripe about, "People aren't shy about stating their complaints," Sullivan relates. "They know it's in our training to be service oriented, so if they think something could be handled different, they say so. Because they know we don't want to do evil."

If you do get an interview, it's because the company concluded you're qualified for the job. Now the question is, Do you fit the culture? So during the interview process Google will ask whether you'd like a fast-paced environment where things aren't fully baked and if you'd like to create new things.

To make sure the place is right for you, Sullivan encourages you to talk to someone who works there. "That's the real-life lens you can trust."

their jobs because of mistreatment, mismatched values, a lack of challenges, and intolerable politics. Others left a job they loved because they wanted higher compensation. Then they took a job that paid better, but they hated the company, management, or culture and wished they were back with the old company—which looked pretty good now, even with the lower compensation.

Yes, you want to be compensated fairly. Yes, benefits are important. For some people they're reason enough to take a job. But for many they're not enough to keep them in a place where they're so unhappy it's making them sick.

Some companies have a reputation for low pay. Others are known for paying well. You can get a sense of this by checking with people who have worked at a firm or talking to a recruiter. But let the company tell

No-travel-no-matter-what Policy

Massachusetts-based HiWired has a policy called "Home Week" to make sure executives and sales staff who travel a lot don't burn out. The policy: One week each month no one is allowed to travel for business—no exceptions. Even to customer meetings.

This designated no-travel-no-matter-what week is set months in advance. So it lets employees meet and collaborate at the office and make plans with family—and not have to cancel—because they know for sure they're not traveling.

The policy came about because of the values of the company founders. Cofounders and presidents Singu Srinivas and Michael Wexler decided their technology services and support firm would have policies that gave workers "time for soccer games and other family activities."

you what the job pays. When it comes to internal promotions, sometimes you do need to broach the subject. In general, my rule is, when it comes to talking about future pay or past salary, don't ask, don't tell.

For the record, how a company motivates people through pay can tell you something about their priorities and philosophy—and sometimes it's not a favorable impression. One of California's largest health insurers, Health Net, Inc., set goals and paid bonuses to employees based in part on how many individual policyholders were dropped and how much money was saved, the *Los Angeles Times* reported on November 9, 2007. It paid its senior analyst in charge of cancellations more than twenty thousand dollars in bonuses between 2000 and 2006, "based in part on her meeting or exceeding annual targets for revoking policies."

Developing a sixth sense includes pay, but is mostly about getting a feel for how a company functions, their guiding principles, and their code of conduct, and whether that fits closest to your ideal.

Develop Your Sixth Sense About a New Career, Too

You'll never know for sure if a career you're considering will be just right for you, either—until you're actually in the trenches. But everything we've talked about concerning evaluating a different company or job also applies to making a career change. Once you have your ideal figured out, visit with people in the profession; watch, learn, follow them around, and ask lots of questions.

The biggest mistakes people make in this process are:

1. They only talk to one or two people in the profession. Based on that, they make up their mind that the career is perfect or the stupidest idea they ever had. They end up in a career lamenting, "This isn't what I signed up for" or never digging deep enough to know whether it could have been a match made in heaven.
2. They decide to change careers because "it sounds fun!" This is like seeing a haircut on someone else and saying "I want that same haircut," even though it doesn't fit your head or highlight your best features. Not a good idea (see my haircuts from 1987 and 1999 and you'll know what I mean). There's a lot more to discover before you know whether a career is actually fun—and before you know everything else that matters.

But don't expect people to be your personal encyclopedia in finding out. Before you ask someone to take time to talk to you, brush up on the field you're considering so you can have an intelligent, focused, and fruitful conversation. Read trade publications, check out the *Dictionary of Occupational Titles*, *The Big Book of Jobs*, and www.bls.gov for details about a particular type of work and its associated working conditions, qualifications, advancement opportunities, earning potential, employment opportunities, and related occupations.

The Fix Is Not In

Remember way back in Part 1 when I talked about the way you once entered the work relationship with your employer: You, the employer, are going to give me certain things in exchange for what I do as well as I can?

Well, that has not gone the way of the once beloved IBM Selectric typewriter. It can still be the way things transpire if you are willing to do the following, which any reasonable professional who wants to be less pissed and more powerful would do:

- Get very clear on precisely what you want.
- Do your homework to find out if what you want is likely to be offered.
- See the company and job for what they are, not what you want them to be.
- Discuss and ask for what you want at the right time and place.

This is not to say you'll get everything. But there is a lot to be said for being crystal clear about what you want, being nervy enough to ask for it, and *then* making up your mind—based on as much information as you could garner—about whether you'll take the job. That's power. And you will have earned it.

TAKE YOUR FIFTH QUIT-BEING-PISSED OATH

I hereby promise myself to quit being pissed off and start being powerful by defining my ideal work and career situation, then digging deep, observing, minding my gut in the interview process, and developing my new sixth sense so I'll know the right situation when I see it.

SIGN HERE _____

DATE _____

Step 6

Go Twist and Shout and Shake Things Up

We began with a day in your life in the workplace. With how pissed you are and the longing you have for a relationship of exchange between you and a company that goes something like this: You give your time, talent, skills, knowledge, and education, and the employer provides a salary, bonuses, and an interesting, safe, nondiscriminatory place to work.

Is it really possible to get that, so that you and the employer can both have what you want and need? Sort of. Quite possibly. And in time (more on this in a minute).

Up until now we've talked about how to achieve some of that by taking care of yourself and your career, suffering less, and prospering more—despite imbalance in the relationship between you and employers, as well as the pressures from technology and the uncertainty of changing times.

Now let's focus on things you can actually *do* to influence—even change—laws, education, and business models that affect you, your work, and your career. And we'll discuss things you can actually *do* to affect your pay, how your days go, and how your overall career and future will work out.

You might be tempted to say, "Why bother doing any of these things (or anything in this entire book, for that matter)? Nothing will change."

Now, why would you go and say something dumb like that? For one thing, you'd be jumping to a broad, overreaching conclusion—and you'd be wrong. Thinking that way may help you justify a decision *not* to take any action. But if you *don't* jump to the conclusion that nothing will change, you'll have to do something about it.

For another thing, you'd be forfeiting your right as a human being with the ability to reason, influence, communicate, choose, change, fix, and put your stamp on relationships, policies, and institutions. Why would you throw away your standards and every scrap of your intelligence and stand on the "why bother?" principle and useless glass-is-empty, woe-is-me attitude that gets you nowhere?

Taking action is a crucial step to moving from pissed off to powerful. It propels you toward making a change, not simply staying mired in being "right."

As I pointed out before, getting mad can be helpful, but moral outrage alone doesn't do much good. But it *can* drive the steps you take next—and do some good if directed at the right people, institutions, and issues.

Now that we've settled that, let's talk about who and what those people, institutions, and issues are.

Why I Say "Sort of, Quite Possibly, and In Time."

Let's do a little reality check.

Experts who study the history of the workplace point out that we are in the midst of a significant and fundamental shift. And that the way laws, business, unions, and education are set up simply doesn't work for the workplace of today and tomorrow.

Take, for example, the fact that over 30 percent of American workers are independent workers. They aren't employed by one company. They are the self-employed, independent contractors, on-call workers, and day laborers. They may toil from home or one-person offices or head out to a different locale every day as temporary workers. Most find their own health insurance and usually pay exorbitant prices or just can't afford it, period. They typically create their own retirement funds, buy their own supplies, and pay for business services like the repair of equipment. Most don't receive protections under laws designed to ensure proper pay and safe, healthy, and nondiscriminatory workplaces. Most don't get disability or unemployment if they can't work. They are about 42.6 million strong, and growing, according to the U.S. Government Accountability Office's 2006 report "Employment Arrangements." Yet most government, education, and business models are still structured to serve a traditional workforce.

This is just one example of how institutions are not set up for today's changing workplace. With that in mind, changes can take place—but in time. Other changes are not related to policies and laws, but completely within your control, which you'll see as you go through the list of things you can do. Also, please know that as we talk about actions you can take, I haven't thought of every issue that may affect you in your career. Therefore, I haven't listed all the ways you can take action. Some of those issues will depend on what kind of work you do. By encouraging you to take action, I hope you'll see other options. For now, though, here are some things you can influence.

Things You Can Do, And How You Can Do Them

Most things are not set in stone. That includes your compensation package, how you're treated, the parameters of your working arrangement, how interviews play out, and how your job and career go. Here are 16 ways to influence those.

I. KNOW WHAT'S EXPECTED OF YOU, AND KNOW YOUR RIGHTS.

Before you take a position in a company, make sure you do this:

Clearly understand your employer's expectations. Ask questions. What functions are you supposed to perform? How do your supervisor and others want you to communicate and get things done? What will be the expected results of the work you do? What are their policies about things like e-mail and Internet use? Read the employee manual or guidelines. And if you do get fired, don't assume there's nothing you can do about it, says Randy Freking, an employment attorney with Freking & Betz in Cincinnati.

"Most people don't realize the extent of their rights that have been created by legislation and courts in the last 30 to 40 years," he says. If you're unfairly fired, you may have legal protection you're not aware of. "Knowing your rights gives you more ammunition to fight unfair terminations or negotiate improved severance arrangements."

One source is the book *Job Rights & Survival Strategies*, by Paul Tobias and Susan Sauter. You can also check out organizations such as Workplace Fairness at www.workplacefairness.org.

If you need help, contact an employment attorney (not a generalist) in your area. There are lots of lawyers around; there are fewer who specialize in this type of work. You can find one through your local bar association or the lawyer referral service at the National Employment Lawyers Association, www.nela.org.

Freking and many of his colleagues are also working hard to change the at-will employment common-law doctrine that I talked about in Naked Truth #2, which in essence means you can be fired pretty much any time and for any reason—as long as the reason isn't prohibited by law. Most employers have at-will employees. So unless you're covered by a union's collective-bargaining agreement or an individual employment contract, you have an at-will relationship with your employer, and you're fair game, says Michael Hanlon, attorney for Blank Rome, LLP, in Philadelphia.

As Jerry, a reader, wrote me in an e-mail: Being an at-will employee is "like they [your company] have their finger on the selector switch ready to fire 24/7."

Freking and other lawyers are trying to advance the law so that someday the at-will employment doctrine is abolished, "with a law on the books that requires an employer to establish just cause before they fire someone," says Freking.

When judges formed the at-will doctrine in the mid-1800s, it was a different time, says Freking. "The nature of our economy and the evolution of the workplace has placed greater importance on a particular job someone has. Alternative jobs aren't as easily found."

"This is not to give a guarantee of employment," he says. "But most people take jobs with the expectation that as long as they do a good job the employer will not arbitrarily fire them. Most employers will claim they have just cause to fire someone. But they should have to establish that."

"For example, if you don't like blue shirts and your employees come in to work with blue shirts, you can't just fire them for that. You need to tell them that when you hire them. The employer has a right to set whatever expectations he or she wants to set. 'Just cause' can include economic conditions. The expectations just need to be set when they hire you. Tell employees up front, and once stated, both sides are held to those expectations."

For now, Freking, other civil rights lawyers, and the National Employment Lawyers Association are developing a grassroots effort to abolish the at-will employment doctrine. Freking and employment attorney Paul Tobias have helped create a Web site to encourage legislators and judges to become more familiar with the issue (www.abolishemploymentatwill.com).

THINGS YOU CAN DO:

▶ Know what your employer expects. Ask questions and read the employment manual.

▶ Know your rights. Read a book like *Job Rights & Survival Strategies*, and check out Web sites like www.workplace-fairness.org.

▶ Learn more about the grassroots movement to abolish the at-will employment doctrine: www.abolishemployment-atwill.com.

▶ If you feel strongly about the at-will issue, contact your state and federal representatives and ask them to support this type of legislation.

2. LEARN MORE ABOUT FORMING UNIONS.

For some workers being a member of a union and having the power to bargain for better compensation is very important. But, first, you have to work in an industry where there is a recognized right to join a union. And if one doesn't exist, and you wanted to start one, the law makes it difficult to do so, says Ross Eisenbrey, vice president of the Economic Policy Institute in Washington, D.C., a nonprofit, nonpartisan think tank that "seeks to broaden the public debate about strategies to achieve a prosperous and fair economy."

Although some 60 million U.S. workers say they would join a union if their workplace had one (based on 2006 research by Peter D. Hart Research Associates), when workers have tried to organize, they have been harassed, punished, retaliated against, or even fired, according to reports.

"The right to form a union isn't worth the paper the National Labor Relations Act is written on if you can get fired from your job for trying to form one," said Robert Reich, former labor secretary and professor at University of California, Berkeley, in his commentary on National Public Radio in February 2007.

It is illegal for companies to fire you for that, he pointed out, but "the penalty for getting caught is a slap on the wrist." He cited statistics from 2005 in which over thirty thousand American workers were awarded back pay "when their employers were found to have illegally fired or otherwise discriminated against them for their union activities."

THINGS YOU CAN DO:

▶ Get acquainted with what unions do and whether this makes sense for your work. See "Freedom to Form Unions" at www.americanrightsatwork.org.

▶ If this issue is important to you, learn more about the Employee Free Choice Act (S. 1041) and tell your legislators to support it. In essence, this legislation would require employers to recognize a union after a majority of workers have stated they want a union. This would be the first such change since 1935. See "Employee Free Choice Act" at www.americanrightsatwork.org.

▶ Learn more about this issue and others related to labor law and workers' rights through such groups as American Rights at Work (www.americanrightsatwork.org), which publishes reports, case studies, and other information.

---

3. LEARN MORE ABOUT PAID FAMILY MEDICAL LEAVE AND PAID SICK LEAVE.

The Family and Medical Leave Act of 1993 (www.dol.gov/esa/regs/statutes/whd/fmla.htm) provides various protections for workers who need time off from their jobs because of medical problems or the birth or adoption of a child. Employers with 50 or more employees are

If you work for one company on Monday and another on Wednesday, migrate from project to project, or toil independently from home, you are one of about 42.6 million workers in the United States with issues that Sara Horowitz can address.

If you're a mobile worker who needs to find health care and other insurance at rates you can afford, figure out your taxes, and establish your own retirement plan, Horowitz offers a solution: the Freelancers Union (www.freelancersunion.org), of which she is executive director, and which has over sixty thousand members.

Whether you're freelance, temporary, part time, self-employed, or a consultant, the Freelancers Union is set up for you. But it's not your traditional trade union. First, there's no cost to join. Second, this nonprofit organization brings together independent workers—computer repair professionals and computer system designers, project managers, sales professionals, musicians, nannies, writers, consultants, and coaches—"for mutual support and advocacy in a spirit of friendship and cooperation," says Horowitz.

You only pay for what you need, such as health, dental, life, or disability insurance plans—at group rates—and you have access to educational events as well as discounts and networking opportunities.

The union speaks on your behalf to elected officials and government to advocate taking a new look at traditional social insurance programs such as unemployment insurance, workers' compensation, antidiscrimination protections, OSHA, and transportation and child-care tax breaks.

required to allow a worker to take up to 12 weeks of unpaid leave for medical reasons related to the worker or a family member or to care for a newborn or newly adopted child, without reducing the worker's pay or benefits when he or she returns to work.

But according to experts, many workers don't take this time off, because they can't afford to leave their jobs without pay. As a result, there is a movement to expand the act so that workers would be paid during that leave. Some cities and states already have legislation mandating paid family leave.

Additional proposals and legislation such as the Healthy Families Act would require certain employers to provide a minimum of seven days of paid sick leave annually. See the National Partnership for Women & Families for more information: www.nationalpartnership.org.

Back in Step 1 I talked about "family-responsibility" discrimination, which has to do with workers suing employers for alleged mistreatment due to family-caregiving responsibilities. If you want to know more about this, see the Center for Work Life Law Web site: www.worklifelaw.org.

THINGS YOU CAN DO:

▶ Get acquainted with paid family medical leave through groups working on this and other proposed legislation: www.nationalpartnership.org.

▶ If it's important to you, contact local and state legislators—not just federal—and tell them how you feel.

---

4. LEARN MORE ABOUT BULLY BOSSES.

You'd think there would be some way to protect yourself against bosses who cross the line of common decency by ranting and raving, lying, threatening and humiliating you, and basically acting as if they can do or say whatever they please. Federal law does prohibit discrimination and harassment, but it's based on specific protected categories such as race, color, religion, sex, pregnancy, national origin, disability, and age, says David Ritter of Neal, Gerber & Eisenberg's labor and employment practice group in Chicago.

The way it stands now, unless you fit within a protected category, you have little recourse other than to complain to management if you are mistreated by a boss.

However, there is a movement afoot to help with this issue. Today there are Web sites and groups to support you if you think you are a victim of a bullying boss. One such place is the Workplace Bullying Institute (www.bullyinginstitute.org).

There's also "anti-bullying" legislation that's been introduced in some states. Proponents of the bill argue that "sometimes, harassment or bullying is not based on some particular bias like sex or race," but is the result of "nothing other than a boss's management style or just a general dislike of one employee or another," explains Ritter. The legislation will also require employers to prevent and correct bullying.

The Healthy Workplace bills prohibit workplace bullying, eliminating the "protected category" requirement.

THINGS YOU CAN DO:

▶ Learn more about what constitutes a bullying boss—as opposed to just a tough one—who crosses the line of common decency. Read books such as *Brutal Bosses*, by Harvey Hornstein.

▶ If you want to know more or learn how to become a "citizen lobbyist," go to www.workplacebullyinglaw.org.

▶ As we talked about in Step 5, check out company policies and procedures regarding harassment.

---

5. EXPLORE DIFFERENT WORK ARRANGEMENTS.

You are probably thinking, "I'd love to spend more time with my family and friends and doing my hobbies. But that means I'd work less. How can I possibly do that? That would mean less money, and I can't afford less. I'm not one of those people averaging $8,367 a week!" (This is the figure I mentioned in Step 1 from the Bureau of Labor

Statistics' September, 2007 report, representing the average weekly salary in investment banking.)

I realize you might be closer to the 70 percent of Americans who say they live paycheck to paycheck. Or you're somewhere in between. You might also be thinking, "Are you crazy? My boss would never consider a flexible-work arrangement, and even if I have one, others will think I don't work as hard." Or, "I'll never advance if I don't put in a full day every day and unless I am there when someone needs me."

Before you jump to conclusions, please consider this: You have more influence and choice than you may think. So let's look at what seems an unlikely—but is a doable—duo: flexibility *and* a good job.

The long and short of it: Employers need you.
More than 25 percent of the working population will hit retirement age by 2010, which means we will have a potential worker shortage of nearly 10 million people, according to the U.S. Bureau of Labor Statistics, as cited by the Sloan Work and Family Research Network. Put another way in their research, since the next generation of workers (Generation X), which would naturally replace these older workers, only account for 29 percent of the workforce, there are not going to be enough workers to meet labor force requirements.

So employers need you, whoever you are. Younger, older, man, woman, someone with a family to raise and other relatives to tend to—you are needed.

The other good news is that the best way to get you in the first place, and then to keep you, is to offer more flexible work options. That means there are all kinds of boundaries and arrangements you can negotiate. Possibilities include traditional part-time work arrangements, of course, but also:

- telecommuting
- intermittent work
- compressed workweeks
- job sharing
- self-directed work
- arriving early and leaving early, or arriving late and leaving late
- seasonal and temporary work schedules
- phased retirement

And your chances for getting such nontraditional work arrangements will just keep getting better as workers age and retire. All in all, more companies are looking at ways to move away from the eight-hours, only-at-the-office model.

At IBM, for instance, each of the 355,000 workers is entitled to take as much vacation time as they want, leave early, or take a long weekend when they want—no one keeps track. According to a *New York Times* article, the company's "vacations-without-boundaries" system lets everyone make informal arrangements with their supervisors. Workers are guided mainly by their ability to get their work done on time.

When talking about telecommuters at IBM, General Manager Dan Pelino said, "We don't care where and how you get your work done, we care that you get your work done."

This self-directed arrangement and vacation policy works great for workers like Luis Rodriguez, who often works from home or on the road, said the article. "Calling colleagues or checking e-mail while visiting relatives . . . is a fair trade" for being able to work from home and be with his children, he said.

Here's the catch: You may have flexibility. Just be careful you're not constantly connected. You can end up putting in longer hours because, with things being so flexible, you don't think about all the time you're putting in. Make sure that just because you're not in the office, you're not always working. Such work arrangements, though, are real and possible options.

"That would be nice, but this would never happen at my company," you might be saying. Not necessarily. A job you're considering may not have been advertised or structured with a flexible schedule. Or the one that you have now may not be set up with such an arrangement. Maybe no one else at your company is doing it. So what? Does that mean you can't be first?

I encourage you to get over the hang-up that prevents you from even *thinking* about how to create an arrangement that does work for you and your company or a company you want to work for.

Having said that, let me be clear that I'm not saying *every* employer will accommodate you. Alternative work arrangements just don't fit some industries, companies, and jobs. (I talked about companies and bosses that do support flexibility and how to know them when you see them in Step 5.) But just because "it's not in the job description," as one man told me when he interviewed for a new position, doesn't mean it's not on the negotiating table.

There's also little chance you'll ever get it as long as you think you can't have a good job in your field with an alternative work arrangement. That goes for people like Joyce, a 48-year-old marketing professional who told me, "Maybe I could find a job answering phones or something, but that's it."

Even if it's unheard of for someone in your company to have a challenging, responsible role in which they start work at 7:30 a.m. and leave at 1:30 p.m. or duck out to take classes or care for a family member, it doesn't mean it *can't* happen.

Take Patty Giura. I came across her a few years back when I read an article in the *Pittsburgh Post-Gazette* profiling the firm she worked for. She not only headed Alpern Rosenthal's entrepreneurial services group, but she was a partner. And she was one of about 15 part-timers on staff. Another worker at this firm, Elisabeth Leach, is a part-time manager of marketing and business development who was promoted to principal when she was pregnant.

You're not alone in thinking that a similar situation can't happen to you or that having a flexible schedule will keep you from progressing. In a study conducted by the Families and Work Institute in New York, nearly 40 percent of workers reported being afraid they'd jeopardize their jobs or career advancement by taking advantage of flexible options.

What's changed is that companies are wising up, and the tide is shifting. They know jobs will outnumber workers, and they need to change policies. Even though many employers haven't been focused on accommodating a different type of workforce—they may have even discriminated against them—the ones with an eye to the future are paying attention. This goes for accommodating younger workers, too—Generation X, in particular—who insist on more flexibility.

Yes, it is a country for older men and women.
Some companies are not only worried about worker shortages, but they're concerned about losing older workers' wisdom. You've probably heard of people who, after leaving their industry or company, were asked to come back (sometimes in a contractual role). The company couldn't do without their years of experience and knowledge, which turned out to be crucial to certain processes or working with particular clients.

A company may also be in need of older workers' loyalty. An article in *The New York Times* discussed a trend in which companies like Hewlett-Packard are reaching out to retirees they're trying to "galvanize into an auxiliary army of senior marketers, good-will ambassadors and volunteer sales people." Yes, they're working for free (I'll get back to the working-for-free part in a minute). Why would a retiree do that? As one of them explained in the article, he feels great loyalty to the company. But my point is why the company wants them. Companies like Hewlett-Packard say the move "reflects a renewed emphasis on grass-roots marketing in the Internet era . . . seeking to turn its retirees into a valuable asset that other, younger tech companies lack."

The company's chief marketing officer Michael Mendenhall said in the article, "We're moving forward with an effort to capitalize on the fact that we have these great brand stewards. When you look at the importance of great word of mouth and great third-party endorsement—who better to do that than your own employees?"

I'm not suggesting you work for free. I'm saying that given the times we're in, older workers have value that companies want, and you have clout in a way you may never have had before. This is one of those ways. So look at how you might be paid for that. Seize the opportunity. Employers need you.

So with companies looking at how to not only attract you but to keep you working longer, you also have more clout than you think when it comes to defining your boundaries. This goes for traditional work arrangements as well. But here also, you have to ask for it.

One of my clients, who works in information technology, was on call all the time. She missed family dinners and her kids' softball games and got little sleep. We talked for months about how she needed to change this, but she worried the company would object. She finally laid down the law with her boss and said she wasn't going to be available 24 hours a day and offered an alternative plan for handling client calls. Her boss was fine with it.

So if you're job hunting or want to revamp your work arrangement, get over the fear that if you ask for X, Y, or Z, you'll be evicted from the room or send the employer into shock. Instead, think about what could be. Then write a proposal. Outline an arrangement that—especially if you're not working in the office—includes the following:

- how you'll be evaluated and how your productivity will be measured
- how your supervisor will know you're achieving your goals
- how your supervisor will stay updated and informed about your work
- how, if need be, you can be reached if you're not in the office

After there's an understanding between you and your employer about your role (or after the conversation between you and a would-be employer is going well, and you seem to be the right person for the job), share what kind of arrangement you are looking for. I've found that reasonable employers listen to reasonable proposals.

THINGS YOU CAN DO:

▶ Notice if you've got it in your head that "I could never have a flexible arrangement *and* a good job," and decide to get over this belief, which isn't helping you get what you want.

▶ Think about what you have—knowledge, relationships, maturity, a great track record, brand loyalty—that employers need and value.

▶ Write a reasonable proposal outlining an arrangement that works for you and your employer.

▶ Be prepared to bring it up at the appropriate time with your employer or a would-be employer.

6. Decide what you'll divulge—or not.

If you've ever been checked out by a company considering you for employment, you know it can get up close and personal. It can involve the company testing your urine or saliva to see if you do drugs, analyzing your handwriting, or sitting you down in a cubicle to complete a personality test that asks such things as how you feel about entering a room full of strangers. It's not that the company thinks you're lying about what you say in the interview; it's that the company thinks you *could* be lying about who you are.

You can't blame them, really. Background checks have become more aggressive since 2001. Companies want to know who they're hiring for security and safety reasons and because mistakes can be costly. It's expensive to bring you on board, train you, and give you what you need to do your job. Not to mention the liability. Employers can be liable for "theft, sexual assault, robbery, and wrongful death because of an employee's misconduct," says Edward Andler, author of *The Complete Reference Checking Handbook*. He tells employers to "assume that possibly one-third of the people" working for them got their jobs "by creatively presenting their backgrounds and capabilities" through out-and-out deception or exaggeration, to be considered or be competitive. Employers have ways to find out if you're exaggerating your credentials or lying. They can do background investigations via information available in public records. It's fairly easy to confirm whether you're a licensed CPA, attorney, teacher, or health-care professional through professional associations—which may also share whether you're in good standing or whether there are violations or complaints filed against you, says the author.

Companies can also check your financial status and credit standing—if you let them (more on that in a minute). According to Andler, "many job candidates overstate their compensation." Dozens of job hunters tell me they believe doing that helps to get more money in their next job. He says companies are beginning to check applicants' pay history, even demanding W-2 income forms. I'm not sure how they can "demand" that if you simply refuse—which I would. What you were paid at your last job is not relevant to whether you're the right person for the next job. So don't talk about it. But if you feel absolutely compelled to discuss it, don't lie. Give ranges.

Just as you want to know about the company you're potentially getting involved with, the company wants to know about you. They're being encouraged to dig deeper—and are. "Many states now have laws that protect employers when giving out information about a past employee," says Andler.

So don't misrepresent yourself. At the same time, make sure they aren't out of bounds with questions about age, disabilities not related to your ability to do the job, religious holidays, family and marital status, national origin, race, or religion. These things are none of their business. If they do ask inappropriate questions, it's up to you to find a way around answering them while not blowing the interview.

And that brings me to the issue of your finances. When you're talking to an employer about a new job, they may ask about your credit. But it doesn't have to go any further than that, because they can only get to this information if you grant them permission.

So, yes, they can find out when you opened your Visa and Nordstrom charge accounts and if you're keeping up with payments (thanks to the Fair Credit Reporting Act)—but only if you give them written permission to access this information.

That kind of data is detailed in your credit report (not to be confused with your credit score). Besides the date on which you opened up an account, the balance you owe, and how often you pay, a credit report includes your full name, address, former names and addresses, date of birth, social security number, and public records such as tax liens, judgments, and bankruptcies. All of this can be accessed as part of preemployment screening, says John Ulzheimer of Credit.com, author of *You're Nothing but a Number*.

The employer wants to know this information because credit reports tell a story (somewhat) about how you manage responsibilities. Says Ulzheimer, "This is of interest to employers, as are other employee attributes they investigate through other methods of screening," such as drug and personality tests.

Certain industries are more interested in your money matters than others. Financial services companies review credit reports as standard practice, he says, because you will "have access to highly sensitive financial and personal information." Credit review would likely be part of the interview process for any job where money is handled.

The theory is that "'the flesh is weak,'" says Ulzheimer, with the employee giving in to temptation if buried by crushing debt and hounded by collectors.

If an employer does ask to have access to this information, you can certainly say no. One man told me he'd respond to the request by asking, "Why? Are you giving me a loan?"

If you do say no, you risk not getting a first or second interview. The employer may wonder what you have to hide. They may see you as unco-operative. They can read all kinds of things into it. Ulzheimer says that if you don't want an employer to have access to your credit report, "then so be it," but you're "not likely to make it to the next level of screening."

I'm not suggesting you give employers the A-OK to view your credit. I'm just pointing out the mind-set of the employer. So if you are asked for this data, you might ask what in particular they'd be looking for. If you're squeamish about divulging such personal information, knowing what they're looking for might help you supply it some other way.

If you have excellent credit, "I wouldn't think you'd mind some-one taking a look, as it will likely give you an advantage over competing applicants with poor credit," says Ulzheimer.

On the other hand, maybe you want to be judged by your proven abilities and experience as to whether you're right for a particular job. In that case, I could understand why you would mind someone snoop-ing around personal information that may have nothing to do with how you'd handle a job.

THINGS YOU CAN DO:

▶ Know what interview questions are out-of-bounds, and don't offer irrelevant information that could give interviewers a reason to disqualify you from the running.

▶ Decide how you feel about divulging such personal informa-tion as finances and what you are and aren't willing to share.

▶ Figure out how you will tactfully set boundaries with interviewers who cross into dangerous territory.

Another viewpoint on the equality issue

It's "the perceived lack of economic opportunity that makes [people] unhappy," according to Arthur Brooks in an article published by the American Enterprise Institute for Public Policy Research, where he was a visiting scholar. So he envisions "a land of both inequality and opportunity, in which hard work and perseverance are [key]." He sees this vision promoting "policies focused not on wiping out economic inequality, but rather on enhancing economic mobility." This would include "improving educational opportunities, aggressively addressing cultural impediments to success . . . and protecting the climate of American entrepreneurship."

7. Take matters of pay into your own hands.

I don't need to remind you that income inequality exists, in part because, as Peter Morici, professor of international business at the University of Maryland and former director of economics at the U.S. International Trade Commission says, "We need a certain amount of it to encourage people to work hard."

If you want to make more money, that's understandable. In simple economic terms you do that with work that the market rewards more handsomely. Generally, the market rewards work that is more difficult to do and that involves training that is more arduous.

That rule of thumb doesn't always apply, however. Look at certain athletes who didn't get a higher education and who make millions. (Granted, their bodies take tremendous punishment, but still...) And there are some very highly compensated CEOs who don't have a college degree.

The more specialized the skills you learn and the more difficult the training, the higher the dividend, says Morici. "Doing the more difficult and less popular things will reward you. Accounting is more tedious and not necessarily rewarding. It's not fun learning the tax code. But it's a marketable skill. If you do what the average guy does, you'll only get what the average guy gets."

When it comes to getting more money for the work you do, you can influence the value others see in you and how much they're willing to pay you by how well you market yourself in your job search. You can also influence how much your company is willing to pay you by proving your increased value.

THINGS YOU CAN DO:

▶ Know salary ranges in your particular profession and where you fit—which can depend on where you live and how much experience and education you have.

▶ Become a better negotiator. Don't talk about money until you've established that you are indeed Boy or Girl Wonder, and you know the employer knows it because they've offered you the position. Remember that negotiations begin from the minute you establish contact. So establish your professionalism (and therefore your value) at every opportunity in the interview process.

▶ Before you ask for a raise, make a list of all the ways you've gone above and beyond your duty and made a difference at your company (this is your increased value).

---

8. LEAD YOUR CAREER DEVELOPMENT BY THE NOSE.

Nearly 70 percent of people said they get few opportunities to discuss their career development with their bosses, according to a MRINetwork 2007 survey. The company's president, Michael Jalbert, cited the trend that more businesses and employees tend to view career development as the employee's responsibility, but suggested that "with increasing pressure on candidate supply, this trend will begin to go the other way again."

That may be. But are you going to wait around to see? I say, first, don't depend on the trend going the other way (it may not). Second,

"The market isn't about fairness, it's about skills and power," explains Ross Eisenbrey, vice president of the Economic Policy Institute.

"The same worker in Houston with the same skills can make $6 an hour and the one in Hoboken make $15 an hour. The difference is the higher wage has been bid up by the power of the union through bargaining."

Nurses on average have less formal training than teachers, he says, but, "Why do some nurses who start at hospitals make $60,000? Because the supply is not there to meet the demand. Teachers don't have as much power because they're dealing with the public sector and it's difficult to keep raising wages."

don't wait for your boss to give you the time of day. And third, even if the trend changes and employers make it more of a priority to discuss your career development, it's *still* your responsibility. Why would you put something as important as your career development in someone else's hands? Others may guide you. But it's not their job to make sure you're using your best skills, enjoying your work, and following a path that lets you contribute your fullest.

Knowing how you're doing and what you need in your career development* is your thing. Besides, if you're one of those independent workers, you may not have a regular supervisor. If you do have one, you may not respect what he or she says. He may not have the smarts to advise. Or she may be one of those bosses who spends all of five minutes covering your progress and "areas for improvement," giving

---

*Discussed in Step 4 with "How'm I doin'?," and Step 1 with your beliefs.

R-E-S-P-E-C-T,
FIND OUT WHAT IT MEANS TO ME

To members of the Writers Guild of America, their 2007 strike was more than a fight over pay; it was a battle about respect. Respect for the fact that without writers, there would be no scripts for television programs and movies. It was about respect and acknowledgment that they are an important part of the process of creating programming.

Five weeks into the strike, a news analysis by Michael Cieply in the December 10, 2007, issue of *The New York Times* referred to Patric M. Verrone, president of the Writers Guild of America West, whom the article paraphrased as saying, "[Writers] were looking to restore a sense of leverage and status that had been lost as ever-larger corporations took control of the entertainment business."

Although this particular strike focused mostly on electronic media rights, in the past the Writers Guild has had to fight for creative rights and practices related to the respect and dignity of writers, Charles Slocum, assistant executive director of the Writers Guild of America West, told me.

For the writers, these include such things as being given proper credit, being allowed to stay connected to their script as a project goes through the production process, being invited to premieres of the movie they have written, and getting a DVD of the movie they worked on when it's completed.

To bring home the point that without writers you don't have a creative product, the guild has used such campaign slogans as "Where It Begins" and "Somebody Wrote That."

you nothing to go on. Even if you get regular, meaty performance reviews, the *next* step is still up to you. And there's always a next step. What if you don't understand your supervisor's so-called constructive feedback? My clients show me their annual reviews all the time, asking me to interpret what their employers mean when they say the person "needs to broaden mutual interdependence" or "should seek work to increase ability to drive results." Beats me what they mean.

It would be nice if supervisors would refrain from writing things like "high on the scale of production focus but low on actively creating a culture of deliverability," and just say what they mean. But if you do get it, it's your job to ask what the heck they mean.

Even if the feedback is helpful, you need to decide if it is useful based on what you want in your career. *The eternal quest for self-improvement is in your hands.*

While we're on the subject, what if you don't agree with the review and the next steps? Most likely, you don't have to sign it. But it's still up to you to let them know. Most reviews have a section for your comments. This is where you'd state your reasons in writing. If your review doesn't have this section, you can write the reasons in a separate memo to your supervisor and send a copy to human resources and your supervisor's boss, says Manny Avramidis, global vice president of human resources for the American Management Association.

Then a meeting would take place to discuss your concerns with your supervisor, human resources, or perhaps your supervisor's boss. Who attends the meeting will depend on the reasons you chose not to sign.

THINGS YOU CAN DO:

- Don't wait for your boss to tell you how you're doing. Ask, and follow up.

- Ask your supervisor what your review means if you don't understand it. Get clear on expectations and how you will be evaluated.

- Put your comments in writing if you disagree with a performance review.

- Figure out how you're going to improve or develop professionally. Investigate classes or getting a coach, and present your ideas to your manager.

9. RIDE ROUGHSHOD OVER YOUR MOOD.

If you ever went to work in a bad mood because some nut on the freeway cut you off, or you ripped your stocking climbing into your car, or no one responded to your umpteenth call and e-mail at the company you were trying to get into, did the whole day go to pot? It can, unless you say to yourself, "I'm not going to let (whatever happened) ruin my day!"

Mood can be changed in as little as five seconds, says Neil Fiore, psychologist and author of *Awaken Your Strongest Self: Break Free of Stress, Inner Conflict and Self-Sabotage*.

If you start the day in a bad mood, you tend to stay in a bad mood, concludes Dr. Steffanie Wilk, professor of management at Fisher College of Business, who's been studying employees in the service industry in particular. The mood could even be a result of feelings left over from the day before.

Season, lack of sleep, hunger, pain, environment, stress, time urgency, noise, hormones, adrenaline, others' moods, and your own thinking affect mood, says Anna Maravelas, therapist and author of *How to Reduce Workplace Conflict and Stress*.

But changing how you think is the most powerful influence and the easiest to control, she says. "Plus it's free. You can do it looking out the window."

10. MEET YOUR NEIGHBORS AND BECOME A NAME DROPPER.

Today there is no reason to claim, "I can't get anywhere in my career because I don't know anybody." (Not that there ever was.) With all the online groups that help you connect with people in your community, job hunters, and those with similar interests or causes, it's a cinch to find people and share information.

By the time you read this, more of those online social and professional network sites will have sprung up, so I'm not going to attempt to list them all. MeetUp.com is one that, as they say on their site, helps "people find others who share their interest or cause, and form lasting, influential, local community groups that regularly meet face-to-face." Group topics run the gamut from politics, cars, finances, and film to pets, religion, work, and career.

But you certainly don't have to use one of these sites to stay connected to the outside world. The old-fashioned way includes introducing yourself to neighbors, taking classes, initiating lunches with peers, attending professional association meetings and conferences, and volunteering. You will be amazed at the number of people you can call on in time of need or tap for references, or who can come to you as a resource when you just make the effort to develop real relationships.

11. PREACH ETHICAL BEHAVIOR.

Ethical misconduct in general is very high these days—it's back at pre-Enron levels, according to the 2007 National Business Ethics Survey. But the good news is the number of firms that have formal ethics and compliance programs is on the rise, says Patricia Harned, president of the Ethics Resource Center, and having these programs does make a difference. It's also something you can fish around for when interviewing with a company, as discussed in Step 5.

The survey also found that less than 40 percent of employees are "aware of comprehensive ethics and compliance programs at their companies." So companies may not be doing a good job of promoting these programs. But people also may not be checking to see if a company has such a program. I have not yet met a job hunter who has checked this out before I mentioned it.

Although the "number of companies that are successful in incorporating a strong enterprise-wide ethical culture into their business has declined since 2005 . . . what seems to matter most is the extent to which leaders intentionally make ethics a part of their daily conversations and decision-making," says the survey.

This is the part that you can affect. Because, as Harned says, making ethics a part of daily conversations and decision making includes supervisors who "emphasize integrity when working with direct reports" and peers who encourage each other to act ethically.

So whether you're a leader by title, a supervisor, or an employee, acting ethically yourself and encouraging others to do so is something you can do every minute of the day. This also affects what we discussed in Step 3: having a brush with greatness.

Once, as I was walking down the hall of a company, I overheard a conversation between two associates who saw a basket of tempting sweet rolls glistening with glaze sitting on a cart. One associate pointed them out to the other and said something like, "No one would know if we ate those." The other associate replied, "But we would."

Making ethical decisions starts with the small things.

THINGS YOU CAN DO:

▶ Make a conscious choice about how you want to operate in all your dealings with co-workers, managers, clients, and customers.

▶ Encourage others to act with integrity. When you notice or sense something that feels off, talk about it with the appropriate person in your company.

---

12. KNOW WHERE YOUR RETIREMENT MONEY IS.

In a commentary on National Public Radio in July 2007, former secretary of labor Robert Reich talked about how corporate and government pension plans are increasingly investing in high-risk hedge funds and private equity funds "with money that was previously invested conservatively on behalf of their beneficiaries."

He added, "Few if any pension plan managers have any idea of the specific risks they're taking, because hedge funds and private equity funds don't have to disclose them. And the people whose pensions are at stake—teachers, policemen, civil servants and other working Americans—haven't a clue." His suggestion: "At least call your plan manager and find out how much of your savings are being invested in hedge funds and private equity."

By the time you read this, regulations may have changed, and who knows where your savings could be invested. The point is, you should know where your money is.

"Times are changing, and the ultimate responsibility lies with the individual when it comes to sound investing," says Rania Sedhom, a principal in the employee benefits consulting firm Buck Consultants in New York.

She advises you to first examine the monthly, quarterly, or annual statement you get from your plan administrator and research the funds you're invested in. Then ask your financial planner (if you have one) any questions you have about the statement and about the investment's risks, returns on investment, and fees. Next, go ask someone you trust who is a good investor the same questions, and finally, go back to your plan administrator and ask the same questions again.

Why all the questions? First, you'll get educated. And by asking multiple people you'll "hear the answers explained differently, and assuredly feel more confident in making decisions if more than one person is in agreement," says Sedhom. Whether you have options available to change those investments will depend on the type of plan that you have.

THINGS YOU CAN DO:

▸ Stay tuned in to how your money is doing by reading your monthly, quarterly, and annual statements.

▸ Find out and understand where your money is invested.

▸ Get advice from several people—your financial planner and someone you trust and who is a good investor.

▸ Make any changes you can that help you feel comfortable about your retirement money.

---

13. SING, DANCE, DRAW, OR PLAY AN INSTRUMENT—JUST BE MORE THAN YOUR JOB.

Journalist Eilene Zimmerman interviewed me in 2007 for *The New York*

Times column Career Couch about how important it is to your career to incorporate hobbies into your life. The essence of one of my messages was that your hobby can help you professionally as well as personally.

Thomas Friedman explains how this can work in an example in his book *The World Is Flat.* He tells the story of G. Wayne Clough, president of Georgia Institute of Technology, and his approach to getting more students to apply and to graduate.

Clough realized that some of the best engineers he had collaborated with over the years knew how to think creatively. He "also noticed that an 'awful lot of the talented students were interested in creative outlets other than what they were experiencing in the classroom.'" His observations led to admissions policies that focused on "recruiting and admitting good engineering students who also played musical instruments, sang in a chorus, or played on a team," writes Friedman. And that has led to "producing not just more engineers but more of the right kind of engineers."

The point is that "'people who have other interests tend to be able to communicate . . . be more social . . . ask for help more readily when they need help . . . help others more who need help . . . tend to be able to tie things together from different disciplines and fields,'" said Clough.

So stop going around saying you don't have time for other things. You will if you *make* time. Having an interest in art, music, trains, collecting, gardening, woodworking, singing in a choir, acting in amateur plays—whatever it is—builds confidence and helps you relax and, ultimately, be better professionally. And all of that makes for a more productive and satisfying career.

THINGS YOU CAN DO:

▶ Decide that having interests outside of work is a priority.

▶ Get involved in an activity that lets you lose your sense of time and get out of your routine.

14. Give free-flowing ideas a chance.

At the 2007 National Conference on the Creative Economy, keynote speaker Thomas Friedman echoed the conference theme: "Creativity and a broad foundation of learning are the fulcrums by which individuals, communities and nations can propel themselves to prosperity."

After the conference, participants completed a survey on what companies and communities can do to be more creative in the next five years. The top recommendations for companies included encouraging the free flow of ideas, expanding flex time for employees, and expanding professional development opportunities.

Who knows how much the company you work for now or later will take the initiative to do any of these. If you own your firm, it's in your hands. Even if you work for someone, you can influence policy.

THINGS YOU CAN DO:

Ask yourself:

- What can I do to influence the free flow of ideas at our company?
- What can I do to help our company expand flex time?
- What can I do to help our company see the importance of expanding professional development opportunities?
- What will I do to expand my own professional opportunities?
- What will I do to be more creative in my work and career?
- What will I do to broaden my learning and learning opportunities for others?

---

15. Look on the break side.

There may come a time in your career when you just need to get away from what you're doing to see things more clearly. You don't have to take a long break. But if you could take time off—by taking a sabbatical or even quitting your job—it might help you get to the next, better place.

INVEST IN A HAPPIER WAY OF LIFE

"Tim Kasser, an associate professor of psychology at Knox College, in Galesburg, Illinois, studied two hundred people who embraced Voluntary Simplicity, a movement focused 'less on materialistic values—like wanting money and possessions and status—and more on what we called intrinsic values or goals,'" according to an article in *The New York Times* by M. P. Dunleavey, author of *Money Can Buy Happiness*.

"The three main intrinsic values were being connected to family and friends, exploring one's interests or skills and 'making the world a better place,'" the article continues.

These people don't live in the forest without toilets and microwaves. They've just made a conscious decision to work fewer hours, which might mean making less money.

"The study found that when people invested more in intrinsic values, like relationships and quality of life and less in consumption, it seemed to increase their happiness," the *Times* recounts.

Of course, you need to support yourself or have a chunk of change to get through a time-out (but not necessarily a big chunk). And you need to be at a point in life where it makes sense.

Bonnie Harris and Brook Silva-Braga are two people who took the initiative to test the waters for making a change. Neither had a huge amount of money, but each had enough to quit work and take a time-out. One traveled and made a documentary film; the other wrote fiction and studied economics. They were at completely different stages in life. Silva-Braga was 25 and working as a producer at HBO Sports. He had saved $20,000 when he decided to quit and visit 26 countries, on four continents, in a year. Harris, 46, was a vice president on the fast track with $30,000 in savings and in options money from a career in a publicly held IT consulting firm. She set out to finish her undergraduate degree in economics and write a novel.

"I did write the novel, self-published it, and although it's probably terrible, it's a finished project," says Harris. Now she's working on her masters in communication and has started Wax Marketing.

Silva-Braga, who had packed five pounds of clothing and thirty pounds of video equipment, chronicled his trip, turning it into a documentary, *A Map for Saturday*, a personal saga of his travels, which he sold for a second chunk of change. He decided, "In the Internet age, you can give yourself whatever job you want. I launched www.theinterviewpoint.com."

If you think it was easy to decide to just pack up and leave their former lives, you're way off. Both had the same pressures and what-ifs you would at the thought of giving their familiar lives the old heave-ho—even for a short time.

There's pressure from those practical folks in your life. "People thought I was nuts to leave a six-figure job at the time," says Harris.

There's the money issue. "I worry about money all the time, but that part is getting better," she says, adding, "Fear has never kept me from doing things. I just try to make sure I am not being careless, but also try to be realistic about my fears, which are usually not things that are likely to happen."

There's the career issue. "I really liked my job and started interning with HBO when I was 19, so there were friendships and professional relationships that I didn't break lightly," says Silva-Braga. "The best reason not to go was the professional impact of leaving the job"—a worry that inspired him to make his documentary.

There are lean times. Before Silva-Braga sold his documentary he learned to "cook more of my own meals, take fewer taxis, and be more careful with the little money I had. But I've come to believe that time and money are commodities with an inverse relationship; you can only earn one by spending the other."

Neither has a single regret. "It was the best thing I could ever have done, and I emerged from my 'gap' year a new person, totally rejuvenated," says Harris. "I went from a pessimist to a total optimist."

Even though Silva-Braga was offered an even better job when he returned, he decided office jobs weren't his thing. His new venture lets him travel and discuss everything from Iraq to Kerouac. He also learned at an early stage of his career that "for me, time is a much more precious resource than money."

Mark Twain put it this way: "Twenty years from now you will be more disappointed by the things that you didn't do than by the ones you did do. So throw off the bowlines. Sail away from the safe harbor. Catch the trade winds in your sails. Explore. Dream. Discover." Not bad for a guy who used to work on steamboats.

THINGS YOU CAN DO:

▶ Entertain the thought of taking a time-out.

▶ Figure out your finances to see what's possible and a plan to see what's doable.

▶ Enroll the support of others who will be affected by this change.

▶ Don't regret what you could have done and didn't when you had the chance.

---

16. BE EVERYTHING YOU SAY YOU ARE.

You can spend time creating just the right words that describe your experience and spout them all you want when talking to people, marketing yourself, or creating your resume. But if your actions don't back it up, what good is it?

The point is, if you position yourself as a trustworthy, caring, mature problem solver with integrity, who is also the best in your particular field, you better conduct yourself that way at work and in your community. That includes online and behind the scenes.

An extreme example of someone who did this poorly is Eliot Spitzer, the former governor of New York, who resigned on March 12, 2008, after his alleged involvement in a prostitution operation was discovered. This is a man who cast himself as a crusader of justice and built his career on pursuing with moral zeal such issues as Wall Street misdeeds and two prostitution rings.

For most people, being everything you say you are will not entail such dramatic events. But it will mean managing your reputation. This includes what you *don't* say as much as what you *do* say. Think about this before you post something on the Internet, in a chat room, or on a blog. Human resource folks and employers scour these for data they wouldn't dare ask in an interview. Don't go posting something that can come back to haunt you and destroy the positioning you've worked so hard to create. Knowing how you want to be seen isn't enough. Creating that experience and reinforcing it with people is what will matter every day at work and throughout your career.

THINGS YOU CAN DO:

▶ Before you do something, and before you say something—to an audience of one or one hundred—think of the ramifications of your actions and words and whether this reinforces or detracts from your reputation and how you want to be seen.

▶ Before you post something online or send an e-mail, consider what it says about you, how it may color someone's perceptions of you, and whether it reinforces or detracts from how you want to be seen.

Now Go Do Something

Read up on the issues that matter to you, your job, and your career. Call, write, e-mail, and bug the people and institutions that influence them. Join with others who have the same agenda as you. Use resources that can help if you're struggling. Figure out what kind of work arrangement you want, develop a plan that makes sense to an employer, and offer it up. Set your boundaries. Figure out what you want to learn and get better at, and research the path to get there. Reach out to people. Educate yourself about your money. Have a life outside of work. How's that for starters?

Get choosy about your education

Get an education that "teaches you to ask good questions, not just get good answers to someone else's questions," says Marc Tucker, president and CEO of the National Center on Education and the Economy.

To learn more about changing the American education system to better serve today's and future workplaces, see the report I've referred to several times written by the New Commission on the Skills of the American Workforce, *Tough Choices or Tough Times*, www.skillscommission.org. This, too, is an area that you can influence by first learning more about the issue and then contacting your legislators to act on the recommendations in the report.

As Tucker suggests: "Let others know you care . . . to work to build better educational opportunities for yourself, your colleagues or employees. That is how America works."

I haven't thought of everything. But whatever is within your reach to influence and change so that you can be less pissed and more powerful, go do it.

Yes, companies need to do their part. To find a way to revamp their businesses and retrain managers to encourage and reward your creativity. To make it possible for you to take care of business *and* your life with different terms than the old ones. To find ways to collaborate with you so that trust, respect, and cooperation prevail, and goals get met. To be more receptive to the vast number of older workers hungry to do good work.

The pendulum seems to have swung far to one side, with profit at the expense of people, community, and even the company. As one of my clients who worked for a large corporation put it, "In the continuous effort to bow down to the gods of Wall Street, bad long-term decisions

This guy's taking action

Corporate lawyer Robert Hinkley has a goal: "To build consensus to change the law so that it encourages good corporate citizenship rather than inhibiting it."

In an article on Resurgence.org, first published in *Business Ethics*, he says to do that "we must challenge the myth that making profits and protecting the public interest are mutually exclusive goals."

He wants to add 26 words to corporate law and create what he calls the "Code for Corporate Citizenship." According to the article, "Directors and officers would still have a duty to make money for shareholders . . . *but not at the expense of the environment, human rights, the public safety, the communities in which the corporation operates or the dignity of its employees.*"

He adds, "We must remember that corporations were invented to serve humankind. Humankind was not intended to serve corporations . . . Many activities cast the fundamental issue as one of 'corporate greed.'" But, he continues, "corporations are incapable of a human emotion like greed. They are artificial beings created by law. The real question is why corporations behave as if they are greedy. The answer lies in the design of corporate law." And that design, he argues, can be changed.

get made, limiting companies' ability to think strategically and forcing them to think quarter to quarter and make merely tactical decisions."

But that's another book.

Yes, policies, programs, and systems need fixing, too. We need to better prepare and support children and adult learners. To have more collaboration between employers and schools. We need curricula that emphasize interpersonal and problem-solving skills and business ethics, among other things. A required course in basic economics would be nice. We need to rethink policies and systems that discourage and burden people who want to work longer. All kinds of systemic issues need work. But that's another book, too.

The conversation about creating better businesses and policies has to keep moving forward. For now, look at what *you* can do to give it a boost. Make your voice heard. Quite possibly, we can begin to get that balance back in the relationship between you and your employers, so you can both have what you want sooner rather than later.

TAKE YOUR SIXTH QUIT-BEING-PISSED OATH

I hereby promise myself to quit being pissed off and start being powerful by looking at how I can twist and shout and shake things up on issues that affect my job and career.

SIGN HERE _____

DATE _____

RESOURCES

Abolish Employment at Will (grassroots effort)
www.abolishemploymentatwill.com

American Rights at Work
www.americanrightsatwork.org
Reports, case studies, and information on workers' rights, current labor law, and ways to get involved in defending workers' rights to organize.

Center for Work Life Law
www.uchastings.edu/?pid=3624

CorpWatch
Information on everything from a company's business strategies, operations, and financial status to its environmental and social record, plus articles about some issues I've touched on in this book, including:
executive pay: **corpwatch.org/article.php?list=type&type=201**
things you can do about corporate excess: **corpwatch.org/article.php?id=3931**
consumerism and commercialism: **corpwatch.org/article.php?list=type&type=188**
"Hands-On Corporate Research Guide": **www.corpwatch.org/article.php?id=945**

Freelancers Union
www.freelancersunion.org

National Employment Lawyers Association
www.nela.org

National Partnership for Women & Families
www.nationalpartnership.org

National Whistleblower Center
www.whistleblowers.org/
Nonprofit educational and advocacy organization dedicated to helping whistle-blowers by offering information, public education programs, advocacy, and national referral services.

New Commission on the Skills of the American Workforce
www.skillscommission.org

Qvisory Tools for Life
www.Qvisory.org
Nonprofit organization started by Service Employees International Union that proposes to offer health insurance and advocacy to workers under 35.

Workplace Bullying Institute
www.bullyinginstitute.org

Workplace Fairness
www.workplacefairness.org/

Summary: All's Well That Intends Well

I was working on Step 6 when I needed to go out of town for a few days. So I drove to this particular city—which will go unnamed—and parked at a meter, and when I got back to my car there was a ticket flapping under my car's wiper blade. Yes—again. Unlike the meter in the other city (which will still go unnamed), this one didn't flash any weird mishmash of letters on its screen when I plugged it with enough change to cover two hours. I just didn't get back in time.

Within hours of getting home I went online to see if I could pay the ticket electronically, which I could by completing the online form. I began entering the license plate number as it had been typed on the ticket. And then I stopped. "That doesn't sound like my license plate number," I thought. I walked outside to look at my car's plate and wrote down the numbers to compare. Sure enough, it had some of my numbers, but it wasn't my license. Should I pay it anyway? Was this my shot at redemption? Was this too good to be true? To find out, I called the customer-service phone number on the ticket.

"It's close to my license, but not mine," I told the woman, who sounded a lot more chipper than I thought a customer-service representative for a city's parking violation division might sound.

"They may have put the ticket on the wrong car," she told me.

"But the license they wrote has *some* of my numbers . . ." I began. She interrupted me. "If the numbers don't match your license exactly, they'll never find you," she said abruptly, and nothing more. "But, what if—" I began again. "Look, I'm not going to tell you *not* to pay it, I'm just telling you the way things are."

The way things are. Sound familiar? That's where *we* began back in Step 1. With the option to stay frustrated by how-things-are-like-'em-or-not situations, or the option to work with them—and feel more powerful about your career and life.

Tomorrow and next week, odds are good that you will collide

with all kinds of like-'em-or-not scenarios. Managers who don't know squat about managing, bosses who are dead ringers for Attila the Hun, and policies that wouldn't make sense even to a third-grader. You'll encounter people who will madden you, and unexpected decisions that may rock your career.

I won't tell you what you should do, either. I don't have to live with the consequences of your decision. You get to decide how you want to *think* about those things and what you want to *do* about them. Like my dealing with my first* and now second parking ticket, it's really our choice, isn't it?

If, though, you want to get back to working steadily toward the ultimate sweet success of the American Dream, these six steps are a good place to start.

Even in a workplace that seems to have gotten way out of whack, I have confidence that with your best intentions you can make it work. I am definitely not guilty of bilking parking meters. But of being an optimist? I stand guilty as charged.

---

* I did not pay this ticket. I decided that I would live with the consequences of this travesty of injustice—whatever they may be.

Acknowledgments

This book was made better thanks to all the people who shared their brushes with greatness, stories, ideas, and knowledge: Doug Brueckner, Howard Cohen, Scott Csendes, John Eckberg, Randy Freking, Don Hauptman, Claudia Julian, Barb King, Scott Ledyer, Annette Meurer, and Pam Saeks. And thanks to those who skillfully kept the process moving forward: my editor Rahel Lerner, my agent Linda Konner, and Brian Rowe, who keeps my Mac humming. And to those who referred me to others, including Paul Calico, Louise Kursmark, and Donna Hart. And, finally, to the readers of my column who shared their upsets and their insights.

A very special thank you to Carolyn Kaufman, who so generously shared her time and expertise on the human mind, Randy McNutt for pointing out better ways to say things, Chris Colwell for offering his smart perspective, and Greg Newberry, who has read every word of every one of my books and always has that special Greg touch for making them better.

Index

A

addiction
  busy-bee, 93–97
  rush-to-do-whatever, 104–7
  technology, 87, 91–93
  thrill-of-it-all, 102–4
adoption, 19, 225, 226
ADP Screening and Selection Services, 147
AFL-CIO, 45
age discrimination, 35–36
Age-O-Matic.com, 18
Aldrich, Nelson, 104
all-or-nothing thinking, 81–82
Alpern Rosenthal, 231
always on call. *See* Availability 24/7
American Bar Foundation, 106
American Dream, 15, 105, 258
American Federation of Teachers, 30
American Psychiatric Association, 91–92
Anderson, Jenny, 27
Andler, Edward, 234, 235
anger, 43, 58–70, 221
  health effects of, 83
  pent-up, 118
  personal effects of, 65–66
  sources of, 61–65, 67–70
  See also Attitude Implants; Pissed-Off
    Vortex
anxiety, 83, 93, 103
Apatow, Judd, 129
"Are You Acting Like a Wimp?" exercise,
  126–27
Aristotle, 59
Aronson, Elliot, 80
"As I Think of People" exercise, 186
Aspland, Robert, 36
astronauts, 79
Attitude Implants, 70, 71–84
Attitudes in the American Workplace (2007
  poll), 134
at-will employment doctrine, 45–46, 223,
  224
automation, 19, 47, 48, 49, 60

Availability 24/7 (Step 2), 9–11, 17, 21–22,
  85–111
  alternative plan, 233
  "Balancing Act" exercise, 108–9
  contributing factors, 90–109, 230
  "Do Nothing but This for 5 Minutes"
    exercise, 95–97
  "Is It You or Them" exercise, 88–89, 93
avoidance, 128–29
Avramidis, Manny, 241

B

background checks, 234–36
bad mood, 242–43
Balaker, Ted, 48
balance, 94, 107–9, 255
  "Balancing Act" exercise, 108–9
Baranski, Celeste, 107
"Be a Terminator" exercise, 144–46
beepers, 9, 21
Begley, Sharon, 82
behaviorists, 81
being there, 148–52
benefits, 213–16, 225–27
  best companies for, 19, 205–6
  pension plans, 16, 18, 245–46
  reduction in, 16, 19
  See also health insurance
Berger, Russ, 185–86
"Best Places to Work" lists, 18–19
Big Book of Jobs, The, 217
bilingualism, 21
Bivens, Josh, 48
BlackBerry, 9, 21, 86, 87
  addiction to, 91–92
  turned off, 93, 111
Bolton, Michael, 185
bonuses, 30, 203, 216
bosses
  bullying by, 227–28
  career development discussions with,
    238–42

incompetency of, 22–25, 46–47, 50, 115
  personal problems with, 155
brain research, 98
Brooks, Arthur, 237
Brutal Bosses (Hornstein), 228
Buckmaster, James, 205–6
bullying boss, 227–28
bureaucracy, 55–56
Bureau of Labor Statistics, 54, 228–29
Bush, George W., 31
Business 2.0 (magazine), 157–58, 161
Business Ethics, 254
BusinessWeek, 48, 196, 206
BusinessWeek/Harris poll, 254
Busy-Bee Addiction, 93–97
Butler, Joey, 163

C

Caine, Michael, 174
Calvin Klein (co.), 32
CareerBuilder survey, 20
career change, 36, 167
  sixth sense and, 217
career coach, 176, 241
career development, 176–86, 190–218,
  241
  assessing company's culture and,
    190–91, 194–98, 203
  bad politics and, 211–12
  clearly defined goal and, 218
  comparison shopping and, 212–16
  continuing education and, 177–78
  facing discontent and, 151
  flexible arrangements and, 233
  free flow of ideas and, 248
  hobbies and, 247
  initiative and, 238–42
  journal keeping for, 177, 179
  keeping up and, 179–80, 191
  mundane but necessary issues in, 177
  personal contacts and, 183–86, 242–43
  preparedness and, 154–87
  problem solving and, 179–80
  rush to get rich and, 106
  rush to next level and, 105
  sixth sense and, 190, 198–200, 212,
    216
  special strengths and, 165–69, 175,
    190–94, 191–94
  staying relevant and, 182
  staying valuable and, 180–81
  superworkers and, 102–4

Things You Can Do, 241
threats to, 155
time-out break from, 248–51
trade publications on, 217
verbal presentation and, 169–74
  See also ideal career; job hunt
Career Rage, 9–11, 14–15
  issues fueling, 17–37
  See also Pissed-Off Vortex
Career Survival Kit. *See* Preparedness
cell phone, 21, 87, 109
  multitasking and, 97, 98
  as obsession, 90–91, 92
  turning off of, 93, 111
Center for Internet Addiction Recovery, 93
Center for WorkLife Law, 227
Center for Work-Life Policy, 22, 46, 102
CEOs, 27, 51, 148
  different styles of, 208–10
  excessive compensation for, 9, 29–31,
    76
  of ideal companies, 203, 205–6
Chacko, Tom, 15, 16, 17
Chaison, Gary, 16
challenges, 161, 168, 198, 214
change
  career time-out and, 248–51
  of mood, 42
  preparing for, 154–56
  willingness to, 137–39
childbirth leave, 225, 226
child care, on-site, 19
China, 48
Cieply, Michael, 240
Clay, Phillip, 148
Clough, G. Wayne, 247
"Code for Corporate Citizenship," 254
Cohen, Randy, 128
Cole, Kenneth, 178
collaborative environment, 214
collective bargaining, 223, 224
company culture, 115, 119–20, 121–22,
    192, 202–12
  assessment of, 17–19, 190–91, 194–98,
    202–3
  bad politics and, 211–12
  birds-eye view of, 202–3
  career development aid and, 177
  compensation and, 213–16
  complaints about, 17–37
  decent leaders and, 204–7
  ethical conduct and, 25–27, 207–8
  fitting into, 208–11, 214–15

good work environment and, 18–19,
   214–15
management style and, 198
social betterment and, 254
company finances, 19, 25, 26–27, 28, 155,
   162–63, 195, 197
comparison shopping, 213–16
compensation, 19, 203, 213–16
  for bringing in new business, 162
  CEO excessive, 9, 29–31, 76
  executive packages, 29–30, 103
  givebacks of, 16
  inequities in, 29–30, 54–55, 76–77,
    228–29, 237–38
  job dissatisfaction vs., 215
  market factors and, 237–38
  negotiation of, 14, 16, 238
  in previous jobs, 234
  quality of life vs., 249, 250
  rush to increase, 106
  self-marketing and, 237–38
  sixth sense and, 216
  for skills, 76, 237–38, 239
  truths about, 47, 155
  See also benefits
competency, 140
competitiveness, 109, 140, 160, 203
Complete Reference Checking
  Handbook, The (Andler), 234
completion. *See* following through
confidence building, 161
confrontation, 128–37, 140
  "Fraidy Cat" exercise, 135–37
continuing education, 177–78, 203, 248
Continuum, 202
conversations, 130–37, 185–86
  difficult, 132–35
  direct, 129, 130–34, 140
  face-to-face, 110, 134
corporate scandals. *See* ethical standards
corporations. *See* company culture; company finances
corruption. *See* ethical standards
Costco Wholesale Corporation, 206
Craigslist, 205–6
creativity, 17, 47, 101
  company competitiveness and, 140
  company encouragement of, 214,
    247–48
  educational level and, 178
  hobbies and, 247
  respect for, 240
  self-censorship of, 117, 140

Things I Can Do, 248
  worker premium on, 201
credit report, personal, 235–36
Crucial Conversation Training, 120
crying, 134
CTPartners, 196
culture shock, 208–11, 215
current events, 211–12

D

David, Susan, 141
decent leadership, 204–7
Declaration of Independence, 46
defensive realism, 74
deferred prosecution agreement, 51–52
delayed gratification, 147
deliberate practice, 142–43
De Mello, Anthony, 84
democracy, 44–45, 60
depression, 83
Desmond-Hellman, Susan, 161
Diagnostic and Statistical Manual of
  Mental Disorders, 92
dichotomous thinking, 81–82
Dictionary of Occupational Titles, 217
Diddly, Bo, 104
Dietz, Steven, 150
difference. *See* making a difference
different viewpoints, 129–32
different work arrangements, 228–33
disasters, natural, 154–55, 211
discontent, facing, 151
discrimination, 203, 225
  age, 35–36
  in firing, 45–46
  protected categories, 226–27
disillusionment. *See* Naked Truths
diversity, 203
"Do Nothing but This for 5 Minutes" exercise, 95–97
Do the Right Thing (Parker), 205
drug testing, 234
Dunleavey, M. P., 249
D'Urso, Anthony, 155
Dux, Paul E., 98

E

Economic Policy Institute (EPI), 30, 31, 48,
  224, 239
Edmondson, David, 147–48
education, 177–78, 203, 237, 248, 253

Eisenbrey, Ross, 31, 224, 239
electronic portfolio, 174
Ellis, Albert, 62
e-mail, 9, 31
  to avoid difficult conversations, 134
  connecting with, 110
  as interruption, 99–100, 109
  set time for handling, 101
  See also Blackberry
emergencies. See Preparedness
Emerging Workforce Study, 201
Employee Free Choice Act, 225
"employment at will," 21
enjoyment of work, 9, 10
Enough Already (Step 2). See Availability
  24/7
Enron scandal, 51, 244
entitlement, attitude of, 77–78
environmentalism, 19, 25, 203, 204
career development and, 179
equal rights, 46
essence of you, 161, 170, 175
ethical standards, 19, 35, 207–8, 245
  acting on, 251–52
  advocacy of, 244–45
  company deviations from, 25–27
  disregard of, 50–52
  politically smart choice and, 120–21
  Sarbanes-Oxley Act and, 51, 56
  short-cuts to greatness and, 147–48
  Things You Can Do, 245
Ethics Resource Center, 51, 207
ExecuNet, 30, 33, 35
executives
  compensation of, 29–30, 103
  hyperactive, 102–4
  job hunt complaints about, 33
  on-call, 21–22
  See also bosses; CEOs
Exercises, 59–70
  acting like wimp, 126–27
  availability 24/7, 88–89, 93, 95–97,
    108–9
  confrontation, 135–37
  following-through, 144–46
  ideal career, 192–93, 212–13
  mediocre job, 124–25
  personal contacts list, 186
  personal image, 176
  personal value to company, 158–61
  speaking up, 122–23
  staying relevant, 182
  thinking about how you think, 59–70

value to company, 158–61
work addiction, 95–97
work/life balance, 108–9
expectations, employer's, 222–24
Explain It to My Mother, 169–74
extramarital affairs, 53
extreme jobs, 22, 102–4

F
Facebook.com, 35
failure, fear of, 144–45
Fair Credit Reporting Act, 235
fairness, 239
Families and Work Institute, 231
Family and Medical Leave Act, 225–26
family disaster plan, 154
family leave, 225–27
family responsibility discrimination, 45–46
Farrell, Patricia, 144
fatigue, worker, 105
fear
  of failure, 144–45
  of speaking up, 114–22, 138–39, 140
feedback, 17, 203, 241
FEMA, 211
Fierce Conversations (Scott), 119
financial records
  of company, 19, 25, 26–27, 28, 155,
    162–63, 195, 197
  of job applicant, 235–36
financial sector, 54, 106, 235–36
  corporate responsibility and, 254
  pension fund investments and, 245–46
firing
  for fudged credentials, 147–48
  lack of preparation for, 154, 155
  legal rights and, 45–46, 222–23, 225
  top ten reasons for, 45
  See also job loss
flexible work program, 94, 203, 205,
    229–33, 248
  Things You Can Do, 233
Flippen, Flip, 80
Flores, Fernando, 141
focus, 101, 149–51
following through, 143–46
  "Be a Terminator" exercise, 144–46
Ford Motor Company, 21
forgiveness, 80
Fortune (magazine), 142
  "100 Best Companies to Work For"
    (2008), 18–19

"Fraidy Cat" exercise, 135–37
Francis, Freddie, 139
Francis, Simon, 196
fraud. *See* ethical standards
Freelancers Union, 226
Freking, Randy, 45, 222, 223–24
Friedman, Thomas, 133, 247–48
friendships, 110
fringe benefits. *See* benefits
frustrations, 56–57, 81
Fulbright, James, 165

G

Gallagher, BJ, 147
Gallup Organization, 110
Genentech, 19, 161
General Mills, 19
General Motors, 21
Generation Next (documentary), 47
Generation X workers, 229, 232
Georgia Institute of Technology, 247
"Get It on Paper," 174–76
Get UnStuck! (Seeley), 143
Giant Leap Consulting, 164
Gibson, Charles, 176
Gilbert, Daniel, 72
"Gist of You," 165–69, 191–92
Giura, Patty, 231
givebacks, 16
global economy, 49
Global Positioning System, 31
gloom, realistic, 72
goals
    in career development, 218
    of company, 158
    personal attainment of, 107, 143
Gold, Stuart, 91
golden parachutes, 31
Goldman Sachs Group, 54
good intentions, 257–58
Google (co.), 196
    working conditions, 18, 214–15
Google (search engine), 34, 35, 197
Gordon, Ellen M., 211
Gould, Elise, 31
Government Accountability Office reports, 51, 221
government employees, 51
government regulations, 55–56
Greatness (Step 3), 113–52
    "Are You Acting Like a Wimp?" exercise, 126–27

barriers to, 114–41
    "Be a Terminator" exercise, 144–46
    characteristics of, 141, 148–52
    deliberate practice and, 142–43
    "Fraidy Cat" exercise, 135
    "Half-ass Job" exercise, 124–25
    "Looking Back at Monday" exercise, 122–23
    no short cuts to, 147–48
    Quit-Being Pissed oath, 152
    trajectory of, 127
    willingness to change and, 137–39
Great Railway Strike (1877), 15
green practices, 179, 203, 204
group pressure, 120–22
grudges, 74–76
Guth, Robert, 195–96
gut reaction. *See* Sixth Sense

H

"Half-ass Job" exercise, 124–25
handwriting analysis, 234
happiness, 249
harassment, 227, 228
harmony, disturbers of, 109
Harned, Patricia, 51, 207–8, 244
Harris, Bonnie, 249–50
Harris Interactive, 134, 201
Harris Poll, 204
Harry, Deborah, 180
Hauptman, Don, 78
Haymarket Square Riot (Chicago), 15
health, 83, 92, 103, 104, 105
    breakdown of, 155
    paid sick leave and, 225–26, 227
health insurance, 9, 16, 17, 31
    cost of, 30–31
    for independent workers, 221, 226
    working to keep, 18
Health Net, Inc., 216
Healthy Family Act, 227
Healthy Workplace bills, 228
Hearst Corporation, 32
hedge funds, 245
Helmet, James, 25
Heritage Foundation, 51
Hewlett-Packard, 232
Hinkley, Robert, 254
historical work conditions, 15, 16, 223
HiWired, 216
hobbies, 246–47
Home Depot, 30

honesty, 164
Hornstein, Harvey, 228
Horowitz, Sara, 226
hostility, 83
hours of work, 15, 19, 22
How to Reduce Workplace Conflict and Stress (Maravelas), 243
Hudson surveys, 21, 22, 292
Hurricane Katrina, 154, 211
hurricane risk, 154, 156
hyperactivity, 102–4

I

IBM, 16, 230
"I Can Do 4 Things at Once" Myth, 97–102
ideal career, 192–207, 209
  questions to ask, 197–98
  sixth sense about, 190, 198–201, 212, 216
  "What Fits You Like A Glove?" exercise, 192–93, 212–13
  what to look for, 202–3
ideas
  comfort with, 178
  free flow of, 247–48
  giving up of, 127
  sharing of, 117
  See also creativity
Ignited (ad agency), 209
I Met Him/Her on a Monday Form, 200–201
impulse disorder, 91
inappropriate interview questions, 236
income inequity, 29–30, 54–55, 228–29, 237–38
  as incentive, 237
  stop fretting about, 76–77
incompetent bosses, 22–25, 46–47, 50
  affecting quality of work, 114–15
  "Think About How You Think" exercise, 59–61
independent workers, 221, 226, 239
India, 48
inflation-adjusted wages, 19, 30
initiative, 141, 238–41
innovation, 117, 140, 178, 179
  company emphasis on, 214
instinct. *See* Sixth Sense
integrity. *See* ethical standards
internalized complaints, 118
Internet
  addiction to, 91–93

personal information found on, 34–35, 53, 61, 78, 165, 251–52
  See also Web sites
interruptions, 99–101
interview, job, 33–34, 194, 196–97, 199–203, 215, 251–52
  company's ethical standards and, 208, 244
  I Met Him/Her on a Monday Form, 200–201
  inappropriate questions in, 234, 235
  open communication and, 209
  sixth sense about, 199–200, 210, 211
intuition. *See* Sixth Sense
investments. *See* financial sector
"in-your-face" system, 138–39
irritability, 83
"Is It You or Them" exercise, 88–89, 93
Isley, Ron, 180

J

Jalbert, Michael, 238
jargon avoidance, 170–71, 172–73, 241
  specific examples, 171
Jefferson, Thomas, 109
job description, 17, 123–24, 140
job elimination, 28, 47–48, 184
job hunt, 9, 10, 21, 165–74, 238
  all-or-nothing thinking in, 81–82
  comparison shopping in, 213–16
  complaints about, 18, 32–36, 49–50
  front desk treatment and, 194–95
  making a difference and, 167–68
  personal contacts and, 183–86
  personal information and, 53, 61, 163, 164–65, 234–36, 251–52
  realistic scenario for, 82
  references and, 34, 147–48, 234
  research about, 191
  resume and, 148, 174–75, 234
  snap decisions and, 147
  special strengths and, 165–67
  verbal presentation and, 169–74
  "Why Do I Matter?" exercise, 158–61
  wimpish behavior and, 126–27, 140
  See also interview, job
job loss, 17, 21, 27–29, 49
  Naked Truth exercise, 60, 61
  scenarios behind, 155
  See also firing; job hunt
Job Rights & Survival Strategies (Tobias and Sauter), 222
job satisfaction, 101, 141, 182

job security, 16, 46, 60
    belief in entitlement to, 77–78
    job satisfaction vs., 141, 182
    staying valuable and, 180–81
job sharing, 19
joy, 59, 165–67
joyful skills, 166–67

K

Kakabadse, Nada, 87
Kase, Larina, 74
Kasser, Tim, 249
Kaufman, Carolyn, 62, 79, 199
Keep a Watch Over You, 176–86
keeping up, 179–80, 191
King's Daughters Medical Center (Ky.), 19
knowledge, 159, 165, 167, 172, 177–78
Know the Gist of You, 165–69, 175, 191–94
Know Where Things Stand, 162–65
Know Why You Matter, 157–61, 175
Koch, Ed, 164
Kolligian, Kory, 202
Korn/Ferry International survey, 21
Kremen, Gary, 107
Kristof, Nicholas D., 127
Kubrick, Stanley, 151

L

Labor Department, U.S., 179
law school graduates, 106
layoffs. See firing; job loss
Leach, Elisabeth, 231
leadership, 204–7
Lee, Kai-Fu, 196
Legacy.com, 24
legal rights, 46, 222–25, 227–28, 235
Lewis, Michael, 26
liability, employer, 234
"Lies My Company Told Me," 17–18
long-term thinking, 147–48
"Looking Back at Monday" exercise, 122–23
Lopez, Carina, 76
loyalty, 26, 232
luck, definition of, 176

M

making a difference, 107, 115, 117, 159,
    167–68, 192, 198
Manilow, Barry, 180
Map for Saturday, A (documentary), 250

Maravelas, Anna, 243
market forces, 237–38, 239
Marois, René, 98
Massachusetts Institute of technology
    (MIT), 147, 148
Match.com, 107
Mayfield, Max, 154
McBrearty, James, 15, 16
meaningful activity, 107, 114
meaningful relationships, 183–84
Medical Group Management Association,
    106
mediocrity, 123–25
    "Half-ass Job" exercise, 124–25
meetings, 17, 93, 100
    fear of speaking at, 114–22, 138–39
MeetUp.com, 243–44
"me-first" worker, 77–78
Mellencamp, John, 180
Mendenhall, Michael, 232
mentors, 176, 203, 242
mergers and acquisitions, 19, 155, 156, 157
microexpressions, 199
Microsoft, 195–96
Midler, Bette, 180
military, 172–73, 204
millionaires, 106, 107
mission statement, 18, 207
mistakes
    admittance of, 80
    career change, 217
Mistakes Were Made (but not by me)
    (Tavris and Aronson), 80
misunderstandings, 132–33
Molly Maguires, 15
Money Can Buy Happiness (Dunleavey),
    249
mood, changing of, 242–43
Morici, Peter, 237
Morris, Bob, 72
motivation, worker, 253
MRINetwork survey, 238
multitasking, 28, 97–102
    arguments against, 100–101
    testing self, 102
Murdoch, Rupert, 161
musicians, 180

N

Nagele, Charles, 121–22
Naked Truth #1, 44–45
Naked Truth #2, 45–46, 223

Naked Truth #3, 46
Naked Truth #4, 46–47
Naked Truth #5, 47
Naked Truth #6, 47–49, 155
Naked Truth #7, 49–50
Naked Truth #8, 50–52
Naked Truth #9, 53, 163
Naked Truth #10, 54–55
Naked Truth #11, 55–56
Naked Truth #12, 56–57, 98, 172–73
Naked Truths (Step 1), 41–84
  Attitude Implants, 70, 71–84
  snubbing, 57–58
  "Think About How You Think" exercise,
    59–70
  working with, 58–70
Nardelli, Robert I., 30
National Business Ethics Survey (2007),
  51, 244
National Center on Education and the
  Economy, 178, 252
National Conference on the Creative
  Economy (2007), 247–48
National Employment Lawyers Association,
  222, 223–24
National Hurricane Center, 154
National Labor Relations Act, 225
National Partnership for Women & Families,
  227
Necessary Evil (album), 180
negative realism, 72
negotiation of pay 14, 16, 238
Nelson, Willie, 180
Nerds On Site, 206
neuroscience, 98
New Commission on the Skills of the
  American Workforce, 140, 252
New Positioning, The (Trout), 175
news sources, 179, 195–96
9/11 terrorist attack, 155
No Child Left Behind Act, 55
non-responses, 49–50
"Not Exactly Branding" exercise, 176
no-travel-no-matter-what policy, 216
Nurick, Aaron, 128–29
nurses, 55

O

older workers, 255
  as assets, 232
  discrimination and, 35–36
  entitlement expectations of, 77–78

opportunity, 176, 237
optimism, 72, 250
Opton, Dave, 32–33
Orwell, George, 116, 170
"Our Country" (song), 180
outside interests, 246–47
  career time-out and, 249–51
outsourcing, 9, 47–49, 60, 61, 155

P

pager, 21
paid family medical leave, 225–27
Parker, James, 205, 207
paternalistic employers, 16
Paterson, David A., 53
pay. See compensation
Pelino, Dan, 230
pensions, 16, 18
  fund investment, 245–46
perfection, 81, 143
performance review, 17, 22–23, 203,
  239–41
  disagreement with, 241
personal characteristics, 168, 169, 191–92
  job fit with, 198
  "Not Exactly Branding" exercise, 176
  reputation and, 163–65, 251–52
  See also strengths
personal contacts, 183–86, 243–44
  "As I Think of People" exercise, 186
personal feelings, 53, 60, 61
  changing bad mood and, 242–43
personal information, 164–76
  countering inaccurate/negative, 164–65
  Internet postings, 34–35, 53, 61, 78,
    165, 251–52
  misrepresentation of, 148, 234
  privacy boundaries and, 234–36
  resume and, 148, 174–75, 234
  skills and strengths, 159, 165–67,
    172–73
personality testing, 234
personal life
  anger's effects on, 65–66
  balance in, 94–95, 107–9
  blurred work boundaries with, 22, 92–93
  career time-out and, 248–51
  company background checks and, 234–36
  company monitoring of, 31–32
  company protection of, 216
  family responsibility discrimination and,
    45–46

hobbies and, 246–47
intrinsic values and, 249
joyful skills and, 166–67
office friendships and, 110
paid family leave and, 225–27
success definitions and, 107
See also Availability 24/7
personal relations
assessing company's, 194–95
avoidance and, 128–29
career advancement and, 183–86
decency and, 204–6
expectations for, 98
extreme jobs and, 103–4
importance in business of, 63, 163–65
self-justifications and, 80
sensitive approach to, 129, 130–32
of value to company, 155–56, 159
personal strengths. *See* strengths
pessimism, 72
phone calls
compulsion to answer, 99
e-mails vs., 110
job hunt and, 195
nonresponse to, 57–58
as work interruptions, 99–100, 101
See also BlackBerry; cell phone
Pissed-Off Vortex, 42–43
getting out of, 43–45, 60, 66–70,
220–55
perspective and, 79
preserving status quo and, 117
pride in work and, 114, 115
Quit-Being-Pissed Oaths, 84, 111, 152,
186, 218, 255
specific issues and, 17–37
pity parties, 72
Planet Dog, 19
planning. *See* Preparedness
Plante & Moran, 19
politics, 127, 211–12
"Politics and the English Language"
(Orwell), 116, 170
Porter, Gayle, 87
portfolio, 174
positioning, 175–76
power, 84, 111, 161, 239, 255
powerlessness, 42
practice, 142–43
Preparedness (Step 4), 153–87
Keep a Watch Over You, 176–86
luck and, 176
"Who Knew?" strategy and, 156–76

pride in work, 114, 115
priority setting, 100, 101
privacy boundaries, 234–36
problem solving, 178–79, 181
procrastination, 132, 143–44
Procter & Gamble, 195
productivity, 49, 105
professional contacts, 243
professional credentials, 148, 234
professional development, 248
profits, 9
promoting within, 17
Putzier, John, 77

Q
Qualcomm, 19
quality of life, 249–50
quality of work, 114–15
Quest-for-Balance Fallacy, 107–9
Quicken Loans, 18
Quinones, Miguel, 163
Quit-Being-Pissed Oaths
availability 24/7, 111
career development, 218
greatness, 152
preparedness, 187
shaking things up, 255
thinking about how I think, 84

R
RadioShack, 27, 148
Rath, Tom, 110
realistic attitude, 72, 81, 82, 84
Reality Check (Weiner), 124
references, 34
verification of, 147–48, 234
Reich, Robert, 225, 245
Reina, Dennis and Michelle, 74–75
Reinhold, Barbara Bailey, 18
relocation, 16
reputation, 163–65, 251–53
enhancement of, 253
resourcefulness, 178–79
respect, 240
resume, 148, 174–75, 234
Resurgence.org, 254
retirement, 229, 230, 232
pension and, 16, 18, 245–46
rich, rush to get, 106, 107, 109
rights. *See* legal rights
risk management, 27

"Risk of Staying Put" exercise, 182
risks, 118, 140, 141, 154
   career development, 182
   pension fund investments, 246
   preparing for, 154, 162–63, 186
Ritter, David, 227, 228
Robinson, Lynn, 199
Rodriguez, Louis, 230
Ronstadt, Linda, 180
Rush-To-Do-Whatever Addiction, 104–7

S

salary. *See* compensation
Sarbanes-Oxley Act, 51, 56
Sauter, Susan, 222
savings and loan crisis, 50
Scott, Susan, 119
Sedhom, Rania, 246
Seeley, John, 143
self-employment, 221, 226
self-improvement, 241
self-justification, 80
self-marketing, 237–38
self-revelation, 169–74, 251–52
sensitivity, 129, 130–32, 134
services-based economy, 16
severance packages, 31
Shake Things Up (Step 6), 219–55
   action plan, 252–55
   bullying bosses, 227–28
   career development initiative, 238–42
   different work arrangements, 228–33
   employer relations, 222–25
   ethical behavior advocacy, 244–45
   free flow of ideas, 247–48
   mood control, 242–43
   outside interests, 246–47
   paid family leave, 225–27
   pay negotiation, 237–38
   personal contacts development, 243–44
   privacy preservation, 234–36
   reputation management, 251–52, 253
   time-out break, 248–51
   union formation, 224–25
sick leave, 225–26, 227
sickness. *See* health
Silicon Valley, 106, 107
Silva-Braga, Brook, 249, 250
Sinegal, James, 206
Sixth Sense (Step 5), 189–218
Skaggs, Boz, 180

skills
   assessment exercise, 158–61
   education and, 177–78
   pay commensurate with, 76, 237–38, 239
   self-analysis of, 177
   special strengths and, 165–67
   transferability of, 172–73
   underutilization of, 17
   as value adding, 54, 159
sleep deprivation, 22, 95, 103, 107, 243
Slocum, Charles, 240
small businesses, 204
snap decisions, 147
snoozer words, 171
social pressure, 120–22
social trends, 179
South Korean Internet addiction symposium, 92
Southwest Airlines, 205, 207
speaking about self, 169–74
speaking up, 114–41
   daily reminders about, 138, 138–39
   misunderstanding and, 132–33
   reasons for avoiding, 119–22, 127, 128–29
   sensitive approach and, 129, 130–32
specialized skills, 54, 165–67
speed addiction, 104–7, 109
Spitzer, Eliot, 53, 251
Srinivas, Singu, 216
Stamberg, Susan, 136
Stanford Daily Online, 32, 34–35
status quo, 116–18, 121–24
   challenging, 121–22
   initiative vs., 141
   reasons for not challenging, 120–21, 127
Steelcase and Opinion Research survey, 32
Stein, Ben, 54, 76
steroids, 148
Stewart, Rod, 180
stock options, 18
stock values, 9, 31, 50
strengths, 165–69, 190–94
   job fit with, 198
   unique, 161, 170, 172, 175
stress, 20–21, 106
   bad mood and, 243
   body's reaction to, 18, 83, 92
   from multitasking, 101
   from technology, 93

strikes, 15, 240
Stumbling on Happiness (Gilbert), 72
subprime mortgage crisis, 18, 27
success
    definitions of, 107
    fear of, 144
suffering, 58, 59, 70
Sullivan, Stacy, 214, 215
superworkers, 102–4, 106, 107
supply and demand, 239
survival kit. *See* Preparedness

T

talents, belief in, 161
talking about yourself. *See* verbal presentation
Tavris, Carol, 80
teachers, 30, 55
technology
    addiction to, 87, 91–93
    job market effects from, 19, 47, 48, 49, 60, 61, 155, 180
    management of, 101, 110–11
    multitasking with, 28, 97–101
    speed of work with, 104–5
telecommuting, 19, 205, 230
terrorist attack, 155
text-messaging, 91
theft, company, 26–27
Things You Can Do
    bullying boss, 228
    career development, 241
    employee rights, 224
    ethical standards, 245
    flexible work arrangement, 233
    paid family medical leave, 227
    union formation, 225
"Think About How You Think" exercise, 59–70
thinking
    all-or-nothing, 81–82
    long-term, 147–48
    new ways of, 67–70
Thrill-of-it-all Addiction, 102–4
time-out break, 248–51
Tobias, Paul, 222, 224
Topps Meat Company, 155
Tough Choices or Tough Times (report), 252
Toxic Work (Reinhold), 18
Train Your Mind, Change Your Brain (Begley), 82

transparency, 206
travel, business, 22, 216
Travels with Alice (Trillin), 105
Treasurer, Bill, 164
Trillin, Calvin, 105
Trout, Jack, 175
trust, 17, 19, 80, 183
Trust & Betrayal in the Workplace (Reina and Reina), 74–75
Trust Your Gut (Robinson), 199
Tucker, Marc, 252
Twain, Mark, 250–51

U

Ulzheimer, John, 235, 236
unions, 15, 16, 223, 240
    freelancers, 226
    right to form, 224–25
    wages and, 239
unique strengths, 161, 170, 172, 175
unpopular opinions, 121
Usana Health Sciences, 148

V

vacation time, 21, 87, 90–91
"vacation-without-boundaries" system, 230
values, intrinsic, 249
value to company, 54, 139, 180–81, 237, 238
    knowledge and, 159, 165, 167, 172, 177–78
    older workers and, 232
    "Why Do I Matter?" exercise, 158–61
verbal abuse, 210–11
verbal presentation, 169–74
    practicing, 173–74
Verrone, Patric M., 240
Vital Friends (Rath), 110
voice mail, 99, 101
Voluntary Simplicity movement, 249

W

Wade, William H., II, 172
wages. *See* compensation
Waitley, Denis, 148
Wall Street, 106
Walsh, Brian, 51
Warshauer, Matthew, 105
WashingtonPost.com, 27

Wayne, John, 174
wealth
    rush for, 106, 107, 109
    superworkers and, 102–4
Web sites
    citizen lobby, 228
    company finances, 197
    family leave, 227
    freelancers, 226
    Google corporation, 214
    job types, 217
    outsourcing, 48
    resources list, 256
    social/professional, 243–44
    stress effects, 18
    U.S. Labor Department, 179
    workplace fairness, 46, 222, 223, 224,
        225, 228
Weiner, David L., 124
Weirdos in the Workplace (Putzier), 77
Wexler, Michael, 216
"What Fits You Like A Glove?" exercise,
    192–93, 212–13
whistle-blowers, 25–26
white-collar crime, 50–52
"Who Knew?" strategy, 156–76
    Explain It to My Mother, 169–74
    Get It on Paper, 174–76
    Know Why You Matter, 157–69
    Quit-Being-Pissed Oath, 187
"Why Do I Matter?" exercise, 158–61
Wilk, Steffanie, 242–43
Wilkins, Kay, 6, 156
wimpish behavior, 126–27, 140
wireless technology, 91
Wolff, Edward N., 106
women
    avoidance and, 128
    fear of speaking up by, 120–21
    superjobs and, 103
word choice, 170–71, 172, 241
work environment and, 19, 192, 198,
        204–7, 214–15
worker shortage, 229, 232
workers' rights, 222–26
Working America, 45, 46
working-for-free, 232
work/life balance fallacy, 107–9
Workplace Bullying Institute, 228
Workplace Fairness, 222
Work+Life Fit Reality Check, 94
workweek, compressed, 19
World Is Flat, The (Friedman), 133, 247

Wright, Frank Lloyd, 136
Writers Guild of America strike, 240

Y
Yahoo Hot Jobs, 92
Young, Kimberly, 93
younger workers, 77
You're Nothing but a Number (Ulzheimer),
    235

Z
Zimmerman, Eilene, 246–47

What are your chances of going from
PISSED OFF
to
POWERFUL?

. . .

Take this test to find out where you stand now
and what it takes to have a rewarding career—
despite what's wrong in the workplace.

Yes, there is plenty to be upset about. And there are many
forces you don't control. But you can go from feeling helpless and
betrayed to hopeful and in control if you're ready, willing, and
prepared. This test will show you where you stand now and how far
you have to go to get from pissed off to powerful.

. . .

Visit my Web site for
this special link
for readers of my book at:
www.andreakay.com/worksabitchtest